Computing for Non-specialists

We work with leading authors to develop the
strongest educational materials in computing,
bringing cutting-edge thinking and best learning
practice to a global market.

Under a range of well-known imprints, including
Addison-Wesley, we craft high quality
print and electronic publications which help
readers to understand and apply their content,
whether studying or at work.

To find out more about the complete range of our
publishing please visit us on the World Wide Web at:
www.pearsoneduc.com

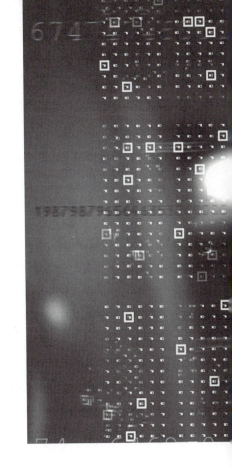

Computing for
Non-specialists

Nanda Bandyo-padhyay

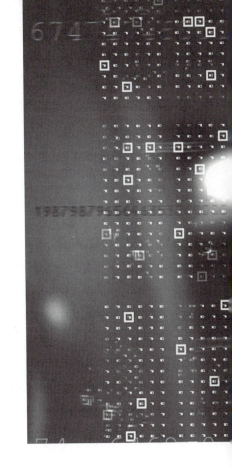

Addison-Wesley

An imprint of **Pearson Education**

Harlow, England · London · New York · Reading, Massachusetts · San Francisco
Toronto · Don Mills, Ontario · Sydney · Tokyo · Singapore · Hong Kong · Seoul
Taipei · Cape Town · Madrid · Mexico City · Amsterdam · Munich · Paris · Milan

Pearson Education Limited
Edinburgh Gate
Harlow
Essex CM20 2JE
England

and Associated Companies throughout the world

Visit us on the World Wide Web at:
http://www.pearsoneduc.com

First published 2000

ISBN 0 201 64861 X

British Library Cataloguing-in-Publication Data
A catalogue record for this book can be obtained from the British Library.

Library of Congress Cataloging-in-Publication Data
Bandyo-padhyay, Nanda.
    Computing for Non-specialists/Nanda Bandyo-padhyay.
        p.cm.
    ISBN 0-201-64861-X (pbk : acid-free paper)
    1. Computers. 2. Computer programs. I. Title.

    QA76. .B265 2000
    004--dc21

                                                                99-054345

10 9 8 7 6 5 4 3 2
04 03 02 01 00

Typeset by 30
Printed by Ashford Colour Press Ltd., Gosport

CONTENTS

Chapter 3:   Input, output and external storage

Chapter 4:   Computer software

Chapter 5:   Common business applications

Chapter 6: Computer programs

Chapter 7:   Communicating data

Chapter 8:   Information superhighway and the Internet

Chapter 9:   Developing a computer system

Chapter 10: Computers and humans

Chapter 11: Security of computer systems

Chapter 12: Computerization of our society

A Companion Web Site
accompanies *Computing for Non-specialists*
by Nanda Bandyo-padhyay

Visit the *Computing for Non-specialists* Companion Web Site at *www.booksites.net/bandyo*. Here you will find valuable teaching and learning material including:

For students and lecturers:

- answers to revision questions
- new food for thought articles
- information on new technologies
- notes on further reading
- links to other sites/resources.

The rationale behind the book

As an increasing number of universities are adopting the modular structure of course delivery there is a growing population of students who are taking combined and interdisciplinary courses. Often they follow a degree structure in which information technology (IT) is a Major, Minor or a Joint in combination with a wide variety of subjects such as Education, Law, Languages, Business Studies, Sociology – in fact anything that the timetable allows. They need to have an overview of all the relevant technology and, at the same time, understand the impact of IT on social, economic, organizational and human matters. Many of these students come into higher education via non-traditional educational routes with a view to building an academic profile that prepares them for today's job market. This book is written to serve the needs of such students.

The aims

As the title suggests, *Computing for Non-specialists* is aimed at students doing a 'non-specialist computing degree' who come with no previous knowledge of the subject. It covers what students 'need to know' in order to become confident users of computers and to understand the issues surrounding the use of computers in today's society. The main objectives of the book are:

- to give students an up to date and wide coverage of the technical concepts behind a computer system without unnecessary details;

- to equip students with an understanding of the issues surrounding the choice, use, maintenance and the future of computer systems.

The book is not designed to help students to gain hands-on IT skills: there are many books in the market to do that. Neither does this book attempt to serve the needs of those following a Computer Studies or Computer Science degree with a view to becoming a professional in the technical aspects of the subject. It is written with the belief that many of today's students fit in-between the above two groups. They need to include some elements of information technology in their studies which goes beyond just using computers into gaining a clear, broad and non-trivial understanding of information technology to prepare them for further challenges as a user, an academic or a provider of technical services. This book puts the emphasis on just the right amount of information to enable students either to take up a job involving IT at an administrative level and build on it for future development or proceed to a higher academic level with a view to specializing in a particular aspect of the subject.

The content

The structure of the book reflects the two main objectives. The first seven chapters give the basic facts behind the technology. They cover what constitutes information technology, where computers came from, what particular role each component fulfils, how they all work, what choices in technology are available and how to distinguish between them, and how to make computers work for us. An attempt has been made to give as much technical explanation as possible without sacrificing the basic principles of clarity and simplicity.

Having informed readers of the technology itself in a straightforward and uncomplicated way the last five chapters go on to meet the second aim, thus discussing the more intellectual issues of communication, security, health and safety, social impact and so on. These chapters are designed to equip students to think critically of subjects such as how computers can be used by individuals and organizations to gain competitive advantage, how to build a computer system that is acceptable to its users, what the best ways are to utilize the power of information technology but avoid its pitfalls, and what social issues we need to consider in order to find a balance between these two extremes.

Each chapter begins with a list of objectives and an introduction to the topics covered. Attempts have been made to address as many features and developments of the topics concerned as possible thus giving a very wide and up to date coverage. However, in order to comply with the needs of non-specialist students, the topics have been covered to a limited depth. The sections on further reading at the end of each chapter give indications of where more information can be obtained.

It is anticipated that most target students are going to experience the use of personal computers and common window-based software. The examples and illustrations are designed with this in mind with less emphasis on mainframe or other large computers and less common applications. 'Further investigation' questions (indicated by a magnifying glass) are inserted in the margins at appropriate points for students who want to go into deeper levels of the topics. These questions expect readers to find more information themselves in order to understand the subject at a greater depth. The chapters conclude with a summary.

Readers who wish to know more than what is covered in each chapter should find the books and articles mentioned in the further reading sections very useful. With this in mind, Internet references are often included assuming that students will have made themselves familiar with the Internet at an early stage of their studies. Sets of revision questions at the end of each chapter are designed to check that readers have understood and can remember the basic points. These are followed by a 'Food for thought' section which includes an article from a magazine or newspaper on a relevant subject. Discussion questions based on the article encourage students to think critically about the topics covered in the chapter and use their own initiative, individually or in groups, to explore deeper into the subject by independent research. This section is ideal as the basis for seminar discussions for an undergraduate course.

Teaching and learning guides

Students manual

This includes answers to the revision questions. Answers to the discussion questions are not provided because this would reduce the academic value of the 'Food for thought' sections.

Web site for instructors

This includes a bank of additional articles for 'Food for thought' together with questions, updates on materials covered in the book, some lecture notes (in due course) and a forum for discussion on the book's topics.

It is expected that the book will be revised every three years. Comments and discussions raised through the websites will be invaluable in the revision. The author expects to be able to use the book for her own undergraduate course which is also going to be an important source of feedback. It is hoped that eventually this book will fill an important gap in academia.

Nanda Bandyo-padhyay

ACKNOWLEDGEMENTS

Many people helped me to make my idea of a book a reality. I am grateful to Roisin Battel for editing the first, very unpolished draft of the book chapter by chapter. She used her command of the English language, her knowledge of the subject and her patience to make suggestions without which the book would not be completed. My sincere thanks must also go to Linda Stepulevage for making comments on a number of chapters and helping me with valuable material on certain topics. Thanks to the Department of Innovation Studies of the University of East London for the support and encouragement I received. Thanks also to Malcolm Richardson for his help with a number of the images. I am very grateful to Rick Branston and his staff in the IT department of the University of East London for allowing me to take photographs of their computer equipment and for taking a lot of trouble while I did so.

I must also thank staff at Pearson Education Ltd. for guiding me and co-operating with me at all levels especially Tina Cadle, Karen Sutherland and Kate Brewin. I am enormously grateful to Jackie Harbour who accepted my proposal and maintained her faith in me through the early and the most crucial part of the project.

I am thankful to my daughter Bidisha for being my inspiration. Finally, above all, I thank my mother for showing me how to fight against all odds.

We are grateful to the following for permission to reproduce copyright material:

An extract in Chapter 1 "Why there is no point in fighting progress" from *Computer Weekly*, 25 April, p 22, Reed Computer Group (Schofield, 1994); an extract in Chapter 2 "A chip off the new block" in *Computer Weekly*,

28th September p 20, Reed Computer Group (Fawcett, N. 1997); an extract in Chapter 3 "Mixing and matching opticals" in *Computing Canada*, 3 March, V 23 n 5 p 38, Plesman Publications (Kaufmann, J. 1997); an extract in Chapter 4 "Has Linux come of age" in *Computer Weekly* 14th January p 28, Reed Computer Group (Sweeting, P. 1999); an extract in Chapter 5 "Packages: one size fits all?" in *Information Week*, 2 October, n 547 p 136 CMP publications (Schofield, M. 1995); an extract in Chapter 7 "European banks play their (smart) card" from *BYTE* Magazine, April, printed with permisison from (Amdur, D. 1997); an extract in Chapter 8 "Intranet Design: hack through the tangle of the corporate intranet" in *Info World*, © 11 August, Infoworld Media Group, a subsidiary of IDG Communications, Inc., reprinted from InfoWorld, 155 Bovet Road, San Mateo, CA 94402 (Cate Cororan. T, 1997); an extract in Chapter 9 "A lesson to be learnt from the Indian culture" in *Computer Weekly*, 31 March, Reed Computer Group (Howard, A. 1994); an extract in Chapter 10 "Ergonomic Inaction: Congress puts OSHAs ergonomics standards on hold", January, published on the internet by CTD Resource Network, Inc. (Mogensen, V.); an extract in Chapter 11 "They want to be safe" in *Computer Weekly*, 18th June p 38, Reed Computer Group (Bicknell, D. 1998).

Figures 1.6, 1.7, 3.1 3.11c from Dell Computer Corporation Ltd. printed with permission; Figures 1.3b, 1.5, 3.11a, 3.11b, 3.12a-d original photographs are taken from the Computer Centre of the University of East London with permission; Figure 3.6 from web site www.computerware.co.uk reprinted with permission from Rik Alexander at Computerware; Figure 3.7 image of a Touchscreen from web site www.aut.sea.siemens.com reprinted with permission from Ken Fisher, Manager – Engineered Products, Siemens Energy and Automation Inc.; Figure 5.2 a newsletter, is printed with permission from Professor N. Miller, University of East London; Figure 9.3 "Complete DFD hotel booking" from *System Analysis, System Design*, p 211 Alfred Waller Ltd. Publishers (Mason & Willcocks, 1994); UEL web sites printed with permission from the web designer.

Whilst every effort has been made to trace the owners of copyright material, in a few cases this has proved impossible and we take this opportunity to offer our apologies to any copyright holders whose rights we may have unwittingly infringed.

Trademark notice

Acrobat and Photoshop (Adobe Systems Incorporated); AIX, As/400, OS/2, PS/2, PowerPc (International Business Machines Corporation (IBM)); Alpha, PDP, VAX, VME, VMS (Digital Equipment Corporation); Internet Explorer, MS-DOS, Windows 95, Windows 98, Windows 2000, Windows NT, Word for

Windows (Microsoft); HP-UX (Hewlett Packard Company); Intel Pentium, Pentium (Intel Corporation); iMac, Macintosh (Apple Computer Inc.); Elite (Netpower Inc.); NetWare (Novell Incorporated); Replica (Sybase Incorporated); Smartsuite (Lotus Development Corporation); Spectrum (Sun Microsystems Inc.); Unix (Licensed through X/Open Company Ltd.); WordPerfect (WordPerfect Corporation).

Introduction to information technology

Introduction

Information has been an essential part of our lives from the beginning of time and some kind of technology has always been used to handle it. At first, human beings used sticks and stones to draw on cave walls and on dusty ground to communicate with each other. They used drums and smoke signals to send information from one place to another. From this beginning they eventually progressed to pen and paper, they discovered printing technology for mass storage and introduced mail services to send information over long distances. It may seem unlikely to us today, but no matter how simple, all these methods are forms of technology which were considered to be a step forward at the time of introduction.

With time, as society progressed, the amount and complexity of information required by humans increased. Consequently, the level of sophistication of the technology used also increased to keep pace. With an ever growing demand for accurate and up to date information, new technologies were introduced to facilitate the way we record, process, store and transmit information. Pen and ink proved inadequate to record the vast amount of documentation involved in business transactions, and typewriters were invented. Calculating machines were developed to cope with the tedious mathematical calculations required in some commercial tasks; and tape recorders and dictaphones were used for long term storage and transmission of information.

Today, organizations handle large amounts of information. Let us use the example of a library: it needs to store information on books, borrowers, staff, equipment used, accounts, and much more. For a very small library such information can be written down, and provided there is a well planned system, it can also be accessed reasonably easily. However, many libraries these days are very large and the information they have to deal with is varied and vast. More than pen and paper are needed to organize this information in a way that enables the library staff to find it quickly. Progressively advancing technology has been used to handle such information, for example catalogues, index cards, microfiche readers and now computers. All these devices can be categorized as 'information technology' because they are all technical devices used to handle information, although some of the devices are technically much simpler than some others.

What is information technology?

Information technology (IT) is any technical device used to collect, store, process, access, manage and communicate information. There is a wide variety of machines used to do these tasks, such as computers, telephones, fax machines, televisions and so on. Information technology encompasses all of these; however in this book we will concentrate on computers and the devices associated with them. We will see what role computers play in performing the tasks mentioned above and how the use of computers affects our personal, social and professional lives. With this goal in mind, in this chapter we will consider the proliferation of computers in our lives at home and outside, take an overview of the origins of computers, and discuss the basic technical concepts behind the technology with a view to developing these concepts further in later chapters.

Computers in our lives

Although readers of this book are not expected to have any previous knowledge of computers, it is highly likely that most of you have some experience of the use of computers, either directly or indirectly. You may have used them at school or at work at a reasonably serious level or you may have been at the receiving end as a customer in a bank or a supermarket where an operator handles information on a computer in order to serve you. There are many other ways computers have entered our lives and made almost all of us, at least in the developed world, computer users one way or another. In the following section we will discuss how computers have penetrated all parts of our lives in a variety of ways.

Computers are now common desk-top machines for applications such as wordprocessing for dealing with text (traditionally done by typewriters), databases for handling filing systems, spreadsheets for handling facts and figures, graphics for producing images, accounts programs for handling a company's finance, and so on. They are now commercially available and are so widely used by businesses, educational institutions and individuals that it is very likely that many readers of this book are already acquainted with some of these applications. We will take a more detailed look at some of these applications in later chapters.

In the early 1990s, the advances in computer technology were faster than ever before. On the one hand, manufacturers of machines and applications introduced increasingly sophisticated products onto the market, while on the other, companies, large and small, continued to see the benefits of investment in IT. Now computers are no longer only the means for running business applications, they have entered all walks of our lives, and recently, have begun to blur the distinction between our work, home and social lives. Advances in technology, coupled with parallel innovation in the development of sophisticated computer programs, have revolutionized the concept of both work and leisure.

Nowadays computer technology can handle data[1] of almost any kind: text from a keyboard, sound from a tape and images from a camera. It has the power to process complicated data, the capacity to provide the large amount of space such data requires, the network technology to transmit it and the sophistication

---

1   The term 'data' is used to mean 'raw facts' such as a membership number, a price, a quantity, a grade, etc., which, by themselves are not very useful. A computer accepts such data items, combines them, processes them as asked and produces 'information'.

necessary to mix data of different kinds. Recent developments in application areas such as multimedia and virtual reality, coupled with advances in network technology, have revolutionized the influence of IT in modern living. Continuing miniaturization of the physical components of a computer has resulted in tiny silicon chips which can be used in small gadgets allowing computer power to be utilized in almost all areas of our lives. Scientists are now using the properties of an atom which can exist in two states – either in the same or the opposite direction of a magnetic field. What is more, an atom can stay in both these states at the same time. Thus, using a molecule consisting of more than one atom, a number of operations can be performed simultaneously. Research is also being carried out into using DNA, the basic biological building block, coated with silver to replace physical wire for electrical conduction. This would reduce the size of a chip to a small fraction of its current size. Since DNA can store an enormous amount of information in a very small space, it has been predicted that if/when this technology works (it is still at the beginning of its experimental stage), 'the content of the entire U.S. library of Congress would fit on a chip the size of a speck of dust' (*BYTEXTRA*, July 1998, p. 3) with predictable effects on the price and versatility of computers (see the list of Further reading for more information on this).

The following is a brief introduction to some of the ways IT has been integrated into our personal, social and occupational spheres.

Computers at home

Initially, many computers entered homes as children's games. But the trend spread fast, from simple games to more sophisticated ones. Soon they became a favourite pastime both for children and young adults. This group of people showed an almost natural ability to adapt to computers; software developers saw the opportunity for the market and developed increasingly challenging games as well as educational programs which made learning fun. Many parents were then tempted to buy computers for home use and this, in turn, led to a situation where people of all ages and backgrounds saw the benefit of computers not only for young people but also for adults who used them for personal and business purposes.

Another side of the use of computer technology at home came via the introduction of computer controlled household goods. Initially silicon chips were used in items such as calculators and watches to make them small and versatile; with time the technology became widely integrated with all types of personal and leisure products. Now we can have a microwave which tells us how to set and run it by displaying instructions on a tiny screen; while driving on a busy road we can get a program to detect traffic jams and find the easy route for us; we can have a personal organizer to keep track of our appointments and important dates, and store handwritten notes rather like a secretary; and we can control our lights and curtains in our homes while away on holiday.

Computers at work

Computers are now an integral part of most offices, the way telephones and type-writers were for a long time. Large organizations have been using computers since the 1960s or 1970s for processing business transactions in the areas of finance, inventory and so on. Smaller organizations adopted computers gradually as their size and cost came down, leading to the current situation where businesses of all sizes are dependent on them. Almost all employees now use computers or computer controlled instruments because they are an indispensable part of every aspect of most businesses. The following list (which, in no way, is complete) gives an idea of the variety of the types of applications which are facilitated by computers: controlling the movement of a satellite, working out the payroll of a company, controlling the processing in a chemical plant, testing product qualities, making medical diagnoses, teaching children at school, making weather forecasts, writing letters, answering customer queries and designing cars. Our dependence on computers is so high that in the 1990s a vast amount of effort was put in to combating the so-called millenium bug[2] in order to avoid a variety of predicted disasters.

Mixing data by multimedia

Multimedia is the convergence of information generated by media (devices) of all kinds, such as cameras, audio tapes, and computer disks. Text, graphics, narration, music, still and moving pictures and animation can be computerized (turned into electronic signals), mixed with each other and held on a CD-ROM, a device similar to a music CD used for storing data. This, together with powerful software, allows users to create high quality presentations which not only can be very useful for the entertainment industry, they can also have valuable applications in training. Using a powerful computer equipped with speakers, a sound card and a large amount of

---

2 Most computer programs written in the 1990s and before catered for two digits to represent a year. Thus 1998 is written as 98. This means that the year 2000 will appear as 00 and could be confused with 1900, causing unimaginable problems for date-dependent programs. Some such programs are used by a computer's ROM, a storage space inside the computer out of reach of ordinary users, holding programs responsible for starting a computer when switched on. These programs, unless corrected, could cause the most serious problems.

storage, you can run a program interactively. For example, you can get an overview of the life and work of Beethoven; you can see the composition of the Ninth Symphony on-screen and choose which bits to play; you can replace volumes of printed encyclopaedias by one CD-ROM with the added benefit of search by keywords and demonstrations by moving pictures and sound. Multimedia has made educational programs enormously interesting by mixing the video of the instructions given by a teacher with other materials such as text, diagrams and computer demonstrations. It also allows users to adapt programs to their own levels by running them interactively by choosing different routes. This has opened up the scope for the use of multimedia techniques to large scale education and training by creating virtual classes supported by networked computers often in users' homes without the need for the presence of a teacher. As is evident from the above example, multimedia offers the convergence of different industries such as computers, electronics, communications, education and entertainment.

The virtual world

We have known of the existence of flight simulation programs used for the training of airline pilots for more than 10 years; this was the beginning of virtual reality. As its name suggests, virtual reality means entering an imaginary environment as if it were real. It is made possible by creating a three-dimensional graphic representation of a real world situation and mapping the reactions and movements of a human being into that world. The user has to wear headgear and attachments to other parts of the body, and the software is made to register the movement of the eyes, limbs and head of the user. This makes it possible for users to feel as if they are inside the environment displayed on the screen because as they change position the graphics reorientate to suit the new perspective. Thus a person can visit a virtual library, take a close look at the books on the virtual shelves and even pick up a book and read it. Virtual reality can be used in the medical field by allowing trainee doctors to perform operations on virtual patients; also a doctor situated far away from a real patient can see the computerized image of the patient and perform an operation by controlling robotics equipment remotely via his or her computer screen. Obviously this is an expensive technology only affordable by very large organizations at the moment. Also, concerns have been expressed about the safety of the headgear used. However, the cost of the technology is coming down fast and alternatives to the headgear are likely to be invented which should enable virtual reality to find its way into many common applications such as shopping, by taking a virtual walk in a supermarket, architecture, by allowing a designer to see the result of a design from within a virtual building, regular medical operations, and so on.

Linking people electronically

The true value of computers cannot be realized fully by using an isolated system, limited by the technology accessible to that system only. We need networks linking a number of computers together to allow them to share resources. This could be a simple intra-company network used for sharing data within an organization, or it could be inter-company for exchanging data on a wider basis. Electronic data interchange (EDI) has been used widely by large organizations for some time, for example by the banks for international fund transfer and by multinational companies for fast communication.

Recently, the power of networking has been brought down to the individual level by the introduction of the Internet. Originally developed and still subsidized by the United States government, the Internet is a network of networks connecting worldwide academic institutions, business organizations and now, individuals. It enables users anywhere on the network to send and receive documents, chat to other users, shop, pay bills, book tickets for various events, amongst many other things.

Networks have also transformed the way people hold business meetings and conferences. Video-conferencing is a growing application area, made possible by the combination of networks and multimedia, where data in all forms can travel through the network allowing the transmission of pictures and voices over long distances. Groups of users at different locations can now talk to and see each other on monitors. This has made it possible to hold conferences without the necessity of making expensive and time consuming journeys.

Currently the trend is towards combining computer and communications technologies, for example, digital television, the combination of TV and the Internet, computer and telephone integration (CTI) and much more. Details of all these are outside the scope of this book but you may like to read a computer newspaper such as *Computer Weekly* or *Computing* to stay in touch with such advances.

Computer networks create the potential for the world to become a so-called 'global village' because distance is almost no barrier for communication. However, some would argue that only a fraction of the world's total population has access to computers or is affected by them in any way. On the one hand IT has opened many doors and given some of us new opportunities. On the other, concerns have also been expressed over the social value of such ventures. The scope that electronic communication offers and the concerns it raises will both be discussed in more detail later on in the book.

There are numerous other application areas which take advantage of computers. Amongst these are *robotics* which make computer controlled machines perform functions normally performed by humans, for example in car assembly plants; *expert systems* which work by making computers take expert type decisions by following logic based rules, for example in locating the source of a malfunctioning machine; and *neural networks* which try to copy the complicated way the human brain learns and makes decisions. The obvious goal is to bridge the gap between humans and the machine. Technically this may or may not be possible but whether computers can be made to acquire common sense, emotions or the ability to understand unclear statements remains a matter of continuing debate. Full discussion of all these technologies is outside the scope of this book (see the list of Further reading for more information on this) but we will revisit some of the concepts mentioned here in later chapters.

Try to find examples of some recent applications of computer technology in our everyday lives. How do they affect you?

Computers and information

So, how do computers help in handling information? Let us use the example of a library again because most libraries in the developed world use computers these days. When you join a library you are given a membership card. The card holds a bar code containing your membership number. When you borrow a book, the librarian uses a scanner linked to a computer to read the code which is then used to search a file held on a computer to access your membership details. Each book in the library also contains a bar code. At the time of issuing, these codes are also read by the computer and the information is linked to your details. Thus a computer system stores the information on the books a member borrows, the date they are due back and so on.

Reading the bar codes and processing the information takes a computer a fraction of the time it would take human beings to handle the information manually. There is also less chance of error. The information is held centrally by the computer and can be used by any member of the library staff. Information can be updated easily and accessed quickly. A computerized system can also be used to produce reminders for members holding overdue books, orders to suppliers for new books, reports on the usage of books and so on. Thus information technology enables the library to manage information in a way that ensures efficient running of the organization without having to rely totally on the alertness and efficiency of the staff.

Organizations of all sizes deal with information. In the 1960s, many companies set up data processing departments with large and expensive computers running complicated programs. Today, most computers are small enough to fit on a desk and cost relatively little, but offer enormous processing power. Things have not stopped here: now computers come in increasingly smaller sizes: a small briefcase, a notebook or even pocket-sized. This, together with the increasing amount of information generated by organizations to keep up with the demands of modern living, has necessitated the ever more widespread use of computers.

The evolution of computers

So, how did computers evolve from being large and exclusive machines to the desktop personal computers (PCs) that we are so familiar with today? In order to understand this evolution you need to have an idea of the computer's main parts. A computer is basically a data crunching machine working in three main stages: *input*, *process* and *output*. It accepts raw data (input), works with it (process), and produces useful information (output). It has strict limitations on how or in what format the data has to be given to it but we will not go into those details as yet. At the time of processing, the data is held in a space inside the computer known as its memory and the information produced can be printed or stored in a storage medium such as a disk (see Figure 1.1). The physical

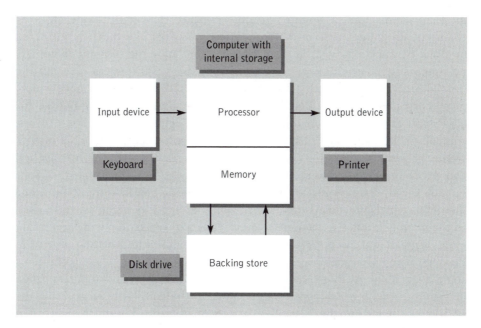

Figure 1.1: The components of a computer system with the shaded boxes indicating physical devices

devices used to do all this, for example, the keyboard to enter data, the computer to process it, the printer to print and the disk to store are known as *hardware*. However, these are simply machines which cannot do anything unless specific instructions in the form of programs and the necessary data to process (such as the membership numbers in our library example) are given to them. *Software* is the term used to refer to data and programs. Programs using specific languages are written by human beings, which also demonstrates the relative superiority of humans over computers although computers can perform tasks much faster and more accurately than their human counterparts. Some programs are general purpose in nature and are meant to operate and control hardware: these are called *systems software*, the most common example of which is an operating system such as Microsoft Windows 98 (or the more recently introduced Windows 2000). Their purpose is to make sure a user can use a computer easily, that data from the keyboard is understood by the computer, that the printer prints when asked to, that if anything goes wrong the user is given a message and so on. *Applications software* on the other hand, runs specific applications such as a game, a library system or a students' registration system in a university. A common example of applications software with which many of you are probably familiar is a wordprocessing program which is used to create documents such as letters, reports, essays and newsletters. We will discuss hardware and software in greater detail later on in the book.

In the 1960s and 1970s computers were large machines often kept in air-conditioned rooms out of bounds to anyone other than skilled operators or engineers. Programmers wrote their programs on paper and these were entered on cards by punching holes in them by data entry staff and fed into computers by operators. After the programs were run, the programmers received the printed results together with a list of any errors (called error messages), which, when corrected, were re-entered. In those days computers were only used for large applications such as payroll, for working out employees' pay-slips, or stock control, for keeping track of goods in stock and so on. Large amounts of data were sent periodically to the computer centre where they were run in 'batches' and the results were sent to the relevant departments. Thus, the members of staff outside the operations section had no direct contact with computers. Some 'dumb' terminals (keyboards and screens without any processing power) linked to the main computer were used by secretaries and typists for wordprocessing letters, reports and so on, or to view a limited amount of information on screen. Printers were sometimes placed in different locations for producing copies of some documents. At that time most organizations used large computers called mainframes which needed special environments and specialist users. From the mid-1970s 'minicomputers' (smaller than the mainframe, but much larger than today's desktop computers) started entering the scene, which changed the situation to a certain extent. Minicomputers were cheaper, smaller in size and less powerful than mainframes but were slightly more robust. Some of them also came with their own keyboards and monitors (screens) and, for the first time, users other than the operations staff had direct access to a computer system. However, they were still expensive items and their maintenance required specialist knowledge. Small organizations were not able to afford computer power and had to stick with manual systems or use the services of other companies for applications such as their monthly payroll.

Personal computers were introduced in the late 1970s to early 1980s. As we have seen, the trend started off with small home computers mainly for playing games. As technology advanced, more powerful machines were manufactured, slowly the prices came down and by the mid-1980s PCs were widely used in homes, educational institutions and in small businesses. PCs have now become powerful and versatile enough to enter organizations of all sizes as desktop machines running common business data processing applications such as wordprocessing, accounts and databases (which are a collection of documents interlinked in such a way that information can be obtained from any of the documents to produce lists and reports), as well as forming parts of a network sharing resources with other computers of various types and sizes. Now the trend is to move away from the centralized systems supported by mainframes towards a system of clusters of networked PCs in turn connected to each other by a midrange (the modern term for a mini) computer or a powerful PC. This is made possible by the enormous growth in the speed and power of PCs in recent times. In the following section we will take a more systematic look at how generations of computers have evolved and how software has moved forward to take advantage of the innovations.

Surf the Internet or look at some computer magazines/newspapers to find the names of some mainframes and minicomputers used today. What types of jobs are they used for?

Generations of computers

The first commercially available computers worked with *vacuum tubes* – electronic *valves* which control the flow of electricity. They were introduced in the 1950s and were called **first generation** computers. Each computer contained a large number of valves and the memory (the internal storage space) was made out of magnetic rings. Together, they occupied a lot of space making computers very large in size.

The language used for programming was machine code consisting of a series of 0s and 1s (also called first generation language). The presence of so many valves caused overheating and they often burnt out after a while and needed replacing. Thus, first generation computers were cumbersome machines, difficult to use and maintain, and extremely expensive. This, coupled with the difficulty of writing programs in machine code, stood in the way of their becoming a commercial success.

Second generation computers were introduced in the mid-1960s following the invention of *transistors*. Transistors served the same purpose as valves but were much smaller in size because they worked by using a semiconductor made of a chemical element with special electronic properties. This was a big step forward because transistors offered higher speed, reliability, efficiency and economy, allowing computers to become both smaller and cheaper. This development was matched with the development in programming languages, first by the introduction of low level languages (called the second generation language) using abbreviations of English words or 'mnemonics' and then, high level languages (the third generation) using English words. The productivity of programmers improved considerably because they could now write programs faster, and of increasing complexity. This made both computer hardware and software economically viable for large organizations. However, computing was still out of the reach of most businesses.

Third generation computers were introduced in the mid to late 1960s following the development of *integrated circuits* (see Figure 1.2). These are electrical circuits etched on silicon chips: small crystals of a semiconductor material. One silicon chip can hold a large amount of circuitry. They can be mass produced

Figure 1.2: An integrated circuit

easily and cheaply, thus reducing the size and cost of computers and consequently making them affordable to many organizations.

The terms 'mainframe' and 'minicomputer' were introduced at the same time. The larger computers with higher speed, larger memory and higher processing power were called *mainframes* and those with lower specifications were known as *minis*[3] (Figure 1.3). The prices and complexity also varied accordingly. This gave the consumer a choice and made it possible for medium-sized organizations such as universities, hospitals and local authorities to computerize their systems. Data processing departments were set up in many organizations and most of them employed their own data processing staff to develop the software they needed. Those who could not introduce computers in their own organizations were able to buy the services provided by a bureau. Some of the minicomputers were small enough to come in the form of workstations and looked similar to today's large PCs.

(a)

(b)

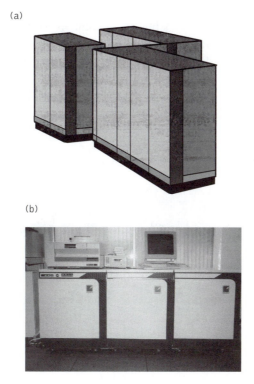

Figure 1.3: (a) A mainframe and (b) a minicomputer

---

3   Currently the term 'minicomputer' seems to be giving way to 'midrange'.

IBM (International Business Machine) has dominated the mainframe market from the beginning (late 1950s) although there were other manufacturers such as ICL who had a significant presence. During the past 35 to 40 years both mainframes and minis have made continuous progress and they still form the backbones of large corporate computer systems and as host (the main supporting) computers in a network. IBM has recently announced the release of its S/390 mainframe which is capable of processing 900 millions of instructions per second. Manufacturers such as Amdahl and Hitachi are also powerful players in the mainframe market. Digitial Equipment Corporation (DEC), now owned by Compaq, maintained a steady presence in the minicomputer market for a long time, initially (in the 1970s) with its PDP range and more recently with brand names such as VAX. IBM also has a large share of the minicomputer market with its AS/400 series.

During the 1970s, rapid miniaturization took place and it became possible to produce a complete processor on one silicon chip (Figure 1.4). These are called *microprocessors* and the computers built with them are known as *microcomputers* and are classed as the **fourth generation** computers. Initially these were marketed as home computers. They had no monitors and had to be connected to domestic television sets for display. Storage devices were magnetic tapes similar to audio cassettes. The Spectrum ZX80 invented by Clive Sinclair was the first such computer commercially available in the UK. Mostly school-age children used them for playing games.

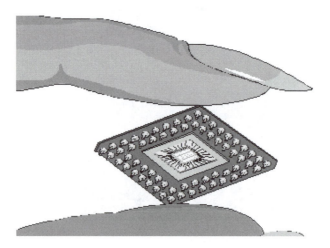

Figure 1.4: A silicon chip

However, as the technology improved, the capabilities of microcomputers also improved and soon complete systems with their own monitors (or visual display units, VDUs), disk drives (the slots for disks) and connections for printers and other hardware devices were introduced. Companies such as Commodore and Acorn introduced their own brand of micros and many programs were written for education and computer-based games. The earliest micros had only about 64 KB (1 KB=1024 characters; this will be explained in more detail in later chapters) of memory which means they could only hold a little more than 64,000 characters, and programs had to be copied from removable (floppy) disks every time they were used since they had no disks attached to them (Figure 1.5). The floppies were normally 5.25" square and they had a storage capacity of about 360 KB. Microcomputers have improved dramatically since those days and have entered all spheres of our personal and working lives, offering enormous speed, storage capacity and processing power. We will discuss the progressive development of PCs in greater detail in the next section.

At the other end of the scale, another range of computers entered the market in the early to mid-1980s. These were **supercomputers** which offer more power and speed than mainframes and can support a large number of networked computers and other peripheral hardware. They contain a large number of small processors and their design is such that a number of instructions can be carried out at the same time, thus increasing the speed by a large extent. Supercomputers are very expensive and are normally used for applications requiring complicated processing and fast response, for example weather forecasting, space research, molecular modelling in the drugs industry, and safety testing in car design. A company called Cray Research was the first to manufacture supercomputers commercially and is now one of the leaders in the hardware and software market in this field. It has had strong competition from some Japanese companies (NEC, for example) with

Figure 1.5: An old micro

their high performance machines at lower prices. NEC also offers the power of supercomputing to smaller businesses by allowing them to use their computers remotely via the Internet for a reasonable hourly rate. However, Cray has managed to maintain its dominance in the market, especially following a merger with another company called Silicon Graphics. Together, they produce computers that range from very powerful desktop versions to large supercomputers. They are in the process of developing a supercomputer called CRAY Origin2000 which allows customers to buy a computer with a small number of processors and to add more as their needs grow (see the section on Further reading for more information on supercomputers). This has added flexibility to the power of Cray and is expected to become the industry standard in the new century.

Look for the names of some companies (other than Cray) which manufacture super-computers. What are they used for?

The so-called **fifth generation** computer is still on the drawing board. Initiated by the Japanese, this is the result of an attempt to reduce the distance between computers and human beings. Based on high level research in artificial intelligence, expert systems (computer systems used to make expert decisions) and natural language development for computers, scientists are trying to make computers which can perform tasks normally expected of humans. A human brain contains a large number of tissues called neurons which carry data through electrical pulses. Neurons work in a very sophisticated way which allows the brain not only to retain a lot of information but also to use experiences to build up a set of rules which allows it to process data even when it is unclear and ambiguous to produce meaningful information. Research has been going on to create a neural network artificially in an attempt to give computers the same capability. The success of this depends to a large extent on whether or not it is possible to mimic the complexity of the human brain. Opinions amongst experts are divided on this matter: some believe that even if it is possible to build a computer which can be taught to make decisions by making logical deductions based on rules supplied by human beings, a machine cannot be taught to imitate the way humans use perception, intuition and context to make decisions or the way they use information to accumulate knowledge. Others think differently. Look at the section on Further reading for more information on artificial intelligence and fifth generation computers.

What do you think about the possibility of making computers behave like human beings? To what extent can they behave (and not behave) like humans?

The journey of the PC

The early microcomputers became very popular because they opened doors to small businesses, schools and colleges as well as home users who, for the first time, were able to afford computer power. A demand was created in the market for micros as business computers. This encouraged large computer manufacturers to get involved. IBM, already a market leader in the larger computer market, saw this as an opportunity and, in collaboration with Intel, the microprocessor manufacturer, introduced a range of personal computers in 1981. The first was known as IBM/XT and was based on a microprocessor called Intel 8086.[4] These computers had 64–128 KB of memory, they used floppy disks which could hold 160–320 KB of data (today they can hold more than a billion bytes) and a monochrome monitor, and yet prices were in the range of £2000–£3500 (today you can get an entry level PC for much less than £1000).

Following this, the IBM/AT series with Intel chips of progressively higher specifications (called 80286/80386/80486), with increasing speed and processing power, were introduced. The design of the processor changed correspondingly and together they offered increasingly better performance in terms of speed, memory capacity, processing power and flexibility. Computers came with an attached disk drive, called the hard drive, equipped to hold large amounts of programs and data permanently, and the capacity of floppy disks also increased correspondingly. IBM made a deal with the software company Microsoft which produced an operating system called MS-DOS and applications software designed to work with Intel chips only. This helped IBM, Intel and Microsoft to establish a monopoly in the market and other companies wanting to enter the personal computer market were forced to follow the same chip/operating system combination. Thus, most PCs during the 1980s became IBM 'clones' to the extent that the term PC became synonymous with IBM-compatible microcomputers. Examples of companies manufacturing such PCs include Compaq, Olivetti, Amstrad and Dell. Software developers joined this race by writing programs compatible with the PC, thus completing the circle.

IBM produced another range of computers in its personal computer series with higher expansion capabilities (scope for adding extra features) and greater speed and called it *Personal computer series 2* (PS/2). PS/2s were expected to take over from PCs but this did not happen, mainly because the PC already had an established market which proved difficult to break into. In 1993–4 IBM

---

4   This followed a brief period of Intel 8088 processors of even lower specifications.

diverted from its old range of Intel processors in the x86 series to a faster and more powerful microprocessor called the Pentium manufactured by the same company. After some initial problems this was accepted as being capable of providing state of the art features and increasingly high processing speeds. The first Pentium was called the Pentium Pro and currently Pentium III is in widespread use. They incorporate a technology called MMX (Multi-media extension) which can process graphical data much faster than before. However, the future of this technology is in doubt and there are other, more advanced technologies in the pipeline, which are likely to replace MMX soon. Other processors in the PC market include Digital's (now Compaq's) 64-bit Alpha (a working name), and Cyrix's MediaGx which integrates multimedia functions into the main processor. Other companies in this game include AMD and Centaur/IDT, both trying to beat Intel[5] by developing technology capable of handling three-dimensional graphics better and faster.

The main exception to the trend started by IBM was led by Apple Computer, Inc. with its *Macintosh* range of computers. These were based on a family of microprocessors (known as the 68000 range) manufactured by Motorola. They used their own operating system with an easy to use screen display, point and click features which enabled users to choose options by selecting icons on screen rather than using written commands and their own brand of applications software. Apple specialized in graphics and desktop-publishing packages (software which allows users to produce documents of professional quality) and has been able to maintain a steady influence amongst a dedicated group of followers, in particular magazine companies and designers, interested in user friendly graphical interfaces with high quality presentation. In the early 1990s, Apple and IBM collaborated in producing a microcomputer which was compatible with both PC and Apple applications: the result was a personal computer called PowerPC. The venture was largely unsuccessful and PowerPC made little impact in the market, first because the collaboration did not work and secondly, it could not stand in the competition against the PC. However, nowadays both Apple and IBM computers often come with the necessary software to allow users to use the other's applications programs. Recently, Motorola has announced the development of a new processor capable of performing complicated operations very fast by handling large chunks of data together. This is a technology called AltiVec to be used in the PowerPC range and expected to rival Intel's MMX. The rivalry between Apple and IBM is an old one and is at the root of many innovative ideas.

---

5 Recently some of these manufacturers have agreed on some common standards in processor design.

There were other companies who produced microcomputers mainly for home users and the educational market. Some well known brand names in this category were BBC Micro, Acorn, Archimedes and Amstrad. These were relatively inexpensive machines and came with a large selection of software, both good reasons for gaining popularity in their intended markets and allowing them widespread entry in schools and colleges. Some companies also manufactured personal computer systems not compatible with IBM, for example, Olivetti's M10 and NEC's 8201A, but they had a very limited exposure to common users and eventually most of them opted for some degree of PC compatibility.

The trend towards making computers smaller and more accessible continued with the PCs (see Figure 1.6). As chips were able to hold increasing amounts of circuitry, laptops, notebooks and eventually palmtops were introduced (Figure 1.7). *Laptops* are PCs the size of a small briefcase with the processor, disk drive and keyboard on the base and a screen inside the cover. They can be battery or mains powered and can use both hard and floppy disks as well as CD-ROMs.

Figure 1.6: A modern PC.

Source: Dell Computer Corporation Ltd

(a)   (b)

Figure 1.7: (a) A laptop (b) A notebook
Source: Dell Computer Corporation Ltd

Together with portable printers, they offer mobile computing and are popular in today's fast and aggressive business market. We no longer have to come back to our desks to work on documents held on disk: we can complete work that we started in the office on our way home on the train (although often to the annoyance of other travellers); sales representatives can have access to up-to-date information in a client's office; and politicians can carry on working while on their way from one country to another. *Notebooks* and *palmtops* are similar to laptops, only progressively smaller in size and thus more mobile and have more widespread uses. You can take a notebook computer to a meeting in order to look at important documents and take notes; some members of the police force carry palmtops to access information on suspected criminals quickly. Initially, the convenience of portability was achieved at the cost of clarity of display, quality of keyboard and memory size, but this is fast becoming untrue.

Do a survey of the 'small' computers in use today, and the way they are used.

How PCs changed the nature of organizations and the concept of users

As technology progressed PCs offered increasing choice and flexibility to users. Monitors capable of handling sophisticated graphics were developed; very high quality and fast printers at affordable prices were introduced; and new and innovative input devices such as mouse, light pen, touch-screen and voice input were brought in for fast and convenient data entry. Now PCs are built with a large amount of memory and come with high capacity hard and floppy disk drives as well as CD-ROMs thus offering a large capacity for storage. We will discuss the precise nature of each of these devices and the options available later on in the book.

Software developers also kept up with innovations by introducing increasingly powerful software capable of taking advantage of the progress in technology. As a result many organizations which previously had used only large computers for their networks began to consider 'downsizing' to PC based systems. Use of PCs in this way offered users the flexibility of using common PC based packaged applications as well as larger, more centralized business systems.

Thus the role of PCs changed from games machines to sophisticated business computers widely used in industry within 20 years. The role of users also changed accordingly. In the past only those with specialist training in computer hardware and software could work closely with computers. As PCs became integrated into homes and educational institutions and software became cheaper and more user friendly, the distance between computer experts and non-experts reduced fast. The main driving force behind the accessibility of a PC to its users has been the software developers. The ease of use of modern applications with graphical representations on screen designed to represent the real world has encouraged many users, previously apprehensive of the technology, to accept computers at work. This, in turn, has led to widespread integration of PCs at all levels of work. Many organizations networked their computers to share hardware and software resources. Large retailers, banks and building societies, hospitals and other such institutions built on-line information systems dealing with the operation of an entire organization and available to the staff for use and update via desktop machines. This changed the pattern of the service industry completely. These days PCs are seen as part and parcel of a modern office and the myth that those who use computers are somehow brighter than the others has disappeared. There is, of course, still a role for computer scientists/experts for specialized jobs such as developing and maintaining new hardware and software, in teaching, research and so on, but ordinary people in all spheres of society and in almost all types of jobs have now become computer users sometimes without even realizing the enormous transition.

How would your working/student life be different if we did not have PCs?

Summary

The term 'IT revolution' has often been used in the past decade to describe the fast development of computer technology and its rapid diffusion throughout our society. It can be argued that another revolution has just started in which information technology has begun to blur the distinction between work and leisure, and wipe out the barrier of time and place mainly through the introduction of widespread national and international networks. Users of IT can access information in almost any form, crossing any boundaries, over any distance. Medical operations can now be performed by a surgeon thousands of miles away from the patient. Colleagues in different continents can hold meetings and students can attend lectures without leaving their homes. Whether this is for best for human society is a matter for argument.

In the past 25 to 30 years computers have progressed from large, cumbersome, relatively slow, specialist machines to small, fast, robust, user friendly tools used in every sphere of our lives. In the past large companies used mainframes for routine data processing tasks and PCs were used by individuals at home or for small businesses. The emphasis has moved towards networked PCs because they offer the flexibility of centralized systems as well as desktop use of common applications such as wordprocessing and databases. Mobile computing is another outcome of the evolution of PCs.

Further reading

For more information on the history of computers read Chapter 1 of *Computers in Your FUTURE 98* by Roberta Baber and Marilyn Meyer, Que Education & Training, 1998. Also *Engines of the Mind: The Evolution of the Computer from Mainframes to Microprocessors* by Jeel Shurkin, W.W. Norton & Company, 1996, gives a history of the inventors of and inventions in computer technology.

More information on supercomputers is also available from Chapter 2 of Barber and Meyer's book. Also, look at the website http://www.fys.ruu.nl/~steen/overview/overview97.html for an overview of recent supercomputers.

Read the following books for more on artificial intelligence: *Reflections on Artificial Intelligence, Legal, Moral and Ethical Dimensions* by Blay Whitby, Intellect Books, 1996, and *Beyond Information, The Natural History of Intelligence* by Tom Stonier, Springer-Verlag, 1992. The latter covers the development of fifth generation computers as well.

Read the article on DNA computing in the July 1998 copy of *BYTE* from www.byte.com. Weekly magazines such as *Computing* and *Computer Weekly*, both of which publish their articles in the CD-ROM called *Computer Select*, are good sources of information. Read them regularly for up-to-date information on all aspects of computing. References to specific items of information taken from the magazines are given in appropriate places in the text.

Revision questions

1. You will find out more about the concepts we introduced in Chapter 1 later on in the book. For the moment, discuss the *basic* difference between the following pairs of terms:

    (a) input and output;
    (b) memory and backing storage;
    (c) hardware and software;
    (d) applications software and systems software;
    (e) first generation computers and second generation computers;
    (f) third generation computers and fourth generation computers;
    (g) machine code and high level language;
    (h) transistors and integrated circuits;
    (i) mainframes and PCs;
    (j) IBM PCs and Apple Macintosh.

2. List some of the computer applications you have come across remembering that not all applications incorporate a typical computer with a conventional keyboard or a monitor.

3. Can you put these applications into any of the categories (wordprocessing, database, and so on) mentioned in the chapter? If not how would you describe them?

4. List the terms used in the chapter that you did not understand and try to find out, either by discussing with other students or by looking at some elementary books, the meaning of the terms.

Food for thought

Computer Weekly, 25 August 1994, p.22
Reed Business Publishing Ltd (UK)

Why there is no point in fighting progress
Jack Schofield

One of the amusing things IBM is supposed to stand for is 'It's Better Manually'. All computer users, whatever their brand of machine, sometimes wonder whether it ▶

wasn't easier doing things the old way. Often it was. Usually, however, computers produce better results, or save work somewhere else.

Journalists – the ones who don't wear anoraks – often suffer from regressive feelings. Someone shows them how to flow their copy into a page layout program, blow up the type to 200%, correct their mistakes and make it fit.

Great, thanks. But could they do all they needed with Locoscript on an Amstrad PCW? Of course they could. Indeed, they could do it with a manual typewriter. But why stop there? Why not cut a quill pen and write an article long-hand, illustrating it with elaborate caps illuminated with gold leaf? That way they would also be directly responsible for the content and appearance of their text.

For a publisher, word processing means you don't need someone to typeset the copy, and there's less need for proof-reading to eliminate typos – so proof-readers have lighter workloads, if they don't disappear altogether.

Writers can simply dump their electronic copy into the typesetting computer. And if they can deliver plain text, why can't they deliver text in the correct typeface, already laid out with headlines and captions?

Photographers used to submit original prints or slides, and publishers would send them away for fourcolour separations to be made for printing. Now photographers can use digital cameras or do their own scanning, make separations and upload files ready for printing. Programs like Adobe Photoshop let them change the colour and contrast of their images, retouch them, move figures around, and paste in bits of other pictures to get the desired result. (And if you haven't got the negative in your hand, how can you tell what they've done?)

For some purposes, half a dozen musicians using real instruments can similarly be replaced by one person with a synthesiser and Midi software, who can cut and paste bits out of previous compositions.

But we're still mixing the old and new systems. The next step might be to bypass the old system altogether. Who needs publishers? Who needs to print things? Why not just distribute them electronically, not as Postscript files (too big) but using a reader like Adobe Acrobat or Farallon's Replica. Why record music and manufacture old-fashioned discs and tapes? Music files can be posted online so that listeners can simply download them and play them on their own computers.

Why go to a car showroom to look at a car? A program could let buyers specify exactly what they wanted (engine size, seats, colour scheme, extras), try it out in a virtual reality simulation, then feed their order direct to the robots on the production line. Every industry has many intermediaries who can be removed by computerisation.

This is the wired society, and it's the way we're heading. Once you've let the genie called Progress out of the bottle, it's impossible to get it back.

Discussion questions

1. Critically review the author's views on how the world of publishing has been changed by the introduction of computers.

2. The article was written in 1994. Try to find out how things have moved since then.

3. Discuss your own feelings about the changes. Who has benefited from them and who has lost? How have such changes affected our lives in general?

4. What do you think about the changes in the music business and in car salesrooms? Describe, from your own experience, some other areas which have been affected in similar ways.

5. Critically discuss the last paragraph of the article.

CHAPTER 2

How computers work

Objectives

After reading this chapter you should have some understanding of:

- the fundamental principles behind a computer;
- what we mean by a computer system;
- the role of the components of a computer;
- how a computer stores data;
- how a computer processes data.

Introduction

Computers are complicated and powerful machines but with a limited ability to do anything without a number of other components working with them. Collectively, they are called a 'computer system'. Without these components a computer would be a useless piece of machinery, as human beings would be without their abilities to think, gather and store knowledge and experience, apply reasoning and, above everything, coordinate these intellectual activities with physical actions. Just as we humans have to be taught, one way or another, how to do all these things and somehow be given the information we need, computers have to be given the data to process and instructions on how to do so. Humans use their brains and their intellectual resources to make decisions and their sensual devices to communicate with the rest of the world; computers use a processor and the data and instructions to produce useful information and the other components to communicate with the outside world. In this chapter we are going to look at what these components are and how a computer works with the resources given to it in order to perform its tasks.

The computer as a concept

Before we go into the depth of the discussion on how a computer works, let us discuss the basic concept on which a computer is built and the principles behind its operation. The word computer comes from the verb 'to compute' which means to calculate, that is, to add, subtract, multiply, divide and so on. A calculator can perform only a limited amount of such tasks using the circuitry built into it.[1] The precursors of the computer were machines that mainly performed arithmetic. In 1642 Blaise Pascal, a French philosopher, invented the first known calculating machine since the Chinese abacus (which is still used in some parts of the world) and the slide rule (also still in use) which could perform more complicated calculations. In 1671 Gottfried Leibnitz, a German philosopher, improved on this by making his machine add, subtract, multiply and divide. Between 1802 and 1804 Joseph Jacquard, a French textile manufacturer, used special punched cards representing the patterns in a cloth to control the weaving action on his weaving machine. Thus mechanical action was automated by Jacquard for the first time. This was followed by Charles Babbage (1792–1871), an English mathematician, who designed a so-called analytical (conceptual) engine to automate calculations in 1834. This was the first machine which incorporated many features of a modern computer including storage facilities for data and instructions. Lady Ada Lovelace, the daughter of Lord Byron and a mathematician and a friend of Babbage, wrote the instructions for it. Unfortunately it was never built.

---

1   Incidentally, today's calculators often contain silicon chips which allow them to do much more than just simple arithmetic.

Many other people contributed to the progress of the concept of automation; you can get more information on this by reading some of the publications mentioned in the list of Further reading. However, the concept of what a computer might be in reality took a leap forward in the mind of Alan Turing (1912–54). Turing was a mathematician and a logician. During the Second World War he worked for the British government on breaking German codes. Turing invented an imaginary machine, in other words, a concept, consisting of two parts: a sliding device with a set of rules built into it, and a sequence of squares marked on a tape of unlimited length with a symbol written on each square (see Figure 2.1). The machine moves along the tape reading each square, responding to the symbol on the square (each symbol has in-built rules) and moving on to the next square in either direction (according to the instructions in the symbol). Responding to the symbol normally involves writing on the square; this could be a new symbol or the same symbol. Since the machine can move in either direction, it can come back and read or update a previously printed square, thus making it possible to use the tape to store a large amount of information. The machine itself is very simple, only capable of responding in a certain way to the symbols, but by combining the symbols on the tape and the corresponding movement of the tape, complicated tasks can be performed.

Thus, the Turing machine introduced a new concept: a simple machine can be made to do complex things if it is given complex instructions broken down into very simple stages. This is the principle that underpins the working of a computer: the machine is the hardware which remains the same but does different things depending on what the instructions, that is the software, asks it to do. Computers were modelled on this concept in the years that followed.

About ten years after Turing described his imaginary machine, a group of scientists and mathematicians in the USA decided to make it a reality. Foremost amongst them was a mathematician, originally from Hungary, called Jon Von Neumann who first suggested the concept of a central processing unit (CPU) and memory. The memory contains the instructions, the data to compute and the results, all coded in the form of binary numbers. The CPU is an electronic device

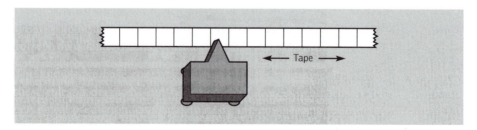

Figure 2.1: A Turing machine

which only understands electronic signals of two types – the presence of a signal which it knows as 1 and the absence of it, which is a 0. These are the two digits used to represent any code handled by a computer. In his design (normally referred to as Von Neumann architecture) Von Neumann suggested, for the first time, that the instructions (the program) and the data should be stored the same way, as binary numbers, and in the same place, the memory. The memory corresponds to the tape of the Turing machine and the CPU is the sliding device.

The Von Neumann computer works by a constant movement of binary numbers between memory and the CPU. One line of a program is fetched from memory by the CPU and is then executed (processed). The result is then sent by the CPU to be stored in memory. Thus if a stored program wants to add 2 and 3 then the program lines would be

1. Bring 2 from memory
2. Bring 3 from memory
3. Add
4. Store the result in memory.

The CPU would fetch instruction 1 in, execute it by bringing number 2 from memory, then fetch instruction 2, execute it by bringing 3 from memory, fetch instruction 3, execute it by adding the two numbers, fetch instruction 4 and execute it by putting the result of the addition (5) back into memory. Thus the operation of the computer is a continuous repetition of fetch and execute, giving it the name 'fetch-execute cycle'. The above was a simple task but complex tasks can be performed on the same principle if they can be broken down into simple instructions as above.

Just as the imaginary Turing machine could do anything depending on what was written on the tape, Von Neumann's computer can do anything depending on what program it is running. So it can work like a typewriter if a wordprocessing program is running, an aeroplane pilot if it is a flight simulation program, an accounts clerk if it is running a spreadsheet program, and so on. The machine itself remains the same, the program is changed according to the task we want it to perform.

Can you describe what steps a computer will need to follow to find the larger of two numbers marked as A and B?

A computer system

Having established the basic concept behind the way a computer works let us consider in more detail how the concept is put into practice and what a computer needs in order to be able to perform its tasks. As stated in the introduction to this chapter, a computer works with a number of elements (including the CPU and memory mentioned above) known collectively as a computer system which consists of the following components (see Figure 2.2):

- the main processing unit: the CPU;
- step-by-step and precise instructions on how to perform tasks: the programs;
- data to process;
- space to store the instructions and the data – before, after and during processing: the storage devices;
- the means to communicate with humans and with other machines: the input and output devices and the data channels (routes).

As mentioned already, these can be placed under two broad headings: *hardware* – to include the physical parts, that is the processing unit, storage, input and output devices, data channels; and *software* – the programs and data.

Hardware

A computer is basically a processor of data. It accepts data as input, processes it, and produces information as output. It also stores data and instructions (as per Von Neumann architecture), some temporarily and some for permanent keeping. It does all of this with the help of the following units.

Central processing unit (CPU)

Known as the processor, this is the main working section of a computer. The CPU consists of two main parts: a control unit (CU), and an arithmetic and logic unit (ALU). The CPU is the equivalent of the human brain in which the CU controls the operations by sending electronic signals to different parts of the computer; the ALU is the space where the calculations take place. Comparing this with the Von Neumann machine, the CU controls the fetch-execute cycle and the ALU is the space which the CPU uses to hold the data during calculations. There are other small storage spaces in the CPU (called registers) which it uses for various purposes during processing.

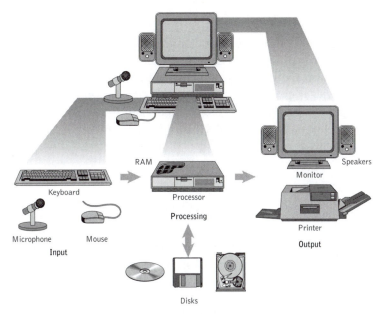

Figure 2.2: A typical computer system

Memory

A computer has an internal storage (referred to as 'memory' in analogy with human memory), the space which holds programs and data for use by the CPU. It consists of two parts: random access memory (RAM), which is used as the working storage by a computer during processing and is emptied when processing is completed; and read only memory (ROM), used to hold some special programs permanently. RAM holds the programs and data being used by a computer at a certain time, rather like your desk which stays empty (in an ideal world) when you are not working but holds your books and notes while you use them. ROM holds the programs the computer needs to perform the basic functions, just as we know how to read to be able to use our books and notes.

The above units (the components of CPU and memory) are connected to each other by channels (each called a 'bus') rather like the nerves in our bodies, and together they control the processing and movement of data within the computer. We will discuss the functions of these units in more detail later in the chapter.

Think about what the programs in ROM do when a computer is switched on and what goes on in RAM when you write an essay using a wordprocessor.

Input devices

The job of an input device is to accept data from users and pass it on to the parts of the computer that process it. The data can be input in a number of ways: as characters typed on the keyboard; by pointing and clicking on an icon on the screen by a mouse; as characters or images read directly from source by scanners; by speaking through a microphone (voice input), and so on. There are other input devices such as light pen and touch-sensitive screens and more new devices are being introduced as computer technology becomes increasingly more powerful.

Output devices

After the data has been processed, it has to be output in a form understandable to humans. An output device is a medium for doing this. The most common output device is the printer but there are also speech output devices, music output devices, graph plotters and so on. One important part of a computer system is the monitor, also called the visual display unit (VDU) which is some-times referred to as an input/output device because it can display both what is input to the system and the result of processing which can then be sent to other output devices such as a printer or a musical instrument.

Secondary storage

This is the storage space external to the CPU and is normally used for storing information for long term use and as a back up. Secondary storage is provided mainly by the use of disks. A sealed unit fixed to the computer called the hard disk drive (although there are separate, connectable disk drives available as well) holds a collection of disks and is used for storing large programs and documents. Information can be added to or deleted from a hard disk but the disk drive cannot be removed easily. A computer also has disk drives for removable disks which can be taken out when not in use. For personal computers these drives are called floppy disk drives and the disks are known as floppy disks. Most modern personal computers also have a drive for a CD-ROM (compact disk read only memory) which is an optically operated disk rather like a music CD. At present they can only be written to once, normally by the manufacturer, and read many times, hence the name ROM (read only memory), and can be used for storing large amounts of data on one disk. Technology for writing to a compact disk has already been developed but is not used as widely as floppy disks.

Recently, DVDs (Digital Versatile Disks), each capable of holding the same amount of information as a large number of CD-ROMs, have been introduced.

Input, output and storage devices are discussed fully in Chapter 3.

Software

As stated before, computers can work only if precise, step-by-step instructions in the form of computer programs are given to them. Also, the data they have to process has to be supplied in the exact format the computer has been instructed to expect. Together, they constitute the software component of a computer system, although conventionally the term 'software' is used to mean mainly programs. As explained in Chapter 1, software used with computers can be put into two categories: systems and applications.

So, how do these units work together? How does a CPU accept the data and what does it do with it? How does it communicate the result of the processing to the user? The following sections should answer these questions for you and give you some understanding of how a computer breaks any problem down to a series of very simple arithmetic operations in order to find a solution.[2]

How computers work

Before we start talking about how a computer works let us remind ourselves what a computer does. A computer accepts raw data via its input devices, processes the data, produces useful information and then outputs the information in a choice of formats, via its output devices. It also stores the information, if asked, in its backing store. Using the library example, the light pen used to read the bar codes on members' cards and books is the input device. The data read is sent to the computer's memory (RAM) which also holds the necessary programs and files containing the relevant data on members and books. Under the instructions of the programs, the CPU processes the data, updates the files and produces output on the VDU. Information is also printed when asked by a user. Copies of updated files and programs are held on disks, the backing store.

In order to perform these tasks computers have to handle data; data handling is the basis of everything a computer does. Computer departments in organizations used to be called data processing departments in the 1970s and 1980s. Nowadays the term 'information processing' is more commonly heard because

2 Hopefully by now, you have got an idea of how a computer works. If you do not want or need to know any more detail, you may like to skip the rest of the chapter and move on to the Summary. However, the following sections are not difficult to understand and should give you a clearer understanding of the concept.

computers have moved on from being number-crunching machines used for a limited number of repetitive and voluminous tasks to being a part of all business systems necessary for the management of an organization.

The first thing we need to do before we can perceive how a computer handles data, is to conceptualise how it stores data. A computer performs all its functions through a combination of four basic operations: add, subtract, multiply and divide (strictly speaking multiplication and division are also combinations of addition and subtraction). Therefore, whatever form the input data comes in, numbers, letters, pictures, music and so on, it is first converted into digits before it can be processed. Hence we need to understand two things: how a computer translates each item of data into numbers and how it handles these numbers.

Representation of data

A computer cannot handle numbers the way we do. It only understands two numbers, 0 and 1, because, regardless of how simple or sophisticated it is, a computer only understands two electronic states – 'on' or 'off'. It interprets the state when an electric current can pass through an electronic valve (called a 'gate' in computer terminology) as 'on', representing the number 1; and when it cannot, as 'off', representing a 0. These two states (0 and 1) are known as *bits* and this system of numbering is called *binary coding*. Each character handled by a computer is represented by a series of bits (for example, 01000001 represents the letter A: Figure 2.3). When we enter data, for example by a keyboard, each keystroke is converted into its appropriate bit string before it is sent through to the computer. The computer processes the data in its bit form and produces output, which, at the output end, is converted back to its human readable form.

There are a number of encoding systems used by computer technology which are used to convert characters to bit strings, the most common being ASCII (American Standard Code for Information Interchange), pronounced 'asskee'. ASCII codes have two versions, ASCII-7 and ASCII-8, with 7 and 8 bit characters respectively. Figure 2.4 shows a table of commonly used characters, their ASCII-8 codes and the corresponding decimal values. Eight bits are said to constitute a byte – thus each character in ASCII-8 occupies one byte of storage space.

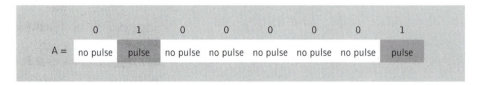

	0	1	0	0	0	0	0	1
A =	no pulse	pulse	no pulse	no pulse	no pulse	no pulse	no pulse	pulse

Figure 2.3: States of 'on' and 'off'

Character	ASCII code Binary value		Decimal value	Character	ASCII code Binary value		Decimal value
A	100	0001	65	0	011	0000	48
B	100	0010	66	1	011	0001	49
C	100	0011	67	2	011	0010	50
D	100	0100	68	3	011	0011	51
E	100	0101	69	4	011	0100	52
F	100	0110	70	5	011	0101	53
G	100	0111	71	6	011	0110	54
H	100	1000	72	7	011	0111	55
I	100	1001	73	8	011	1000	56
J	100	1010	74	9	011	1001	57
K	100	1011	75				
L	100	1100	76	Space	010	0000	32
M	100	1101	77	.	010	1110	46
N	100	1110	78	<	011	1100	60
O	100	1111	79	(	010	1000	40
P	101	0000	80	+	010	1011	43
Q	101	0001	81	&	010	0110	38
R	101	0010	82	!	010	0001	33
S	101	0011	83	$	010	0100	36
T	101	0100	84	*	010	1010	42
U	101	0101	85	)	010	1001	41
V	101	0110	86	;	011	1011	59
W	101	0111	87	,	010	1100	44
X	101	1000	88	%	010	0101	37
Y	101	1001	89	–	101	1111	95
Z	101	1010	90	>	011	1110	62
a	110	0001	97	?	011	1111	63
b	110	0010	98	:	011	1010	58
c	110	0011	99	#	010	0011	35
d	110	0100	100	@	100	0000	64
e	110	0101	101	'	010	0111	39
f	110	0110	102	=	011	1101	61
g	110	0111	103	\\	010	0010	34
h	110	1000	104				
i	110	1001	105	1/2	1010	1011	171
j	110	1010	106	3/4	1010	1100	172
k	110	1011	107	▬	1011	0010	178
l	110	1100	108	■	1101	1011	219
m	110	1101	109	▬	1101	1100	220
n	110	1110	110	▌	1101	1101	221
o	110	1111	111	▐	1101	1110	222
p	111	0000	112	▬	1101	1111	223
q	111	0001	113	√	1111	1011	251
r	111	0010	114	n	1111	1100	252
s	111	0011	115	z	1111	1101	253
t	111	0100	116	■	1111	1110	254
u	111	0101	117	blank	1111	1111	255
v	111	0110	118				
w	111	0111	119				
x	111	1000	120				
y	111	1001	121				
z	111	1010	122				

Figure 2.4: Table of ASCII codes

Using eight bits, this system can represent up to 256 characters. This is useful because as well as the alphabetic (A–Z, a–z) and numeric (0–9) characters, a computer also needs to represent a large number of so-called special characters, for example, comma, space, mathematical functions, graphical characters and so on.

Although a computer works only in binary, it has to communicate with its users in decimal. It is obviously more sensible to let the computer translate input data from decimal to binary and output data from binary to decimal than to ask human beings to deal with binary coding. Normally users do not need to see binary codes but sometimes specialist users dealing with a computer's memory may need to know its exact content. For example, programmers, especially systems programmers, may have to examine the contents of the memory from time to time as part of checking programs for errors. Going through rows and columns of binary numbers would be extremely tedious. To reduce the extent of the problem, memory 'dumps' (copies of the contents of memory) are produced using the hexadecimal (hex) system. This is a base 16 numbering system in which there are single digit or character representations for numbers from 0 to 15 after which the pattern is repeated. Figure 2.5 shows a table of binary, decimal and hexadecimal numbers. It is important to remember that memory content is translated into hex for displaying to human readers but all internal arithmetic is performed in binary.

Binary (base 2)	Decimal (base 10)	Hexadecimal (base 16)
0	0	0
1	1	1
10	2	2
11	3	3
100	4	4
101	5	5
110	6	6
111	7	7
1000	8	8
1001	9	9
1010	10	A
1011	11	B
1100	12	C
1101	13	D
1110	14	E
1111	15	F
10000	16	10

Figure 2.5: Table of binary, decimal and hexadecimal

Storage within a computer

A computer has internal storage (called memory) consisting of read only memory (ROM), random access memory (RAM) and a number of registers.

ROM

As the name suggests this is a storage space the contents of which can be read and used but cannot be altered in any way and is used to store programs and data permanently by the manufacturer. This is achieved by encoding the programs magnetically on a chip thus making the contents indestructible (non-volatile). Using a human analogy, we can compare (loosely) ROM with the part of our memory which enables us to remember basic facts such as how to read and write. In the early days of personal computers, many applications programs came on ROM chips which had to be fitted into the computers. Now, applications are normally produced on disks and can be stored on a hard disk for repeated use. Today's personal computers hold only some essential programs in ROM, for example, the program that starts up a computer when it is switched on so it is ready for use: this program is called the boot program and the process is called *booting*.

There are other types of ROM used by a computer: PROM (programmable read only memory) allows users to apply a special technique to load read only programs themselves for permanent keeping; EPROM (erasable programmable read only memory) allows users not only to load read only programs as above but also allows the process to be reversed and the chip reloaded; and finally, EEPROM (electrically erasable PROM) which can be altered electronically by using a program without the need to remove it from the computer.

RAM

Normally much bigger in size than ROM, this part of the memory holds programs and data currently in use together with the result of the processing. RAM is the working storage of a computer which we have described as being rather like your desk that holds the paper you are writing on, your lecture notes and any other sources of information. RAM is volatile which means that it is cleared when the power is turned off or when processing is completed and programs are closed. So the next time you run a program you have an empty RAM ready to accept new programs and data to work on just like you begin with a clear desk when you start a new task. A computer cannot use programs and data unless they reside in RAM, so everything a computer needs to use has to be loaded into RAM before processing starts.

Most personal computers have dynamic memory – DRAM (dynamic random access memory) – the contents of which leak because of the storage technique used and have to be refreshed. DRAM is simple in construction, inexpensive, it allows high storage density and saves power. Static RAM (SRAM), on the other hand, is built using a different technology and retains its contents. It is faster than DRAM, more expensive, and is used for specific purposes. PCs started off with 8 KB of RAM; today's PCs can have 16 MB (million characters) or more.

Cache

Although RAM is a fast device and allows access to data much faster than secondary storage, in terms of computing speed it can sometimes seem slow. A cache is a faster, smaller and more expensive memory chip (normally SRAM) which is used to hold data and instructions temporarily between RAM and the processing unit. This is used like a reserve to store the next set of instructions and data while the previous set is being executed (run). Because of its cost, only a few cache chips are used in a computer.

Registers

These are small, high speed storage areas capable of holding a small amount of data. They reside in the central processing unit and are used to hold single instructions or data at the time of execution. Examples of some common registers are the accumulator, used for holding data immediately before and after an operation, and the program counter, used for holding the address of the instruction being executed. The purpose of registers will become clearer when we discuss how the CPU executes instructions.

Flash memory

Flash memory was invented as a result of the search for a memory chip that is fast but non-volatile. It allows a user to store data within the computer but the contents do not disappear when the power is turned off. Flash memory is used in some special cases such as aeroplane flight recorders and mobile phones but due to the high manufacturing cost its widespread use is not yet possible.

The memory types described so far provide a computer with integral storage space: they reside inside the computer and are used when a computer executes programs. They are also called primary storage. Secondary storage (also called the backing storage) is the term used to describe external storage, normally in the form of disks, used to hold programs and data when not in use.

Primary storage is similar in concept to our short term memory, with the exception of ROM which is permanent. When we write an essay, for example, we read books and articles and hold the information in our memory while our brain processes it. The information disappears from our memory after a while. In comparison, the books and articles are secondary storage because they hold the information permanently. As you may have realized already, the comparison is not completely fair since we retain a lot of the information for a long time, whereas information held in RAM is totally volatile. This is because human brains are far more sophisticated and complex than a computer's memory. We will discuss secondary storage in Chapter 3.

 Can you think of ways in which humans and computers are alike and/or different?

The role of the CPU

The CPU, which contains a control unit (CU), an arithmetic and logic unit (ALU), a number of registers and other small storage units, is at the centre of data processing. Repeating our human analogy, the CPU is the brain and the CU is the nerve centre of a computer: together they control the flow of data and coordinate its processing by sending signals to the rest of the computer. The CPU has also been compared with a traffic controller who stands at a road junction and controls the flow of traffic. The actual computation is performed in the ALU. With the aid of a number of registers for holding data, it performs arithmetic (add, subtract, multiply and divide) and logical operations (comparisons) on data during processing. The roles of these units will become clearer when we discuss how data is processed.

How a computer processes data

Although most programs are written in high level languages, computers understand only machine code (see Chapter 1). Some systems programs known as compilers and interpreters translate high level programs into machine language.

One high level instruction is often translated into a number of machine instructions each representing only one simple operation. Each machine instruction has two parts, an operation code (commonly called op-code) telling the computer what operation to perform and an operation address (called operand) which tells it where to get the data from. Sometimes the operand is the data itself; this happens when the data is held in the instruction rather than with the rest of the data in a different memory location and is known as *immediate addressing*.

In our example we are going to use some binary numbers. Although it is not necessary for you to understand how binary codes are written, it may be frustrating to see the codes and not be able to tell how they make up the numbers. The following is a very brief introduction to binary coding.

Each position (bit) in binary coding has a number associated with it: starting with 1 (2^0) for the rightmost bit, it goes up in powers of 2. Thus the second bit stands for 2 (2^1), the next for 4 (2^2), then 8 (2^3), 16 (2^4) and so on. A 1 in a bit position indicates the presence of the corresponding number, a 0 indicates the absence. In the following example the second (representing 2), fourth (=8) and sixth (=32) bits are 1 indicating that these values are present, thus making the decimal value of the number 42 (2+8+32).

bit positions:	32	16	8	4	2	1	
a number:	1	0	1	0	1	0	= 42

Can you make up the number 95 using the binary method?

Before a program is executed, the program and the data to be processed are copied into RAM. The program instructions are stored in consecutive locations each of which has a unique address. The data is also stored in addressed locations. Figure 2.6 shows a section of a typical machine language program together with the meaning of each instruction. The language used here is imaginary but follows the same pattern as most machine languages. Study Figure 2.6 carefully before you go on to the next paragraph.

The program (indicated by the shaded columns) would be stored in the main memory starting at a specified address. The data to be used for this program would also be stored in the appropriate addresses. The main memory may look like Figure 2.7.

At the end of the program execution, location 50 will hold the result of the addition. In this example location 10 holds 00000100 (4) and 11 holds

Op-code	Meaning of op-code	Operand	Value of operand in decimal	Overall meaning
00000000	Put the content of the address in the operand into the register called accumulator	00001010	10	Load the content of storage location 10 into accumulator
00000010	Add the content of the operand address to accumulator	00001011	11	Add the content of location 11 to the content of the accumulator
00000001	Store the content of accumulator to the operand address	00110010	50	Store the result in the accumulator into location 50

Figure 2.6: A set of instructions in a fictitious machine language

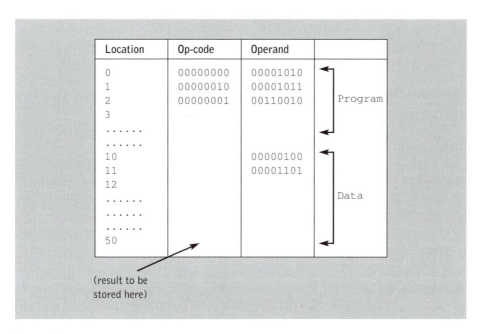

Figure 2.7: The stored program

00001101 (13). Thus, at the end of the program run location 50 will hold 00010001 (17).

It is not very difficult for humans to do this because we can read an instruction, get the data from the operand address and do the calculations in our head. However, in doing this, we are following a number of precise steps but our brains are so used to doing such computations that we are not aware of this. These steps are:

1. Check where the program starts.
2. Start at the first program address (0 in this case).
3. Separate op-code and operand.
4. Understand (decode) the operation to be performed and the address for the data.
5. Look at the address indicated by the operand (address 10) and pick up the data (4) from that address.
6. Hold the data in our (short term) memory.
7. Check the next instruction (at address 1).
8. Separate op-code and operand.
9. Understand the operation to be performed and the address for the data.
10. Look at the address indicated by the operand (address 10) and pick up the data (13) from that address.
11. Hold the data in our (short term) memory.
12. Check the next instruction (at address 2).
13. Separate op-code and operand.

and so on.

A computer has to follow all these steps as well. What our brains can do almost subconsciously, has to be set out for a computer in precise steps because being a machine it cannot work otherwise. However, a computer can follow these steps much faster than a human can. The above example was an easy one but if we had large numbers to compute or complicated instructions to execute it would take us much longer. This is where computers are superior, they can perform any complicated operation much faster and more accurately than human beings.

Let us now see how a computer follows the steps. Each component of the CPU contains registers, some special purpose and some general. Figure 2.8 shows a simplified schematic diagram of the CPU together with these registers.

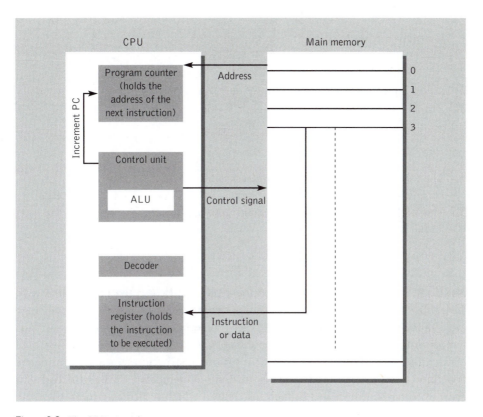

Figure 2.8: The CPU at work

The program counter (PC) is a register that holds the address of the next program instruction to be read. Following a signal from the control unit, this address is sent, via the address bus (a channel through which an address travels) into the PC. The instruction register (IR) holds the instruction currently being executed. At the start of our example program the PC would hold 0 to indicate the program starts at location 0. The control unit sends a signal to memory to send the instruction from location 0 into the IR. The instruction is fetched via the data bus (a channel for data and instructions to travel) and placed in the instruction register. The instruction is then separated into opcode and operand, decoded by the decoder and executed. The ALU and some other registers are used during the execution for temporary storage of data. At the end of this, the result is put into the appropriate location in memory, the program counter is increased by 1 and the process starts again for the next instruction.

For our example program the following steps are taken. The process starts with 0 in the PC.

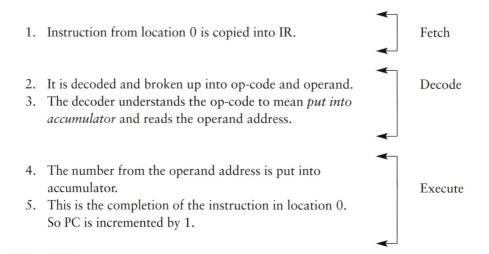

1. Instruction from location 0 is copied into IR.   Fetch

2. It is decoded and broken up into op-code and operand.   Decode
3. The decoder understands the op-code to mean *put into
   accumulator* and reads the operand address.

4. The number from the operand address is put into
   accumulator.   Execute
5. This is the completion of the instruction in location 0.
   So PC is incremented by 1.

Next, the instruction is fetched from location 1 and executed in the same way. This process goes on until the program is completed. The above is one machine cycle called the fetch-decode-execute (F-D-E or simply the F-E cycle) because it is a repetition of the pattern of fetch new instruction, decode meaning and execute instruction. The CU transfers control from one instruction to the next until the program comes to an end. The PC is normally incremented by 1 at the end of a cycle except when there is a branch instruction which indicates a jump to a specific location other than the next. In that case the appropriate location number is put into the PC.

Can you write the fetch-decode-execute steps for a program which compares two numbers A and B to locate the larger one?

What makes one computer different from another

All computers basically work on the same principle, that is a repetition of machine cycles of fetch, decode and execute. Yet, we know computers vary enormously in their power, speed, cost, size and so on. So, what makes them different from each other? If you look at any advertisement for a personal computer, you will find descriptions such as 'Pentium 400 MHz processor', '512 KB cache',

'128 MB RAM', '32 bit local bus', and so on. What do they all mean and how do they affect the performance of a computer?

A computer does what a program tells it to do. The power and efficiency of a computer are determined by the quality of the program and the speed at which it can be executed. We will discuss computer programs in later chapters. The technical specifications you see in advertisements include factors that determine the computer's processing power. Personal computers are based on a piece of silicon (called a chip) consisting of very large scale integrated circuit technology with sometimes millions of transistors on one chip. One such chip holds the central processing unit of a microcomputer and is called the microprocessor. Intel, a company at the forefront of the personal computer market for the past 20 years or so, introduced its first processor Intel 8088 in 1981. This was a 16-bit 4.4 MHz processor that worked with 8-bit bus width. Today's Intel Pentiums are 32- to 64-bit processors with a clock speed up to 450 MHz (with 700 MHz in the pipeline at the time of writing) and can work with a bus width of up to 64 bits.[3] (The meanings of these terms will soon become clearer!)

The factors that determine a computer's level of performance are:

- word length
- clock speed
- bus width.

Word length

This indicates the number of bits that are treated as a unit by a microprocessor. A 16-bit processor has a 16-bit word length, that is it can handle 16 bits (or 2 bytes) of data at a time. As the word length increases so does the speed of a computer as larger chunks of data are moved around at a time.

Clock speed

A clock is required to control the timing of each action of a computer. This is achieved by including an electronic pulse generator such as an oscillating crystal (for example, a quartz) which sends precisely synchronized streams of pulses to different parts of the computer. Megahertz (MHz) are the units used to measure the number of pulses per second (frequency) and are referred to as the clock

---

3   These are typical figures. Manufacturers are constantly trying to improve the performance of their products to gain advantage in a very competitive market. Thus, as soon as one update is released, company researchers start working towards the next.

speed. Thus a 64 MHz processor has a crystal that sends a pulse 64 million times per second. The higher the clock speed, the faster the processor. Depending on the complication of an instruction, different numbers of clock pulses are required by each instruction. If an instruction is such that it takes exactly one fetch-decode-execute cycle then it may need only one clock pulse, whilst another which, when broken down into single operations, takes five cycles, will take longer.

Bus width

Different components of a computer system are connected through each other by channels called bus lines. Bus lines are designed to carry a maximum number of bits called the bus width. A 32-bit bus will allow 32 bits of data to travel together: thus, the higher the bus width the faster the processor.

However, it is simplistic to suggest that each of the above factors is a measure of the speed of a processor. In fact the processor speed depends on a combination of all these factors. It is of no use to have a processor with 32-bit word length unless the bus width is at least 32 bits because otherwise 32 bits of data will be moved around in the CPU at one time but will not be able to move together outside the CPU and into the other components. (There is a technique called clock-doubling which can be used to improve performance, but we will not go into that.) Also, a high clock speed needs to be matched with the speed and power of the rest of the computer system; extensive use of caches has to be made to allow the data transfer between RAM and CPU at the speed required; adjustments have to be made to balance the high power consumption resulting from fast clock speed, and so on.

Find some ads for PCs in a current magazine and pick up some typical specifications. What do they signify?

Various measures are taken to make the most of word length, bus width and clock speed in the latest microprocessors. One method used is *pipelining* in which three separate units are used for fetch, decode and execute operations. When one instruction has been fetched it is sent to the decode unit, while the next instruction is brought into the fetch unit. When decoding of the first instruction is completed, it is sent to the execute unit and the second instruction is decoded, while a third instruction can be brought into the empty fetch unit. Thus, all three units are used to process three instructions simultaneously. Two other techniques used are to break an instruction up into more than three stages thus making each stage simpler and quicker, and using more than one pipeline.

The amount of cache available also contributes to the speed of a processor since this increases the speed with which instructions and data can be transferred between RAM and the CPU. Another technique that was first introduced in the mid-1980s is now gaining prominence and is presenting itself as the challenger to the Pentium processor. This is the RISC (reduced instruction set computer) processor in which each machine instruction is simple and of a fixed length. RISC instructions can be processed much faster than those used in the traditional CISC (complicated instruction set computer) processors. PowerPCs, built initially by the collaboration of IBM and Apple and now built separately by both companies, use a RISC processor.

If a computer has only one CPU, only one instruction can be processed at any time. Using pipelining a processor can handle more than one instruction at one time but the execute unit can only execute one instruction. However, computers can be built with more than one processor which allows the execution of multiple instructions. Some personal computers have extra processors for special functions: for example, maths co-processors are often used to handle complicated mathematical operations to gain extra speed.

Supercomputers are built with a large array of small processors. One main processor examines the entire program and breaks it up into parts which can be processed independently. These are then sent to the processors simultaneously to be processed. At the end of the processing, the results are brought back into the main processor and reassembled. This increases the speed considerably.

In the 1970s and 1980s there was a clear distinction between mainframes, minis and micros. Now the actual technical differences are somewhat blurred. What a mainframe could do 10 years ago can now be done by a PC. Supercomputers, mainframes, minis and micros represent a broad spectrum of decreasing values of word length, clock speed, bus width, memory size, amount of cache, and hence the processing power and speed. Scientists are working on processors based on single electrons technology (SET) which are said to seriously challenge Pentium chips, being capable of functioning like the human brain. More recently we are hearing about the use of quantum mechanics in processor technology which uses the two directions of the spin of an atom to represent two states (as discussed in Chapter 1). If scientists are able to perfect this technology, we should see computers which are much smaller in size and much faster by about 2015 (*BYTE*, July 1998, p.24).

As well as the processor's capability, the performance of a computer system also depends on many other factors such as the speed of data movement from backing storage, the speed of input and output devices, the quality of programs and so on. It is a combination of all aspects of a complete computer system that determines the overall performance to be expected. Look at the list of Further reading if you want to know more about the concepts and terms we touched on in this chapter.

Summary

A computer system consists of a number of hardware and software units, and the successful performance of a computer depends on the extent to which the combination works. Hardware refers to the input, output, processing and storage devices. Inside the computer, there are the central processor and the memory. The processor consists of a control unit, arithmetic and logic unit and a number of small special purpose storage spaces called registers. Programs and data are held in the memory in binary form during processing. Using a continuous cycle of fetch, decode and execute operations, a computer brings instructions and data from storage, breaks them up into understandable parts and executes them. This is done with the help of the various units in the processor.

The speed and performance of a computer depends on its word length – the number of bits treated as a unit, clock speed – the frequency of the electronic pulses generated by a crystal in the computer, and bus width – the width of the channels which connect different parts of the computer. Some techniques are used to improve the speed of a computer, for example pipelining which facilitates the simultaneous operation of the fetch, decode and execute units, the use of more than one processor and the use of RISC technology.

Further reading

Look at the website http://goldenink.com/computersandnetworks.shtml for the history of early computers.

Look at http://obiwan.uvi.edu/computing/turing/ture.htm and the linked pages for more information on a Turing machine.

Read an A Level text, for example, *Computer Science* by Peter Bishop, Nelson, 1991 (or later editions) for information on how computers work at a further technical depth. This will also give you more technical details on representation of data, storage within a computer, execution of program instructions and so on.

Look at the website http://pclt.cis.yale.edu/pclt/PCHW/CPUMEM.HTM for more information on CPU and memory.

An article at http://pcmech.pair.com/cpu.htm gives a good account of the Intel processors from the early ones up to the most recent. Other articles, for example, one at http://www.tomshardware.com/cpu.html give the latest information on CPUs manufactured by Intel and other companies.

An article entitled 'Time for a quantum leap' by Philip Hunter in *Computing*, 29 October 1998 explains the use of quantum mechanics in processor technology and gives further details on the subject.

Read the article on DNA computing in the July 1998 copy of *BYTEXTRA* from www.byte.com.

Revision questions

1. Describe the main components of a computer system and their functions.

2. Describe different types of memory devices (large and small) and their functions.

3. Explain the structure of a CPU.

4. Explain how an instruction is executed by a CPU.

5. Explain the fetch-decode-execute cycle.

6. Explain the significance of each of the following in the operation of a computer:

   memory of a computer   word length
   op-code   clock speed
   operand address   pipelining
   storage locations   RISC.
   bus width

Food for thought

Computer Weekly, 18 September 1997, p.20(1)
Reed Business Publishing Ltd (UK)

A chip off the new block
Neil Fawcett

Neil Fawcett looks at the advances made by Intel which will establish the Pentium II chip in the business market

This week Intel tried to play down speculation over new versions of its Pentium chips.

▶

Reports are coming out of the US that Intel is developing a new version of its MMX multimedia technology codenamed Katmai – that will appear in Pentium II chips in 1998.

The technology should provide vastly improved graphics performance for desktop and notebook machines, with a big focus on 3D imaging.

MMX is a set of instructions that have been added to the Pentium and Pentium II processors, allowing them to handle complex data such as video and audio much more easily. Katmai will add to the existing 57 instructions to improve 3D image manipulation.

Intel is eager to play down any speculation because it believes people are getting confused about its plans for the Accelerated Graphics Port (AGP), which is part of its project to speed up the PC. This could well be true, but Intel's often complex product strategy is open to confusion.

The standard Pentium chip, currently running at a maximum of 200 MHz, is now defunct. It will continue to sell for a while, but Intel is not planning to make any more non-MMX chips.

Short-lived

This leaves the Pentium MMX chip as the entry-level option for users. These days, you would be hard pressed to sell a PC without an MMX-based processor inside, be it an Intel or an Advanced Micro Devices (AMD) chip. However, even this technology is going to be short-lived.

Intel's future lies in its Pentium II chip. Eventually this microprocessor will power everything from notebook PCs to high-end multiprocessor servers running mission-critical applications. But for this to occur, a number of events must take place.

The Pentium II was launched in May, with more of a whimper than a bang. At the time Intel wanted to introduce new technology, but did not want to suddenly move the market over to a chip that it could not manufacture in volume. It also had a stock of Pentium and Pentium MMX chips it wanted to clear.

Now, however, Intel is ready to move over to Pentium II in volume, taking the desktop community with it. Last week, the company launched an initiative to make Pentium II the ultimate chip for games/consumer computers, ramping up its volume manufacturing in the process.

Pentium brought with it some interesting technologies: the new Slot 1 standard for connecting a processor to the motherboard; the Dual Independent Bus, a fast data bus inside the chip which boosts performance; and the Accelerated Graphics Port. However, the AGP only started to gain momentum two weeks ago when the 440LX chipset came out. These chips allow motherboard manufacturers to support this kind of technology, paving the way for graphics card makers to support the new way that graphics are processed by a PC.

The launch of Slot 1, meanwhile, can be seen as a direct assault on AMD. By moving to the new standard, Intel in effect has shifted the industry away from the Pentium Socket 7 design which AMD is supporting with its K6 chips. Slot 1 has also allowed Intel to cut manufacturing costs by taking cache memory off the Pentium II chip.

But Slot 1 has its performance limitations. The cache memory sitting on the cartridge assembly runs at half the speed of the CPU core and can support a maximum memory of only 512 Mbytes.

Intel hopes to remove several of the performance barriers that limited Pentium II when it ships Slot 2 in 1998. The cache memory will operate at the same speed as the Pentium II – so if the chip is running at 300 MHz, the cache is as well. Also, the Pentium II is currently limited to one-way or two-way design. By the middle of next year, Slot 2 will allow for four-way systems design. But there is a problem with this. Because of the increase in speed of the cache memory, a Slot 2 cartridge will generate a lot of heat, which in turn means Slot 2 will be twice the size of its predecessor.

Therefore, Slot 1 will continue to sell as the mainstream way that PC makers assemble desktop PCs and entry-level servers. Slot 2 will become the de facto standard for assembling high-performance workstations and high-end servers.

About the same time as PC makers move to support Slot 2, you will see the performance of motherboards move from 66 MHz to 100 MHz which will bring a major speed improvement.

As a result, the Pentium Pro chip – which has served Intel well in the workstation and high-end server space will die out. Its time is up, and Intel will no longer need it once Pentium II is established in the workstation and server markets.

In order to make its dream of making Pentium II ubiquitous a reality, Intel needs to alter the manufacturing process. Currently, the chips are made using elements as small as 0.35 microns (a third of a millionth of a metre) across.

But Intel needs to move to a 0.25 micron process in order to make the chip even faster and smaller. This super-fast, ultra-small version of the chip is codenamed Dechutes and will arrive by mid-1998. At that time, the processor should be running at speeds in excess of 300 MHz, with rates of more than 400 MHz on the cards.

'When we move to 0.25 microns, you will see the Pentium II family of chips span a whole range of machines, from very fast notebooks to high-end multiprocessing servers,' said Stephane Negre, product marketing manager for Pentium II at Intel in Munich.

He added, 'What has to be understood is that Slot 2 does not mean the death of Slot 1. We will keep both designs. Slot 2 allows us to increase the performance – that is its goal.'

So in 1998 Intel is going to be a busy company, making the world's PC makers work hard to keep up to speed with its advances.

Discussion questions

1. The article mentions many concepts explained in Chapter 2 as well as some new ones. List the new terms you met and try to find their meanings and the relevance they have to the way a computer works.

2. Find out how AMD is performing in the PC market. Do you believe manufacturers such as AMD and Cyrix could ever be a serious threat to Intel?

3. What role did the strategies used by processor manufacturers play in the war to win the PC market? Critically review the effect of such competition on the quality of the technology.

4. What are the consequences of a difference in speed between different parts of a computer?

5. The article was written in September 1997. Find out if the predictions made in the article have come true and what other progress has been made in the processor industry.

Input, output and external storage

Introduction

In Chapter 2 we discussed how a computer processes data and how it moves it around in and out of its CPU and memory to produce information under the instruction of computer programs. We also established that a computer is connected to external (known as peripheral) devices, such as a keyboard, a printer and a disk drive, and that together they constitute a computer system. In this chapter we are going to discuss the external devices in more detail and take a brief look at the alternatives available to computer users.

Input devices

Even if you are not a so-called computer user, it is highly probable that you have used a number of input devices. The cashpoint machines outside high street banks and building societies are common examples. You enter the bank's computer system when you insert your card into the machine. The system identifies you as a valid user by checking the pin code you input and then prompts you to enter your requirements using a display screen and a small keyboard.

Naturally the data we put in is in human readable form. This is first converted into machine code and then entered into the computer system for processing. A peripheral device is operated by a program called a *device driver*, which is copied into the hard disk when the device is installed. Each type of input device has its own program; when a computer is switched on this program is copied into RAM, ready to be used.

There are many different types of input devices available to computer users. In the beginning these were mainly typewriter-type keyboards. With increasing demands for user friendly computing, innovation in easy-to-use input devices has been remarkable, giving rise to many new and sometimes special purpose products. The following is a brief description of some of the input devices available today.

Keyboard

This is the traditional and the most common input device (see Figure 3.1). Following on from the typewriter tradition, it uses a QWERTY layout (named according to the first six characters of the keyboard); together with function keys (F1, F2 and so on) which are used to access special features in one key stroke (for example, F3 summous the Help program in some applications); a number pad on the side (a block of dual purpose keys containing numbers and screen navigation facilities); and a set of special symbols such as #, ~, ¬, and so on.

A number of keyboard designs with improved facilities for speed and comfort have been introduced over the years but none of them has taken over from the traditional design. The reason for this is mainly the cost of replacing existing keyboards and retraining the staff. However, some new keyboard designs have entered the market, for example, Microsoft's new keyboard called Elite which has two sections at an angle to each other with no keys in the middle and a gentle slope to allow the natural positioning of hands (Figure 3.2). There are also cordless keyboards, detachable palm rests and keyboards with special keys for common operations such as scrolling (moving up and down the screen) and so on.

Figure 3.1: A common keyboard
Source: Dell Computer Corporation Ltd

Figure 3.2: A modern keyboard

There are other forms of keyboards in use for some special purpose dedicated computer systems: bank cashpoint machines have small keyboards with numerical digits plus a few special characters; some fast food restaurants (for example, McDonald's) use keyboards or keypads in which one key is dedicated to each item in the menu; keyboards for computer aided design often come with special keys for colours; and there are special keyboards for users with different types of physical disabilities.

Look through magazine articles and ads to find some examples of alternative keyboard designs some of which are commercially available, others not. Comment on these designs.

Mouse

Another input device which has become almost standard with PCs is the mouse, a pointing and clicking device essential for software with a graphical user interface (Figure 3.3).

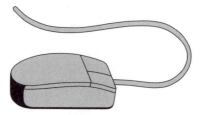

Figure 3.3: A mouse

A mouse needs a flat surface to work. As it is moved on the surface, a ball on the underside of the mouse rolls and a cursor on the screen moves according to the movement of the ball. This allows a user to point to different parts of the screen. Once an icon is chosen this way the selection is made by clicking a button on the mouse. Most mice have two buttons, one for clicking to select and the other for getting context sensitive menus, that is, options related to the task being performed. Sometimes there is a third button meant for specific functions assigned by the user: this works with specially installed programs. It is expected that in future this facility will become common. Usually a cable connects the mouse to the PC. However, cordless mice also exist which operate by transmitting signals to the screen. This is useful when working space is limited. Normally a keyboard and a mouse are used together because no text can be entered via a mouse.

A variation is available in the form of a mouse pen. This looks like a pen and works like a mouse in a very small area. Some mouse pens work by directly pointing on the screen and are used with hand held computers.

Trackball

A trackball (Figure 3.4) is like an upside down mouse; the underside is flat and a ball faces up. The user moves the ball by a finger and this produces movement of

Figure 3.4: A trackball

the cursor. Trackballs offer finer control and are useful when a flat surface is not available which makes them a suitable input device for laptop computers.

Joystick

A joystick used to be the common input device for early home computer games. It is an upright handle-type device which moves in four directions in its socket, with the movement changing the direction of a cursor on the screen (Figure 3.5). It is still used for some video games in entertainment arcades and for some children's software because it allows a user to enter instructions fast without having to type or use precise hand and eye coordination.

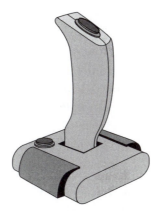

Figure 3.5: A joystick

Why do you think the mouse became so common as an input device while the trackball and joystick did not?

Light pen

This light sensitive pen is another pointing device, which, when taken close to the screen detects the light emitted by the monitor (Figure 3.6). As the pen is held close to the screen and moved, the cursor on the monitor moves with it. A light pen is normally used to point and select from a menu displayed on the monitor. Sometimes it is used with a flat horizontal surface (called a tablet) connected to a computer. Users can write or draw directly on the tablet. A tablet has the same x, y co-ordinates[1] (cross-section of horizontal and vertical positions) as

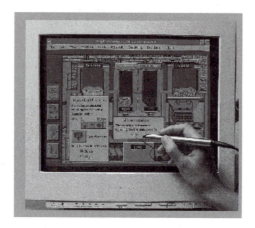

Figure 3.6: A light pen
Source: http://www.computerware.co.uk/index.html

the monitor and any impression made on the tablet is transferred to the screen. This is used widely in computer aided design.

Pen based input is also used with notebook-type computers together with handwriting recognition. The light sensitive pen is used to write directly on a pressure sensitive screen. At present such a device works only if the writing follows set patterns, but work is in progress to facilitate the recognition of free handwriting. Pen based computing will become more common as computers get smaller and will take an increasingly important role in all kinds of everyday functions such as personal organisers and mobile computing, and in use by the emergency services such as the police and the ambulance service.

According to reports in the media (*Daily Telegraph*, 9 October 1998, p. 4) British scientists have developed a 'smart' pen, to be available commercially in two years, which can translate any handwriting to typed text without the need for a screen or paper. Users can write in mid-air and the pen will memorize the writing movements the same way that a microphone recognizes the vibrations of a voice. When the pen is returned to its slot, the stored information can be sent to a computer, printer, mobile phone or a modem (modems are described in Chapter 7). It also comes with a small screen which allows it to be used as an electronic diary or a calculator.

---

1   This term comes from mathematical graphs. Imagine a horizontal and a vertical line from the bottom left-hand corner of the screen. The corner is said to have coordinates 0,0, that is, it has a horizontal (*x*) value of 0 and a vertical (*y*) value of 0. Any other position on the screen has a coordinate determined by its distance from the corner. Thus 10,20 is the coordinate of the position which is 10 points to the right and 20 points high relative to 0,0.

Touch-screen technology

Touch-screen input technology has been growing fast in popularity because of the flexibility and ease of use it offers (Figure 3.7). The computer screen used with this technology is divided into x and y coordinates and the system detects a touch by the coordinate of the point touched which is then accepted by the computer as the selected option. Currently it is used mainly for public information systems (it is more common in the US than in this country) but future possibilities include bank cashpoints, cash tills in superstores and as an alternative to a mouse with a graphical user interface. Some retail stores use it with bulletin boards which hold information on products sold in the shop. Customers are able to select from the choices available on the screen by touching the appropriate names. Further information on the product selected is then displayed on the screen.

Figure 3.7: Touch-screen monitor
Source: http://www.aut.sea.siemens.com

List the examples of the use of touch-screen and light pen you have come across. What future do you think these technologies have as input devices?

Data entry at source

This is a concept used for facilitating quick and accurate data input. Traditionally, in business data processing, data has been collected on a sheet of paper and then transferred into a computer by a VDU operator using a keyboard. Data entry at source works by eliminating the intermediate stage of transferring data from one medium to another by getting a computerized device to send data directly into the computer. The process is much quicker and there is less risk of errors. Such devices are normally used in supermarkets, in warehouses, in banks and other places where speed and accuracy are directly linked to productivity. The following are some of the devices used for direct data entry.

Bar code readers

You are probably familiar with bar codes because they are used on most retail products these days. A bar code is a series of black and white stripes of different widths stuck to an item (Figure 3.8). The bars represent a code that identifies the product to a file held in the store's computer system. The code is read either by a scanner or a pen-like bar code reader connected to the central computer system. The file holds all relevant data related to the product. The necessary details are automatically accessed from the file and the name and price of the item are printed on a receipt. Information such as availability, colour, and so on, is also available on line. This makes it easy and quick to alter information when necessary because changes can be made centrally giving the person at the till access to the most up to date information. This reduces the risk of operator error. The file on the computer system is updated with every sale. The system can also be used to generate orders for items running low in stock, to produce reports on sales patterns and so on.

There are other forms of data entry at source which work on similar principles. For example, many clothes shops use a small card attached to a product. The card holds a magnetic strip which is read directly and the data collected is dealt with in the same way as a bar code. Devices used by retailers for data entry at source are known as *point of sale* (POS) devices because data is entered automatically as each sale is made.

ISBN 0-434-90076-1

9 780434 900763

Figure 3.8: A bar code

Optical mark recognition (OMR)

If you have ever sat a test with multiple choice questions where you put a pencil mark by your chosen answer then you have some experience of OMR. The answer sheet is used as the input medium. An optical scanner identifies the position of the mark by measuring the amount of light reflected from a set of possible entries, the marked positions reflecting less light than the unmarked ones.

Optical character recognition (OCR)

OCR is the process by which a computer recognizes printed (normally) characters. A set of character images is stored in the computer's memory. A scanner connected to a computer is used to scan a document which is then compared against the images stored for recognition. OCR is widely used on credit card slips which are imprinted with the details of the card holder and the shop, the amount spent, the date of transaction, and so on, together with the signature of the owner of the card. One copy of the slip is sent to the credit card company which uses it as the source of input data. A scanner connected to a central computer reads the details from the slip. Card holders' signatures are also stored in memory and the computer recognizes a signature by matching the pattern against the one saved against the account number of the holder.

Handwriting recognition works on the same principle but this has had a restricted use so far because every person has individual handwriting and consequently the number of images required to recognize all varieties is vast. However, research has been going on and considerable progress has been made in this area. Handwriting recognition is important for hand held notepad-type computers but at present the use of a notepad is restricted to such tasks as form filling mainly due to the limitations of the system just mentioned. A number of hardware and software companies are working to introduce a technology based on collecting and analyzing a large sample of handwritten characters and creating a dictionary of characters to be held in a computer's memory (*Daily Telegraph*, 9 October 1998).

Find more information on this technology.

Page scanners

We have seen how scanners are used to scan bar codes, optical characters and so on. Scanners are also used as input devices to scan text and images. Whole pages of text or pictures can be scanned and then saved on disk. After this, the scanned image can be edited and printed. Most scanning programs scan typed text the same way as a picture, that is, by storing characters as a collection of dots (called pixels). This can produce unreliable results because characters (or groups of characters) with similar shapes can be mistaken by the computer for each other; one typical example of this is 'cl' scanned as 'd'. However, work is being done to improve the situation and no doubt soon this problem will be overcome. Scanners have the obvious benefit of using existing text and pictures from printed sheets rather than creating new ones.

Magnetic character recognition (MCR)

Also known as magnetic ink character recognition (MICR), this has been used on bank cheques (Figure 3.9) for a long time. A customer's account number, the sort code (used for sorting cheques), and the cheque number are printed at the bottom of the cheque using ink mixed with magnetic materials. When the cheque is received by the bank the amount is also imprinted on the same line. An MICR reader connected to a computer system then reads the data on the cheque and processes it. If data had to be input via a keyboard it would be impossible for banks to keep up with the millions of bank transactions that take place every day and the error rates would also be much higher.

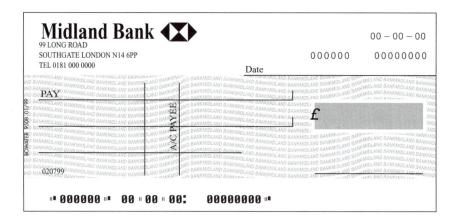

Figure 3.9: A cheque

Smart cards

One of the buzz words of the 1990s, smart cards, the size of a credit card, are incorporated with small microprocessors which hold personal and security data on the card holders. This data is read and checked by a card reader. The data is then sent to a central computer which holds all details on the card holder. Thus a smart card can be used for a number of purposes such as bank transactions, keeping medical and social security details, electronic payment, and so on. Recently, smart cards have been used for handling electronic cash: this involves a user storing money on the card by using a bank cashpoint machine. The electronic money can then be spent instead of cash in shops and other businesses equipped with the appropriate facilities. Although not yet very common in this country, companies such as Mondex and Digicash have introduced this system on an experimental basis in some parts of the UK. The experimental stage is now nearly completed and the future of smart cards in this country will be decided by the outcome. On the one hand, smart cards have great potential because they can provide access to large centralized sources of information and a link between different service areas such as the police, the Home Office, the medical service and so on. On the other hand, many people are seriously concerned about the social consequences of such centrally held data in terms of the preservation of individual privacy and rights. We will discuss such issues later on in the book.

At what stage is the development and diffusion of smart card technology at the moment? Find some articles from the Internet to get a more up to date picture.

Voice input

Voice input systems based on speech recognition technology have been one of the more recent introductions to the input devices market. Initially samples from a large number of speakers are analyzed and a frequency pattern for each sound is stored in the computer's memory. Any word spoken after this is matched against the stored patterns and when a match is found the sound is converted into text and displayed on the screen and/or printed. This has obvious use for people with some types of physical disability but is limited in its scope because of the same difficulty as in the case of handwriting recognition, that is, the wide variation in people's speech patterns. However, the scope is wider in fields where the input can be limited to a number of predetermined words or letters, for example, in hospital operating theatres where doctors can ask for information on patients by using standard terminology. Voice input also offers obvious possibilities for blind people if a Braille printer is available, or for those who have restricted use of their hands.

There are some other less common input devices and research is going on into further developments to make input as quick and as easy as possible. *Image processing*, used in scientific research, is a technique in which pictures taken by a camera can be used as input data. Recently digital cameras have become common input devices because they allow a user to take still and moving pictures which can then be fed into a computer for further processing if necessary. This has obvious use in multimedia productions.

There is also a growing market for suitable input devices for people with disabilities of different kinds, for example some people with severe physical disability can use a pointing device connected to their head. There are even systems where input can be made by blinking at selected points on a screen or by pointing a beam of light on the selected key of a keyboard. Scientists are also working on a device which can sense a person's brainwave when he or she is thinking of an object such as a chair, and print the word on a screen. American scientists have recently successfully inserted a chip inside the brain of a person, enabling him to operate a computer by his thought processes. However, these are very expensive specialist devices often with limited scope and not yet suitable for mass production. Due to limitations of space we will leave the discussion on input devices at this point, but you can read more on the subject by consulting the sources listed under Further reading.

Search for examples of types of input devices not covered in this section. Which way do you think the future of input devices is going?

Output devices

It is likely that you have used output devices in some form or another. The printed receipt that you receive after a transaction made through a bank cashpoint machine is produced by a small printer behind the wall. The small screen you see is also an output device because it displays what you key in as well as the results of the transaction and any messages prompted by the computer system.

Like input devices, output devices also work under the instruction of device drivers which are copied into RAM at the time of use. Processed data in machine code is sent to an output device and converted into a human readable form before it is output.

Visual display unit

Visual display unit, or VDU, is another term used to describe the monitor currently standard with any microcomputer. It is normally made with a cathode ray tube (CRT) which fires electron beams from a gun at the back of the screen. The screen is coated with phosphorus which glows when struck by electrons. Screens are divided into individually addressable dots (following the principle of x, y coordinates), called pixels. The images to be displayed on the screen are created by energizing the appropriate dots on the screen which are then hit by electrons from the CRT. For colour monitors three guns representing red, green and blue fire electrons on each pixel. The number of pixels on a screen determines the clarity of the pictures. The electron beams continuously scan the screen from top to bottom and the pixels energized by the computer are lit up by the electrons and displayed. The scanning happens so fast that although the picture is formed from top to bottom as lines of pixels are serially lit up, the human eye cannot detect the delay. Also, data on the screen is continuously refreshed by being sent repeatedly from memory. The rate at which this is done is called the refresh rate; the faster the refresh rate the less is the flicker on the screen.

Monochrome monitors produce a single colour display on a contrasting screen, for example, white or amber on a dark background. They can also produce shades of the same colour, for example, black and different shades of grey. Colour monitors can be of four different types depending on the number of dots on the screen which determines the resolution of the display. The greater the number the higher is the resolution and the clearer are the pictures. You can visualize the effect of the number of pixels by imagining a character, for example 'N' written by a collection of dots (Figure 3.10) shown here by using bold characters ('0') to indicate the energized dots.

Figure 3.10: A character formed by dots

When there is a large number of pixels on a screen, the dots are closer together which makes the character look less like a collection of dots and more like a continuous line. Some graphics (called vector graphics) are in fact produced by continuous lines rather than illuminating pixels, but they are not very common.

At the bottom of the range of monitors is the colour graphics adapter (CGA) with 320×200 pixels. This was the resolution for the first colour monitors and the images produced were of much inferior quality to what we are used to seeing these days. The next resolution was 640×350 pixels, called the enhanced graphics adapter (EGA), followed by the video graphics array (VGA) with 640×480, and finally by the super VGA (SVGA) initially with 800×600 but increasing continually. Today, typical resolution values are 1280×1024 or 1600×1200 pixels with the ability to handle up to 65,000 colours. The price of monitors varies according to resolution and together with it, the sharpness of the picture. In parallel with the increasing popularity for high quality graphics and multimedia

(a)

(b)

(c)

Figure 3.11: Different types of monitor. (a) PDA (Personal Digital Assistant) (b) Common PC Monitor (c) Flat panel display unit

Source: Dell Computer Corporation Ltd.

presentations, the demand for better display technology has been increasing. This has resulted in an increased demand for larger screens (up to 50 inches, diagonally), antiglare screens, detachable monitors, small footprint (space taken at the base), thin display panels and additional features such as adjustable bases, built-in speakers and cables for connecting peripherals.

The VDUs we have discussed so far are based on CRTs. There is another type with flat screens which are normally smaller and lighter and commonly utilize one or more of the following technologies: liquid crystal display (LCD), plasma display panel (PDP), vacuum fluorescent displays (VFD), thin-film transistor (TFT), electroluminescent displays (ELD), field emission displays (FED) and organic light emitting device (OLED). To learn more about these have a look at the Further reading list. It is worth mentioning that at the moment TFT LCD seems to be the most commonly used for laptop computers and small display screens such as watches, hand held notepads and so on, but some manufacturers are also beginning to incorporate this technology in their desktop computers. Some argue that the quality of an LCD display is not as good as that of a CRT for a number of reasons, including the possible mismatch between the number of dots on a screen and the number of pixels supported by the software, and the sometimes dark and distorted images projected by LCDs. Plasma display has been in existence for a number of years; it produces good results but tends to be very expensive. Although most desktop computers today are made with CRT monitors, flat screen display is expected to become increasingly common.

Printers

From the initial days of computing, printers have been used as the standard output device. Although we have been hearing about paperless offices being on the horizon for the past three decades, printed sheets are still the most commonly used output form today. Printing technology has advanced a great deal in recent years and there is a wide choice in the type and quality of printers for business and personal use.

Printers can be put into two main categories: *impact* and *non-impact*.

Impact printers

Called impact printers because the print-heads make physical contact with the paper with some force, these use an inked carbon ribbon to print. There are two types of impact printers: *dot-matrix* and *character*. Dot-matrix printers form the characters out of a matrix of pins attached to the print-head in the same way that characters are formed by pixels on a VDU. You can get 9- (3×3), 18- (3×6) or 24- (4×6) pin dot-matrix printers. Just as the resolution of a VDU improves with the number of dots on the screen, the clarity of printing improves with the number of pins on a print-head. Character printers, on the other hand, have fully formed mirror images of characters stuck on a drum, chain, wheel or sphere. They give better quality printing.

Dot-matrix printers can be the serial type – printing one character at a time from one end of the page to the other, or the line type – printing a line at a time. Serial printers are often double-sided, that is, the print-head moves from left to right for one line and then comes back as the paper moves up for the next line, from right to left. Line printers have pin head hammers lined up for the whole width of the page on a drum containing lines of characters, each line containing repetitions of the same character. The paper is placed between the drum and an inked sheet; as the drum rotates, hammers hit the paper to print the character required. Thus, when the line of 'A's appears under the hammers, all the 'A's present in the line to be printed are hit by energized hammers. The drum then moves to the next line and all 'B's in the next line are printed the same way (Figure 3.12a). A small storage space in the CPU called the printer buffer holds a line of code and keeps it there until all the characters in the line have been printed. The paper then moves up for the next line to be printed while the buffer gets filled with the next line of output, thus printing at a faster rate than a serial printer. Chain printers (Fig 3.12b) work on the same principle but the characters are on the same line.

Impact printers are the oldest in printing technology. They are normally inexpensive but often rather noisy and slower than the more advanced, non-impact type of printers available today. Another disadvantage of impact printers is that they can only have one set of fonts at any one time. However, impact printing technology has advanced considerably and many of today's printers are quieter and produce prints of reasonable quality economically. Also, using ink cartridges of different colours it is possible to get them to print in colour. One major advantage of impact printers over other more advanced ones is that they can handle continuous stationery and are therefore useful for receipts, prescriptions, invoices, large listings of programs and data and multi-part forms thus making them suitable for businesses which need such stationery as well as large commercial systems based on mainframes and minicomputers.

Non-impact printers

Printers in this category are so called because there is no mechanical impact involved in the printing operation. The most common amongst non-impact printers are *ink jet* and *laser* although other types based on *thermal wax transfer*, *light emitting diode* and *liquid crystal* are also available.

(a)

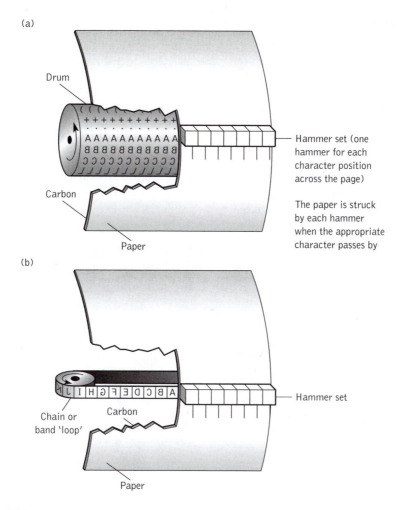

Drum

Hammer set (one hammer for each character position across the page)

The paper is struck by each hammer when the appropriate character passes by

Carbon

Paper

(b)

Hammer set

Chain or band 'loop'   Carbon

Paper

Figure 3.12: (a) A drum printer and (b) a chain or band printer

Ink jet printers Ink jet printers print a line at a time by spraying droplets of ink from nozzles. The images are formed from a matrix of small nozzles in the same way that dot matrix printers use pin heads. A heating element vaporizes the ink in the nozzle forming a bubble that forces the ink out. Ink jet printers are quiet, produce good quality prints and also provide inexpensive colour printing by using different coloured inks. However, the colours are not completely true to what we see on the screen and the paper handling mechanism can be unreliable at times. Also, the prints can get smudged by humidity or wet hands and poor quality paper can affect clarity.

Laser printers Laser printers provide high resolution, smudge-free and very high quality prints because the dots are produced by specks of a toner rather than droplets of ink. They are page printers, that is, they print a page at a time. A drum is electrostatically charged and then a laser beam is used to remove the charge from all but the image of the page to be printed. The charged parts of the drum attract toner particles and throw them on to the paper. The surrounding heat fuses the toner particles to the paper. Figure 3.13 illustrates different types of printers.

Laser printers are often faster than ink jet and they produce better colour. However, they are far more expensive to buy, although cheaper to run because ink cartridges for ink jet printers are expensive. Also laser printers are quite heavy and hence, not very portable.

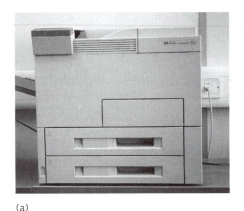

(a)

(c)

(b)

(d)

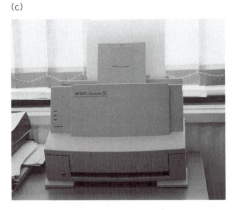

Figure 3.13: (a) Tektronix Phaser 200e laser printer (b) Epson LQ-1070 line printer (c) Hewlett-Packard colour ink jet (d) Epson dot-matrix printer

As you can see all printers have their advantages and disadvantages. Which printer one should use depends on the budget, the quality required, environmental conditions and so on. Thus if you are a student and need inexpensive printing you will probably opt for a dot-matrix provided that noise is not a great problem. On the other hand if you need good quality colour graphics your choice will be either ink jet or laser depending on your budget. If you work for an organization which needs continuous stationery and good paper handling capability, you should choose a good quality dot-matrix printer. But if your company uses a network and needs fast and quality printing, you will most probably have to go for a laser printer. Companies dealing with large computers and commercial systems often choose a combination of different types of printers, for example, impact line printers for routine high volume jobs, serial printers when quality and speed are not very important and laser printers for documents for which presentation is important, such as advertising leaflets or letters to clients. As with all new technology, printers are becoming increasingly cheaper. Only a few years ago laser printers were outside the reach of small organizations and colour laser was only affordable by a few companies. Both of these are now available for a few hundred pounds and good quality printing is within the reach of most users.

Imagine a small garden design company who work in their own office as well as in clients' propeties. What output devices should they buy?

There are other, special purpose output devices. Amongst these are plotters used mainly for sketching architectural plans, design work and charts, especially when they have to be precisely to scale. They use pens which move over the paper under the control of a computer to create images. There are also voice output devices, useful for blind users, and music output products which can simulate different instruments and can work in conjunction with computerized keyboards to create and mix sounds of various kinds.

Information can also be output to a microfiche (sheets of photographic film), mainly used for archives of old literature, library catalogues and so on. These are less common now since CD-ROMs can store a large amount of data which can be displayed on a VDU or printed as necessary. CD-ROMs will be discussed in more detail in the following section.

Search for examples of types of output devices not covered in this section. What are the main uses for them?

Storage devices

We discussed different kinds of storage in Chapter 2, internal (RAM and ROM) and external (called secondary or backing storage). Internal storage (also called primary storage but normally referred to as memory[2]) is expensive and small in size. ROM is out of a user's access for storage, and RAM is volatile and therefore unsuitable for permanent storage of data. We need secondary storage devices to hold programs and data for permanent keeping to be loaded into RAM at the time of use.

Secondary storage is based on two types of technology: magnetic and optical. Magnetic tapes and disks are used to store data magnetically, while CD-ROMs, based on the same technology as audio CDs used in the music business, use optics.

Magnetic tapes

Widely used in the 1960s and 1970s, these have now become less common and are only used for archives and sometimes as back-ups. They look similar to the tape reels used with old fashioned tape recorders and film projection units. They come in widths of ¼" and ½" and in many different lengths. The tape surface is coated with iron oxide and is magnetized as necessary to represent 1s leaving the unmagnetized bits to represent 0s. A tape is a serial medium: data is stored serially from the beginning of the tape to the end and, just like audio tapes, can only be read serially.

Tapes are read by an electromagnetic read-write head that senses magnetic data. Data is brought in equal sized chunks (called blocks) into RAM for processing. Processed data is transferred from RAM and written to tape in the same block sizes by a reverse process. Tape drives are used to read data into and out of tapes. For mainframes and minis these are large devices but for microcomputers they are small units called tape streamers which run ¼" tape cartridges. In the early ages of microcomputers tape recorders of the same type as those used for audio tapes were used but they are rarely seen now. Since serial processing is too slow by today's standards, magnetic tapes are normally used only for keeping large back-up files. One common use is to store copies of all systems files needed

---

2   Storage is the common term used to mean a computer's internal and external storage space. However, often the term 'memory' is used to mean the internal storage, just as we refer to human memory as opposed to backing storage such as in books and tapes.

to boot up a computer system. Then, if the system fails and needs to be reinstalled, the tape can be used to copy the files back, because tapes are faster than disks when non-selective sequential reading is required.

Magnetic disks

These are flat round objects coated with iron oxide. They come in various sizes: large ones about 14" in diameter are used by mainframes and minis and smaller ones, 5.25" and 3.5", called floppy disks, are used for microcomputers.

Similar to a music record a disk surface has a number of tracks on it along which data is recorded (Figure 3.14). Before a disk can be used it has to be formatted which divides the disk into sectors. The space in between two sectors is typically 512 bytes and is referred to as a block. Data is read from and written to a disk block by block. When a disk is to be used it is inserted into a device called the disk drive. An electromagnetic read-write head attached to the disk drive

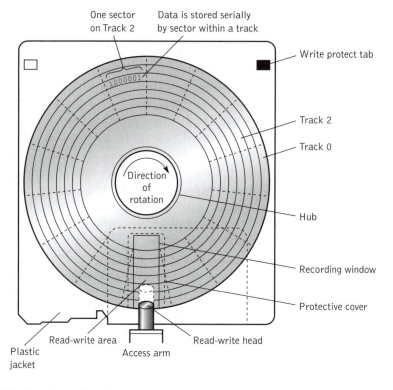

Figure 3.14 Disk with tracks and sectors

floats over the disk surface and writes by printing magnetic spots on the tracks. Data to be read is picked up by the read-write head using a reverse process and transferred to the RAM of a computer. At the time of formatting, a disk is treated by the read-write head as new, that is, the sectors are redrawn thus losing any existing data. This is one way of erasing a disk completely to start anew, but at the same time, formatting a used disk carelessly may result in the loss of important data.

Disks can be fixed or removable. In personal computers the fixed disk is called the hard disk. It normally holds a pack of disks, also called Winchester disks, stacked on a rotating axle. Data is stored on both sides of each disk and a set of read-write heads placed on arms connected to the axle move in and out of the disk pack. Each arm has two read-write heads, one for the lower surface of one disk and the other for the upper surface of the disk below (Figure 3.15). Because the heads can get to any position directly, data can be read from any track and any sector without the need to start at the beginning. This is called random (or direct) access and is much faster than serial access. At present a hard disk on a PC can store more than 2 GB[3] of data which is much larger than the disk space available in mainframes and minis 10 years ago. As increasingly sophisticated programs are introduced into the market, the demand for hard disk storage is also increasing. For example, Microsoft's Windows 98 has initiated the introduction of a 10.1 GB drive by a company called Western Digital. It is envisaged that the increasing demand for graphics and web storage (Internet pages) will double the capacity needed every 18 months (*Computer Weekly*, 24 September 1998).

The removable disks for personal computers are called floppy disks because the disk surface is made of flexible plastic over which an easily magnetizable coating is applied. Most floppies used nowadays are 3.5" in size and are enclosed in hard plastic casing. Typically, they have a capacity of 720 KB or 1.44 MB, although disks with higher capacities are available. Floppy disks are double sided which means data is written on both sides of the disk and the disk drive has two read-write heads, one for the upper surface of the disk and one for the lower.

Floppy disks are much slower than hard disks and obviously much smaller in size. Normally programs and systems files are held on hard disks and floppies are used for storing users' personal files and back-up copies. Similarly, in the mainframe and minicomputer environment, fixed disks are used for programs and files needed frequently, for example, those required for booting up and frequently used programs, whereas removable disks are used for other programs and data as well as for back-up copies.

---

3 1 gigabyte = 1 billion bytes

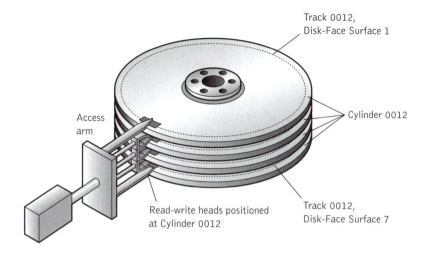

Figure 3.15: Read-write heads for a disk drive

Compact disks

For personal computers optical storage is becoming increasingly popular. CD-ROMs, similar in size to 5.25″ floppy disks but holding a lot more data, are now used for storing large documents such as encyclopaedias and large multi-user databases as well as games, multimedia applications and large programs. The typical storage capacity of a compact disk is 600 MB, equivalent to 200,000 pages of text. One CD has about 16,000 tracks. A laser beam burns pits on the tracks to write to the disk. A CD drive has a laser source which beams light on a CD. If the light comes back with the same intensity then it is recognized as an unburnt bit and read as a '0'; burnt bits of the CD reflect less light and are read as 1s. CDs are normally written to by the software vendors who have the required technology. Users can only read them via their CD drives, hence the name CD-ROM (read only memory). This has reduced the piracy problem for software manufacturers as well as the possibility of using CDs as a source of virus programs.

There are also CD-WORMs (write once read many times) to which users are allowed to write once using optical technology. Once burnt the pits cannot be unburnt, so CDs cannot be erased and written to again. Rewritable CDs are also available although at present the technology is too expensive to allow them to become common. They use magneto-optic technology and are written to by shining a laser beam on the tracks only slightly so that the magnetic polarity of the spots change to indicate 1s, leaving the untouched parts as 0. These disks can be rewritten to by changing the polarity again.

CDs are random access devices and the access time is much faster than floppies although not as fast as hard disk. However, with their high capacity and relatively low prices, CDs have become very popular and a large number of personal computers are built nowadays with CD drives. The multimedia industry is currently benefiting from CD technology because they have storage space large enough to hold text, pictures and sound. They are also secure since magnetic fields have no effect on them and as the drives have no moving parts disk crashes (caused by the read-write head crashing against a disk) cannot occur. They are also robust against the effects of dust, moisture, light scratches, and so on, to a large extent. Recently, a new type of optical disk called DVD (originally known as digital video/versatile disk) has been developed. This is similar in size to a CD-ROM but is capable of holding about 17 GB of data. Currently these are used in video players and by the film industry but in the near future they will be used with computers for ROM, RAM and secondary storage. The advantages of optical storage coupled with the introduction of cheaper and more versatile disks will hopefully make them the most common secondary storage medium of the future.

What is the role of storage technology in the creation of a paperless office?

Summary

In order to perform its functions, a computer needs input, output and external storage devices. An input device is used to enter data into the computer. The most common of these is the keyboard but there are a number of other devices such as a mouse, light pen, and so on which are equally useful in today's computer world where the emphasis is on making the computer a part of everyday life. Output devices, used for displaying processed data in human readable form, also come in a number of forms, the most common being the printer. Printing technology has improved enormously in recent years and now it is possible to have good quality colour printing for a reasonably low price. One of the driving forces behind innovations in input/output technology is the needs of disabled users, giving rise to a number of special purpose devices.

External storage is used for holding programs and data permanently. The devices used commonly are disks: fixed and removable. In the world of PCs fixed disks are referred to as the hard disk and the removable, as floppies. These work with magnetic technology and data stored can be changed at any time. Recently,

CD-ROMs have become common; they are similar to music disks and operate by optical technology. They can hold a large amount of data very securely. Commonly, they are read-only and are used to hold collections of articles, encyclopaedias, multimedia programs, and so on. Technology capable of producing rewritable CDs is already available and as it becomes cheaper, CDs will become increasingly common for storage. Another storage device fast becoming common is the DVD.

Further reading

Look at recent articles in magazines such as *BYTE* (www.byte.com) and CD-ROMs such as *Computer Select*, which stores articles from a large number of magazines, for up to date information on input, output and storage devices.

Look at the July 1998 copy of *BYTE* for innovations on screen displays (www.byte.com).

Buying a Personal Computer: How to Choose the Right Equipment to Suit your Needs, by Allen Brown, How To Books, 1998 gives clear information on PC hardware and software.

There is a press report on page 4 of the *Daily Telegraph* of 9 October 1998 on smart pens which you might like to read.

The weekly magazines mentioned in the Further reading section of Chapter 1 contain useful information.

Revision questions

1. List the types of input devices available today and explain briefly how they work.

2. Compare and contrast the use of different input devices explaining clearly their strengths and weaknesses in different circumstances.

3. Explain the significance of data entry at source for users. How do different input devices serve to achieve the full potential of this mode of data entry?

4. List the types of output devices available and explain briefly how each of them works.

5. Discuss the criteria by which one should select a printer for a PC based system. Using examples of different requirements in different circumstances, explain which printer you would choose in each case.

6. Discuss the contribution made by recent innovations in input and output devices for disabled users.

7. Discuss different types of storage devices, their characteristics, advantages, disadvantages, and specific uses in the computer industry.

8. What is the significance of the CD technology in the market for storage?

Food for thought

Computing Canada, 3 March 1997, vol. 23, no.5, p.38(1)
Plesman Publications Ltd (Canada)

Mixing and matching opticals
Jim Kaufmann

Memory-hungry application software, mixed media development, workgroup and enterprise workflow management, the dramatic growth of the Internet – all have converged to produce an almost insatiable demand for ever-increasing amounts of removable, on-line storage.

To meet the demand, optical storage has evolved from a limited data storage solution into a broad range of diverse technologies – each unique in its capabilities and technological approach. The options, combined with recent technological innovations, lower prices, standards compliance and a steady stream of success stories, will continue to expand the use of optical storage across the complete spectrum of business applications.

With the wide range of optical that are now available, organizations of all sizes can achieve improved data management and increased productivity while lowering their storage costs.

Understanding the differences between the options that are available will help users during the selection process. However the industry has advanced so quickly that it's important to compare the most recent specifications and capabilities of the various technologies when determining which storage technology is the best solution for a specific application.

To meet the market's needs, a number of optical industry standards have been adopted, improved technologies are being implemented, and industry-wide agreements on capacity, compatibility and growth paths have been reached.

Much of the demand for storage capacity growth can be attributed to today's highly competitive, information–dependent business environment where there is an increasing need for companies to exchange volumes of information – internally and with external business partners, vendors and customers. Sharing vast amounts of proprietary information requires both a high degree of data security (so that distributed information cannot be altered) and standardized media formatting (to ensure universal data access).

While initial hardware/software costs are always a consideration, network and IS managers are now taking a harder look at the features and benefits that the various solutions offer and are balancing factors such as flexibility and scalability with accessibility and data life cycle costs.

As a result, rather than choosing a single, all-purpose storage technology, they're often finding that they need to develop a mix of removable and on-line technologies. The objective is to use the most cost-effective approach for each application without sacrificing performance.

At one end of the spectrum are the corporate managers and decision-makers who have come to understand that they need a centralized solution in order to improve communications and reduce management costs. These central repositories require secure, low-cost storage for volumes of on-line data and images that can be accessed by authorized users throughout the enterprise.

At the other end of the spectrum are the users who are increasingly being armed with pre-press, presentation, multimedia development and workstation backup/recovery applications which require fast, reliable access. Because they also require a high-capacity solution that won't create network bottlenecks, a removable storage solution that frees valuable space on the hard drive is best.

In selecting a stand-alone storage system, users have to weigh all of the drive features, including scalability, reliability, write speed and cost of retrieval, along with the cost per MB, before choosing a storage solution. A single feature, such as interchangeability, may be the overriding factor in selecting one solution over another.

Since a scanned image may require from three to 50 megabytes or more of storage, optical disk technology has been proven to be ideal for document image storage and retrieval. A recent study by The Gallup Organization reports that imaging is the leading application for optical disk storage. However with the advancements MO optical has achieved in capacity and performance, optical technology has moved from niche market applications into mainstream business applications.

In addition to advancing the capacity and performance of their products, the key players in the optical industry have realized that the demand can only grow if corporate decision-makers see that the technology complies with industry standards.

No one wants to buy a storage/retrieval solution that quickly becomes obsolete and difficult to support. When they see compatible, competitive products using the same technology, they are convinced that the technology is a long-term solution that can be used to meet their current and future needs.

The right storage mix can be determined with a few key questions: How much information do you need to store? How often will you need to access it? How fast do you want to be able to retrieve it? The final selection is often a two-tiered storage solution that puts the best technology to work for both sets of requirements now (real-time access and near-line access), and provides a growth path for the future.

For example, when fast access to volumes of information is important, network managers can use jukeboxes with one or more 2.6 GB direct-overwrite MO drives for a fraction of the cost of hard disk storage.

If near hard drive performance and low storage costs are needed, a stand-alone 2.6 GB drive can be used in conjunction with the storage matrix. Archived documents or data that doesn't require split-second access can be stored on recordable CDs in a CD jukebox. Regardless of the application, in comparing the cost and performance of the various storage options, it is apparent that optical will play an increasingly vital role in helping organizations meet their burgeoning storage/retrieval requirements.

The author is vice-president, sales and marketing, at MOST Inc.

Discussion questions

1. In today's business world, what are the main criteria on the basis of which storage decisions are made?

2. Why, according to the author of the above article, is optical storage considered the most suitable solution for modern businesses?

3. What does the author mean by the MO (magneto-optic) solution and how does this advance the case for optical storage?

4. What are the reasons why a mixed solution is often found suitable? How is this achieved?

5. Find some more information on storage needs and technology of the future and write an essay on the way the two are likely to converge.

CHAPTER 4

Computer software

At the end of this chapter you should have some understanding of:

▶ What we mean by computer software;
▶ the difference between systems and application software;
▶ the common types of systems software;
▶ the roles systems and applications software play in the running of a computer system.

Introduction

A computer system consists of both hardware and software and it is only by an intelligent combination of the two that the system works. Without hardware, software has no role to play. The performance of a high quality computer program depends on the quality of the hardware available. On the other hand, hardware is driven by software and its performance is largely dependent on the quality of the software. All computers are built on basically the same principles, capable of performing basic mathematical functions. By using specialized software we can turn a general purpose computer into a special purpose one. In this chapter we are going to discuss the purpose of systems and applications software and take a closer look at operating systems – the systems software you are most likely to become familiar with. Applications software will be discussed in some detail in Chapter 5.

Categories of software

As discussed briefly in Chapter 1, software can be put into two broad categories: *systems* and *applications*. Systems software consists of programs which perform the basic operations involved in running and maintaining a computer system. One very common example of this is an operating system, the program that controls the way computer hardware and software work together. Applications software, on the other hand, is written with specific business or personal applications in mind. You are probably already familiar with some applications programs such as wordprocessors or spreadsheets. Thus, systems software runs a system and applications software runs particular applications and needs systems programs to make it work, for example, a wordprocessing program works under an operating system. The following is a brief description of the types of systems and applications software available today.

Systems software

Systems software can be put into five categories:

● operating systems
● operating environments
● utility software
● translation programs
● communications software.

Operating systems

An operating system is a program (or a suite of programs) designed to aid the day-to-day running of a computer system. This is what operates a computer system and enables hardware and software to relate to each other and to the user.

The general functions of an operating system can be listed as follows:

- running programs
- handling input and output
- managing memory
- managing secondary storage
- processing files
- maintaining security
- handling errors
- managing communications between the system and its users.

Operating systems perform other tasks as well but most of them can be broadly put under one or more of those listed above. A detailed description of each of these functions is outside the scope of this book (see the section on Further reading if you want to know more); we shall take a brief look at them in order to have an overview of the role of an operating system.

Running programs This is the main task of an operating system. It involves copying the programs to be run into RAM, copying other necessary files and documents into RAM, starting the program and generally managing the operations till completion. This is a simple task for a single user system running one program at a time and all operating systems are capable of doing this although at various degrees of speed and flexibility. However, they vary enormously in their ability to run programs when more than one user or one program is involved. The following are some of the types of environment an operating system may have to deal with and today most of them come with an ability to handle more than one of these.

- **Multi-user** This is a system with a number of linked computers and peripherals where users share disk space, programs, files and other resources.
- **Multi-tasking** A multi-tasking system allows its users to perform more than one task involving more than one application at the same time. For example, a user, while using a wordprocessing program to create a text based document can call up a spreadsheet program to work on a balance sheet without exiting from the former program. However, at any one time only one program is handled although both of them are open and available.
- **Multi-programming** This is the feature which enables an operating system to allocate the input, output and processor times to a number of programs in a way that optimizes the use of resources. For example, when one program has completed input and processing and is being printed, another program is

processed and a third program is input, thus keeping all three devices busy to reduce idle (unproductive) times. The system works on the basis of a predetermined priority rating; a program with higher priority can interrupt lower priority programs to claim the service of a device.

● **Multi-threading** This is the term used to explain the way a program can do several things at the same time, for example, a spreadsheet program printing a worksheet and at the same time allowing you to create a chart.

● **Multi-processing** As mentioned in Chapter 2, some computers are equipped with more than one processor and need an operating system capable of handling this. A supercomputer works with a large number of small processors while many of today's microcomputers come with additional processors for special purposes such as a maths co-processor for handling complicated mathematical functions.

Thus, when we hear terms such as a multi-tasking or multi-user operating system, it indicates that the operating system under discussion can run programs under those environments. In the past only operating systems for mainframes could deal with such complications, but today the same features are widely available to PC users.

Multi-tasking is a common term in the world of microcomputers. Give some examples of useful applications of this facility.

Handling input and output devices A user communicates with a computer via an input device. This may be to give the system instructions at the time of running, to send data interactively and to load programs and files into memory amongst other things. Similarly, the computer passes information back to a user using output devices. It does this by displaying messages on the VDU or by transferring the results to a printer. An operating system checks that the programs that run these devices are available in RAM and when data is sent in or out they are passed on as quickly and as efficiently as possible.

Managing memory The memory manager part of an operating system is responsible for organizing the internal storage space available to a computer. This is necessary to ensure that programs and data required to exist in the memory at the same time can be accommodated and easily accessed. For jobs requiring only small programs and files it is a simple task. However, if the memory is not large enough either because the program is too large to accommodate all of it or because a number of programs are required to be in the memory at the same time then the management of the memory becomes a major task. In such cases advanced techniques have to be used and the operating system must be equipped to handle them. Some of these techniques involve the use of the hard disk and others require additional RAM chips. One of the techniques used by modern microcomputers is swapping in which some hard disk space is used as the spare for RAM. For running large programs, the operating system swaps files between RAM and the hard disk in order to accommodate the files required by the system at any one time within RAM. This concept, referred to as *paging*, has been used for mainframes for a long time. It is also known as *virtual memory* as it allows users to extend the capacity of RAM beyond its physical size.

Managing secondary storage A major part of an operating system's job is to organize the storage of files on disks. Operating systems are responsible for making sure that the best use of the space available on a disk is made and also that finding files on a disk takes the minimum amount of time. Maintenance of the directory structure on a disk is one of the main methods used in such organization. We will discuss files and directories here to give you a clearer idea of how this works.

- **Files** Every document saved on a disk is called a file. Each of these files is given a name with two parts, a prefix and an extension, separated by a dot. Until recently no spaces were allowed in filenames and the names could only be up to eight characters long. Thus, if you use an operating system of a generation before Windows 98 'chapter_1. txt' or 'chapter 1.txt' would be invalid filenames. But Windows 98 allows filenames up to 255 characters long and with spaces to make them more natural and therefore, user friendly. The following conventions for naming files are accepted by most operating systems:

  - any alphabetic character and digits can be used in filenames;

  - only certain special characters are allowed;

  - extensions can be up to three characters long.

  Thus, 'file1.doc', 'essays.ch1', 'letters', 'chpter_1.txt' are all valid filenames; but, 'file\.doc' and 'essay.chapter' are not. An operating system knows a file by its full name, so 'essays' and 'essays.ch1' are recognized as two different files. The extension can be optional for files personal to users but most programs either demand certain extensions or allocate extensions to files automatically.

  When we wish to save a file we send an instruction to the operating system which then stores the file on a disk in a way that ensures that it can be found easily. It does this by maintaining an index in a reserved space on the disk. The index holds the name and location (the address) of each file stored. When an operating system is asked to open a file, it searches the index for the filename, finds its address and fetches the file.

When there is a large number of files stored on a disk, the index becomes very long and searching it serially from the beginning is time consuming. The process is complicated by the fact that often users cannot remember the exact name of the files. Also, in a multi-user system where many different types of files are stored and many different categories of users have access to the system, it is essential that there are some methods used for simplifying the process. A multi-level *directory* structure ensures that files can be found easily whether a computer is used by an individual or by people sharing a system.

● **Directories** A directory (called a folder by modern PC systems) is a tree-structured index. Just like a tree has branches and each branch has either more branches or leaves, a directory has further subdirectories or files. The top level of the directory structure (before any branching begins) is called the root and is normally specified by the name of the disk drive. Figure 4.1 gives an example of a directory structure on a typical user's disk whilst Figure 4.2 gives a schematic representation of a directory tree.

As stated already a directory is only an index (rather like the table of contents in a book). It does not contain any files, only addresses (called pointers) of where the files are actually stored, together with some other information such as size of the file, date of creation, and so on. Files are not necessarily stored in consecutive spaces on the disk surface. This does not create problems since the operating system can find the exact location from the directory.

To find a particular file, the user has to specify the path name to the operating system written using the specific convention of the operating system used. For example, if a user wants to access chap11.doc (Figure 4.1), the path name for it from the top (the root) is 'c:\book\chap11.doc'.[2] When the operating system is asked to look for a file, either with a full path name (as above) or by asking for a directory one level at a time (first asking for c:, then book, and finally chap11.doc) it looks at the entry in the index for the file, finds the exact physical address and fetches the file. Each directory in such a structure is a subdirectory to the level above. A directory (or a subdirectory) may contain further subdirectories or files and a combination of the two can exist at the same level, for example, ADDRESS and finance under DB in Figure 4.2.

Look at the screen dump in Figure 4.1. Try to identify the purpose of each directory on the left-hand side of the picture and the type of the file on the right-hand side.

---

2 Most operating systems use the character '\' to separate levels in a directory tree. Also in modern systems with a graphical user interface you can open directories and files by clicking on appropriate icons rather than having to write a full path name.

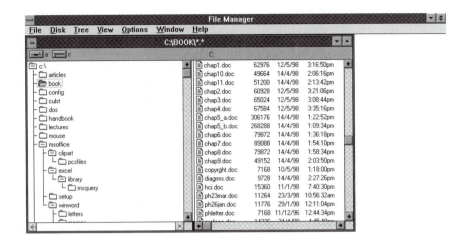

Figure 4.1: A typical real life disk structure

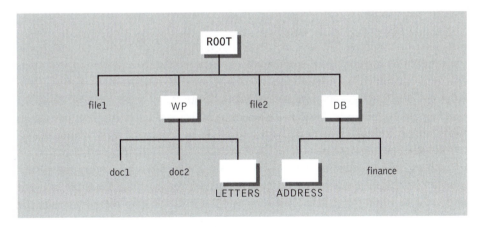

Figure 4.2: A typical user's disk organisation. Here file1, file2, doc1 and so on are used as filenames and WP, DB and LETTERS are directories. LETTERS is a subdirectory of WP and ADDRESS is a subdirectory of DB

Often users of multi-user systems are grouped, and hierarchical access rights are given to different groups thus facilitating security of files. For example, Unix, a common operating system for medium sized computer systems, allocates directories on the basis of the type of use. Thus, there will perhaps be a directory called bin for binary files, one called sys for systems files, another called usr for end-users and so on. Each directory in turn would be divided into subdirectories for further organization; thus, usr may have subdirectories called dept1, dept2 and so on for each department in the organization. In such a hierarchical system normally the system administrators have full access to anywhere down the tree and individuals have access to parts according to their functions in the organization.

When asked to save a file, an operating system looks for a space large enough to hold the file. This leaves trapped unused spaces in-between files; in other words, a disk can get fragmented and has to be compacted by running special programs. If an operating system fails to find the space for a file it informs the user that the disk is full. Sometimes a large file is saved in small parts in scattered positions on the disk with links from each position to the next to enable the operating system to find it later on. This demonstrates how efficient an operating system has to be to manage storage.

An operating system also performs many of the routine tasks necessary to facilitate the use of secondary storage, such as formatting a disk and checking if a disk is suitable for use. Read the sources mentioned under Further reading if you want to know more on the subject.

Processing files As well as organizing the storage of files, an operating system also coordinates how files are processed. You are probably familiar with some file operations through your experience of using a PC. Some common examples are: retrieving files from backing store, copying and deleting files, moving files from one place to another, and so on. Users can perform these file operations by issuing operating systems commands or by choosing the appropriate operation from a list of options available. Before the days of window based operating systems, users had to write commands such as save, copy, rename, delete and so on to do these tasks. Users' lives have been made much easier by the graphical user interfaces of modern operating systems because of the facilities available to point and click at the required instructions, but the operating system interprets the commands and performs the operations the same way as before. We have already seen the steps involved in saving and retrieving files within the framework of a directory structure, and this demonstrates some of the complications involved in file processing.

Maintaining security Security of files is a major concern in any system but it is of crucial importance in a multi-user environment when more than one user uses the same system and stores some of their files on the same disk. Unless security controls are built in, accidental and deliberate damage and loss of files can easily occur. It is the job of the operating system to see that authorized users have the necessary access and unauthorized users are locked out. The most secure way to protect a file is to stop anyone other than the person who created it having any access to it. Normally, in a multi-user system each user is allocated a directory. For example, in a university, a directory called 'staff' may be reserved for all members of staff; this may have several subdirectories, one for each department, with further subdirectories for each person working in the department. Similarly, students may share one directory called 'students' with subdirectories for different subject areas, and eventually, an individual subdirectory for each student. Thus the directory structure allows each user access to his or her own pathway only obtainable by entering the identification code and password allocated to the user. However, in a multi-user system there is often the need for sharing of files and this can be facilitated in different ways, for example by allocating a special identification code to a group of people. Unix allows users to build a security system within each file by choosing who can access the file and to what extent. For example, the creator of a file can allow some users the right to read as well as to alter the file, some just the right to read and others no access at all.

Find out what security features are used in the computer system of your college or place of work.

Handling errors Operating systems are equipped to detect errors and produce appropriate error messages for the user. They cannot correct errors but some efficient operating systems can take certain actions when they detect an error. This may include making automatic back-up copies of all files open at the stage when a problem is detected, closing all open files and so on which ensures that minimum damage is done when a program ends abnormally.

Managing communications between a system and its users In a single user system this is the part of the operating system that provides its users with an interface. An operator gives instructions to a computer by typing in commands or via a graphical user interface; the instructions are interpreted by the operating system and then the necessary actions are taken. In a multi-user system the task is more complicated because it involves the control of simultaneous access by users to the same resources and making sure that there is no deadlock or corruption of one user's resources by another. Efficient operating systems facilitate these operations by various means. You can consult the Further reading list if you want to know about these.

Thus, an operating system is a set of programs which work together to coordinate the overall working of a computer. The tasks described above are all parts of the same set of an operating system's programs and there are considerable amounts of overlap between the areas covered under each named task. Together, the operating system programs provide an environment or an interface for the users which allows them to use a computer system without having to worry about the internal structure and the working of the hardware or software. Thus an operating system shields users from the complications of the technology and organizes the access to resources as quickly and as securely as possible.

How do we choose an operating system?

Operating systems differ in the way and the extent to which they can perform their tasks. The choice depends on a number of factors not all of which are determined by the technical specifications of the operating system alone. A computer system is a combination of hardware, applications and systems software as well as the users; therefore the operating system chosen has to satisfy a wide variety of needs. Amongst these are: the speed with which it can run applications, for example a 32-bit operating system[3] can handle 32-bit processors well; the interface it offers to its users; its compatibility with other applications and systems software written by different software developers; the amount of memory needed to store and run it; security features built into the program; network compatibility; its ability to handle multi-tasking and other modes of program running; the technical support required to run it, and above all the specific needs of the users.

At present there are a large number of PC operating systems on the market and the choice is often confusing and the information available misleading. Some users are now demanding that PCs come with their own operating systems invisible to the user. This would be the ideal solution for non-specialist users because the primary goal of an operating system is to hide the complications of the technology from its user. A US company is currently working on the concept of a Network PC which would use the Internet to download and run programs, thus

---

3   A 32-bit operating system can handle 32 bits of data or program code together.

avoiding the need of specific systems or applications software. This would reduce the price of computers dramatically and would be particularly beneficial to the home computer market.

Some common operating systems

Amongst the many operating systems on the market some are large and powerful ones meant for mainframe and mid-range computers supporting a multi-user environment, and some are smaller ones for microcomputer based systems. Large computers normally have their own operating systems written specifically for the hardware concerned and supplied with the machines by the manufacturers. Examples are IBM's OS/390, ICL's VME and DEC's (now Compaq's) VAX/VMS). Unless you become a programmer it is unlikely that you will have to deal with these operating systems. Most of these are managed centrally with access to users via computer terminals (inexpensive computers with little processing power of their own) in which case either the users are technical people with expertise in systems software or the system is used for a specific application (called a dedicated system) and the operating system is transparent to its users. On the other hand, PC users at all levels have a closer relationship with the operating system and need some awareness of it.

As discussed in Chapter 1, most personal computers currently in use are IBM compatible and are run by an operating system written by Microsoft. They began with the Microsoft Disk Operating System (MS-DOS, also known as DOS) which was written for Intel processors and was strictly a command based program: that is, it worked by a user typing in commands. MS-DOS has been very popular for more than 10 years with its increasingly updated versions. In 1990, Microsoft introduced its Windows program which had a big impact on the use of personal computers. Initially, Windows was a graphical front for MS-DOS, thus making the operating system easier to use. Recent versions of Windows such as Windows for Workgroups, Windows NT, Windows 95, Windows 98 and Windows 2000 are full operating systems in their own rights and progressively offer a range of features such as network compatibility, multi-tasking, multi-threading and multi-processing.

Windows for Workgroups is a version of Windows specifically tailored for workgroup computing, that is, when a team of people work on a computer network to use the same applications and share files in the same way they would do if they were working on a paper based project laid out on a desk.

Windows NT is a full 32-bit operating system (the previous ones being 16-bit) independent of MS-DOS, which supports multi-tasking, multi-user, multi-threading and multi-processing. It also works with a number of hardware systems and claims to support advanced security features. However, it requires at least 16 MB of RAM to run it and is expensive to buy.

Windows 95 was introduced in mid-1996 amongst widespread publicity. It has all the features available in Windows NT and is fully backward compatible, that is, it works with previous versions of Microsoft Windows applications and files. It has a realistic (intuitive) interface thus making it easy to understand for non-expert users and it works fast and reliably. However, it needs at least 8 MB of RAM and 60 MB of disk space to store. It does not have the security protection offered by NT and does not cope with DOS programs well. It was suggested at the time that Windows 95 may be the perfect choice for individual and small business users whereas Windows NT may be more suitable for corporate users. Windows 98, introduced in July 1998, and Windows 2000 introduced recently, offer faster operation, easier file handling and more efficient memory management. However, as is the case with most new products from Microsoft, they have not been without their critics.

Find out how Windows 98/2000 differ from Windows 95.

Other well known operating systems available in the market are OS/2, developed by IBM in collaboration with Microsoft, IBM's PS/2 for its range of personal computers by the same name and Apple's own operating system for its Macintosh range. As explained in Chapter 1, high hopes were placed upon these at the time of their introduction but except for the Macintosh, with its own specialized market, the others were not successful. However, OS/2 has currently made a comeback with an increased 32-bit design and a number of advanced technical and security features. In the meantime, Unix, which was initially designed for the PDP range of minicomputers, has made enormous progress and has even entered the personal computer market. Unix is described in more detail below.

In today's competitive market, it is difficult to give a complete account of the existing operating systems since new programs or versions of older ones are continually being introduced. For example, Windows NT has already developed a version which has incorporated the Unix standard thus making it compatible with Unix based applications allowing Unix users to move to NT easily. On the other hand, Unix is already on its way to producing a 64-bit version of the software, and this will no doubt be followed by the others. Also, increasingly powerful versions of MS-DOS have been introduced because there is a large group of dedicated users who find the speed and control offered by a command based operating system unmatched by the user friendly interfaces of Windows.

Unix operating system Unix is a multi-user, multi-tasking operating system. First introduced by researchers in Bell Laboratory in 1969, it was sold, together with its code, very cheaply to academic institutions. It soon developed a market via the graduates of these institutions and gained popularity for its simplicity and modularity (programs were written in separable chunks to make them easy to understand and alter). With the availability of program codes, versions of Unix were soon written for computers of different makes, including personal computers. This led to the concept of one operating system suitable for different types of hardware. Leading computer manufacturers and software houses became interested in developing a standard version of Unix and formed the Open Software Foundation (OSF). This is an organisation involved in developing a system in which any software would work with any hardware system without the constraint of compatibility. This is called an open system and Unix has been accepted widely as the operating system suitable for this purpose.

Unix is primarily a command based operating system although some recently introduced versions come with a graphical user interface. It has a powerful file handling capability and offers a simple but efficient multi-user environment. Thus it is popular amongst systems developers and those working within a technical environment. However, Unix is not so popular amongst non-specialist end-users because there are a large number of commands which are often not self-explanatory or easy to use. Unix has also had some problems with security and memory management in the past but with the introduction of increasingly updated versions, these problems are soon expected to be eliminated. The overwhelming strength of Unix is in its ability to work across hardware and software platforms. Thus, it can work in a multi-user system which encompasses a variety of sizes and makes of computers; this has created a growing market for it amongst large businesses who are searching for vendor independence for their computer systems.

A number of companies have developed versions of Unix suitable for PCs. Companies such as Sun Microsystems, Santa Cruz Operation, Solaris (SCO) and IBM are amongst many who have updated Unix to improve its performance, flexibility, speed (some parts of it can now handle 64-bit processing), security and above all, usability to make it suitable for today's windows-type environment. IBM's AIX, Hewlett Packard's HP-UX and SCO's Unixware are examples of such operating systems.

In 1992, a new PC operating system called Linux which is similar to Unix in its interfaces but is not based on Unix code was introduced. It has built up a reputation as a totally portable system which is also highly secure, very easy to upgrade and customize, fast and inexpensive (free to many users). It is now competing strongly with other operating systems. You can find out more about Linux from the *Food for thought* article at the end of this chapter.

Find out what you can about the use of Unix on PC based systems.

Operating environments

With the development of microcomputers, computer power has been brought closer to individuals. A large proportion of the western population has access to computers either directly as users or indirectly through the services industry. This has created the need for making computers suitable tools for non-experts. One of the most important features of a modern computer system is user friendliness. In the 1970s and 1980s, the only way for users to communicate with computers was by typing in commands and using specific key-strokes. These are sometimes difficult to conceptualize, and hence, difficult to remember for those without specialist training.

Operating environments hide the complications of software from users by allowing them to select options from menus and graphical interfaces presented on the screen. Initially, this was restricted to pull-down menus available with certain programs (Figure 4.3). In the early to mid 1980s, Apple, with its Macintosh range of microcomputers and Digital Research with GEM (Graphical Environment Manager) incorporated with most of its software, introduced the concept of easy-to-use graphical user interfaces. These are screen displays consisting of realistic pictorial representations of tasks and computer concepts (Figure 4.4). A user with a mouse can point to the appropriate icon (a picture to represent each task) and click to choose the features required. Graphical user interfaces proved very popular and all large software developers jumped on the bandwagon. In the late 1980s, Microsoft, the software company behind the programs working on IBM compatible PCs, introduced Windows. In 1990,

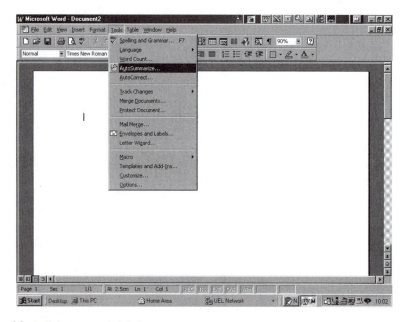

Figure 4.3: Pull-down menus in Windows

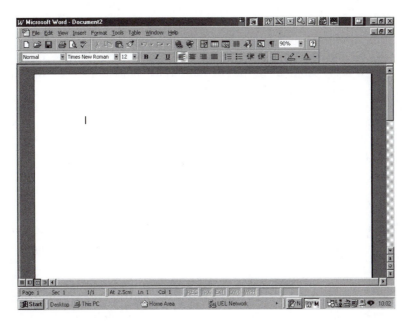

Figure 4.4: Windows screen display with a number of applications and icons

Windows version 3.0 was released and made a big impact on PC users in spite of some major problems with the software. Since then, as explained earlier, Microsoft has been relentless in the way it has dominated the PC market with continuous innovations and extravagant marketing strategies to make a place for itself in small and large businesses alike.

Utility software

Utilities are systems programs designed mainly to perform some routine 'house-keeping' tasks for a computer system. This could be to organize storage on disks, allocate memory space to the operating systems and other programs, perform security checks on disks for viruses and so on. For the microcomputer market many utility programs are supplied with operating systems and, as far as the users are concerned, are not distinguishable from the operating system. Larger systems have libraries of special purpose utilities for various functions which can be incorporated into other programs to save time: one typical example being a utility for sorting data.

Translation programs

In the early days of computing, programs were written in machine code using a series of 0s and 1s (representing electronic switches 'off' or 'on'). This is the only language a computer understands but is difficult for human beings to use. To make programming easier, higher levels of programming languages using mnemonics (English-like abbreviations) and English words were introduced. These are easier for humans but need to be translated to machine code. This is done by translator programs. The translators for high level languages are called compilers or interpreters. Each programming language has its own translator. For example, before a program written in Pascal (a high-level programming language) can be run, a Pascal compiler has to be run to translate it to machine executable form. Translators are covered in more detail in Chapter 6.

Communications software

In today's highly competitive and fast moving world, computers often need to communicate with each other: between computers in the same building, nationwide or even internationally. These computers are connected by cables or satellite networks and they share a large amount of hardware and software resources. Communications software consists of programs which enable the computers in a network to work together. Inter-computer communications is an important topic and is covered in more detail in Chapter 7.

Applications software

As we have seen above, applications software is written to get the computer to perform specific tasks. For example, a payroll program to work out monthly salaries and print employees' payslips; or a database application to maintain students' registration records and performance details. In some cases, and normally for large organizations, these programs are written by in-house programmers and are tailor-made for their needs. Indeed until about 15–20 years ago this was the only option unless software houses (companies which specialize in writing software) could be employed to write programs for their clients. But, with the proliferation of microcomputers came the age of packaged software and now there are applications packages available for almost all types of business uses. Common application areas include wordprocessing packages for text manipulation, spreadsheets for manipulating numbers, databases for data management, desktop publishing (DTP) programs for creating professional quality documents, accounts, computer aided design/manufacture (CAD/CAM) and many more. A large number of programs are also available in the fields of education, entertainment, and other specialized applications. There is also integrated software incorporating more than one application in one package. Many applications packages are commercially available and most are written for Microsoft's operating systems and therefore can only run on IBM compatible PCs (as explained in Chapter 1). Although smaller in size, there has also been a steady market for applications programs for other microcomputers, for example Apple's own brands of applications including very popular DTP packages, Atari's games programs and Archimedes' own range of programs in all application areas favoured mainly by those who grew up with BBCs and Acorns.

More recently the trend in the nature of applications software has been influenced by user friendliness and compatibility across the range. This has resulted in some of the following developments/trends:

- Packages are increasingly written for the Windows environment.
- Many upcoming packages have versions for both IBM and Apple computers.
- Many applications offer facilities previously requiring separate packages; for example, most modern wordprocessing packages provide a considerable amount of graphics and DTP facilities.
- Most applications are compatible with each other, that is, files created in one package can be read by another.
- Most of these packages offer excellent on-line Help facilities.
- Prices have come down dramatically. Also, a large selection of 'shareware' (also called public domain) packages are available. These are often held on one floppy disk or available on the Internet, normally in packed (condensed) format. Shareware programs are very cheap (often £5.00 or less) and users are allowed to make free copies. Such programs are popular with home users and non-specialist enthusiasts.

Using the example of a wordprocessor package familiar to you, identify the features not included in it that you would like to have had. Are there features you do not like?

The above features have made applications packages increasingly popular and have enabled non-specialist users to adapt easily to a wide range of applications at work and at home. Many large organizations are now opting for the packaged solution for the majority of their general purpose applications. As a result many new applications are being developed and this, together with the integration of microcomputers in business and for personal use has revolutionized the role of information technology in our lives. We shall discuss applications software in specific areas in Chapter 5.

Packages versus tailor-made programs

Applications packages offer a number of advantages because they are normally:

● tested and proven by an established market;
● readily available;
● reasonably priced;
● supplied with on-line tutorials and professionally written manuals;
● regularly updated;
● available with special deals such as technical support and after-sales service.

Packages cater for general needs. The coverage is normally very wide, often offering far more than is necessary for most users. This highlights the importance of the adaptability of software, that is, the scope for users to select the level of usage they require. Windows based packages are excellent in this respect because they provide simple methods for accessing most facilities but, at the same time, include many sophisticated features suitable for more adventurous users.

However, some organizations still choose to have software developed to their own specifications because it offers the following advantages:

● Programs are tailor-made to the needs of the users with no unnecessary extras.
● Programs can be easy to use since the terminology and screen displays are directly related to the users' needs.
● Changes to programs can be made easily.
● The organizations are the owners of the programs which means they can make any number of copies.

On the other hand, there are some disadvantages of tailor-made programs, such as:

● They are normally more expensive.
● Errors may be detected after the programs go into live operation.
● Programs may not be as user friendly as commercially available programs and hence, often need extensive user training.
● The quality of an application depends on the expertise of the project development team and may not satisfy the end-users.

Whether an organization opts for a packaged or a tailor-made solution depends on how specific its needs are, the budget, the expertise available in the company and, to a certain extent, the tradition of the organization. In general, most small businesses choose common business packages for most of their applications and larger organizations often use a mixture of the two. The compromise solution of using a software developer to write a tailor-made program is also common.

 Explore the Internet to find which software packages are available for downloading.

Summary

Systems software controls the hardware of a computer system and applications software is used to perform tasks usually done manually before the development of computers. One way of understanding this is that systems software runs the system which is then used by applications software to produce output. The most common types of systems software are operating systems such as Windows NT, Windows 98 (or 2000), OS/2, Unix and Linux. Unlike systems software which has always been written by computer manufacturers or specialist companies, applications software used to be developed in-house. However, many applications are now available as packages and most companies prefer to use at least some of these programs. There are a number of advantages and disadvantages of both tailor-made and packaged programs and the choice of one or the other depends on a number of factors. Many large organizations use their own computer personnel to develop specialized applications in-house but use packages for common applications. Smaller organizations normally use either packages or the services of software houses.

Further reading

Read *Operating Systems* by Colin Ritchie, DP Publications, 1995 for more information on files, memory management and storage management by an operating system.

Look at current articles for recent developments in Windows NT and Unix. The best sources are computer magazines (available on CD-ROMs) and the Internet.

Revision questions

1. Explain the difference between systems and applications software. Use examples from your own experience of using PCs to demonstrate your answer.

2. Describe the main tasks of an operating system. Identify the ones you have experience of with comments on how they help you, as a user, to use a computer system.

3. List the main operating systems in the microcomputer market with a brief description of the features offered by each.

4. Give a brief introduction to other types of systems programs.

5. Compare the advantages and disadvantages of tailor-made versus packaged software.

6. List some typical office tasks for which you think applications programs may be useful.

7. If you are associated with an organization using computers, try to identify the applications software it uses and whether it is tailor-made or pre-packaged.

8. Identify some applications software that most people use these days even when they are not computer users themselves (for example, in banks, shops, libraries and so on).

Food for thought

Computer Weekly, 14, January 1999, p.28(1)
Reed Business Publishing Ltd (UK)

Has Linux come of age?
Philip Sweeting

Will the new kid on the operating system block emerge as a serious alternative to Windows? Philip Sweeting investigates

Linux, it seems, has arrived. It is everyone's favourite buzzword, to the extent that its creator, Linus Torvalds, has just been voted *Computer Weekly*'s IT Personality of the Year. But is there more than just the hype? Is Linux really a viable commercial option?

Last year saw a spate of software companies releasing, or announcing the imminent release of, Linux versions of their key products. They, of course, must respond to market forces. In 1997, Linux was the only non-Microsoft operating system to gain market share. And for 1998, estimates place its increase in share at more than 200%. Cautious estimates of the current Linux user-base range between five and seven million, with some putting the figure at 10 million or more.

Another indicator of the operating system's legitimacy is provided in the field of training. QA, one of the UK's largest training organisations, is to start offering Linux courses from early this year, and doubtless other firms will follow suit.

Linux's success can be tied in with the success of open-source software. The growth of the Internet has made the 'team development' ethos of the open-source movement a practical reality. Indeed, open-source software is vital to the Internet. About 80% of all e-mail is routed using Sendmail, an open-source program written by Eric Allman. And Apache, the freeware Web server software usually running on Linux, had a 50% share of the market, a Netcraft survey found in July 1998 (compared with Microsoft's 22.6% and Netscape's 8.4%).

Team effort

Like the Internet, Linux started life in an academic context. So it will be interesting to see whether the new mindset associated with open source has an effect of similar magnitude to that observed with the Internet, which in the past few years has been taken up on a huge scale by all business areas as they begin to appreciate a new way of sharing data.

Linux is certainly perceived as a product ideal for certain niche markets. Peter Hollands, senior consultant for Dale Strategies, thinks Linux is still 18 months from a viable desktop platform, but it's way ahead of other operating systems in networking, for instance.

The Ministry of Defence is taking the operating system seriously. 'The MoD is selling satellite images over the Internet, and the system is entirely based on Linux.' says Hollands (see www.dera.gov.uk).

'From a defence point of view, we like Linux because we have all the source code,' he adds. If a company wants to extend the functionality of an open-source program or operating system, they can just hire a programmer to do the job – a much easier solution than might be provided by software under any other kind of licence.

For software support, the open-source model provides a very different context. The traditional commercial fears about support are based not on speed, as there is often a faster response for open-source software. Instead it is based on the unorthodox – in business terms – lack of enforceability.

Hollands offers an example of the established way in which open-source support works. A major city bank was using an open-source fire-wall called IP Filter. When a security flaw was discovered, the author provided a fix in two hours, and this was immediately available to all other users of the system.

'This is the big advantage of open-source software,' says Hollands. 'There is a process of "peer-group evaluation", which means experts are independently reviewing the system. If the source code is not available, this process is simply not possible.'

However, as Linux comes of age, more commercial approaches to mainstream Linux support are emerging. The suppliers that sell varieties of Linux – Red Hat (www.redhat.com), S.u.S.E. (www.suse.com) and Caldera (www.caldera.com) – all provide the sort of technical support you would expect with non-open-source software. There are several independent companies that exist solely to provide Linux technical support.

Neil Spencer-Jones, business information systems consultancy manager at the National Computer Centre, recommends adoption of the same caution that would be

▶

exercised in the deployment of any new software. He has some concerns about a 'skills shortage', but the problem is not as pronounced as might be expected, since Linux shares enough of a heritage with Unix for the large existing base of Unix experts to re-train easily.

'Any large organisation that has the resources to test Linux for themselves should do so and look at the business benefits,' he says.

Cost benefits

Quite apart from issues of reliability and speed, there are various cost benefits. Spencer-Jones was involved in a migration to Linux at an NHS Trust where in-house development was due to take place. Since Linux could be run on desktop systems, the cost associated with a separate development server was removed. 'The maintenance of a PC-based server is always less than a proprietary box like from Sun or Hewlett-Packard, for example. The savings in maintenance for one year paid for the purchase cost of the PC boxes,' he says.

Nor does he consider Linux to have any security problems. 'There are no more security issues with Linux than any other operating system. Linux doesn't seem to be in the premier league for problems!'

A key problem associated with open source in a commercial context, says Hollands, is management education. To adopt this approach, 'we must become used to a different culture. We're used to a hierarchical structure for management. The Net encourages a flatter management architecture in terms of how to manage and develop software.'

Perhaps the most dramatic sign that Linux and open-source solutions have a place in the commercial scene comes from the company that has most to lose. Two well-publicised internal Microsoft memos, christened by the Linux community Halloween 1 and 2, compare Linux favourably to NT and describe Open Source as 'a direct, short-term revenue and platform threat to Microsoft'. If Microsoft is sitting up and taking note, then Linux may well be living in 'interesting times'.

Linux pros...

Low cost – software is available cheaply or free, and runs faster than many competing operating systems on lower spec machines.

Open source – means repaid bug-fixes and security patches.

There are Linux releases for almost all hardware platforms, and developers are writing appropriate drivers for devices.

If Linux doesn't do what your company requires, you can hire a programmer to add functionality.

Linux is generally Y2K compliant. The 32-bit representation used by Linux and other Unix-like operating systems may have difficulty in 2038.

...and cons.

While major software firms are beginning to provide Linux ports, this inevitably takes time.

Backwards compatibility – there may be questions of file compatibility with systems previously in use.

The story so far

1980s: Richard Stallman founds GNU Project to provide software whose source-code is made available at no cost.

Summer 1991: Linux created by Linus Torvalds, a University of Helsinki student, after experiments with MINIX.

January 1992: Over 100 users/hackers have downloaded Linux and, with Torvalds, are continually updating the code, writing drivers.

1994: Networking functions added and Version 1.0 of the Linux Kernel released on the Internet under the GNU General Public Licence.

1995: Version 1.2. Ports for Digital and Sun Sparc processors.

1996: Multi-processor support. Version 2.0.

1998: Major software houses, including Oracle, Netscape and Sybase, announce Linux versions of their products.

Discussion questions

1. Summarize the reasons behind the success of Linux.

2. Unix started its life almost the same way as Linux. Find some information on the Internet on the current status of Unix and discuss the relative positions of Unix and Linux.

3. According to your survey for question 2, which of the above two operating systems is going to win in the battle for popularity in the PC market and why?

4. What problems do you think open-source software could lead to? What would be the solution?

5. What is an open system? How do Linux and Unix demonstrate the benefits of an open system?

6. What do you think are the pros and cons for individual PC users of the continual change in the PC operating systems' market?

CHAPTER 5

Common business applications

Objectives

At the end of this chapter you should have some understanding of:

▶ the purpose of business applications;
▶ some typical applications software for microcomputers;
▶ the criteria for evaluating software.

Introduction

Applications software has already been introduced in previous chapters and the functions of some common applications have been mentioned. Programs can be tailor-made (custom-built), that is written to the specification provided by the user organization or they can be pre-packaged (bespoke) commercial programs which are written and sold by software companies.

Normally packaged software is used for common business applications such as creating and manipulating documents with wordprocessing or desktop publishing software, data manipulation using spreadsheet or database programs and finance management with accounting software. Nowadays varieties of packaged software are available and some data processing applications such as payroll or project management for which companies in the past had to opt for a tailor-made solution can now be bought. For more specific requirements or data management involving large amounts of specialist data, organizations still need programs written to their specification.

There are a large number of business applications available; these are normally written for microcomputers and many of them work well on networks. Some of the most common categories used by both individuals and businesses are wordprocessing, spreadsheets, databases, graphics, accounts and integrated packages. Other, arguably less commonly used, applications include desktop publishing, personal data management, groupware and email. We cannot give full accounts of all of these in this book but in this chapter we are going to look briefly at the nature of some common pre-packaged business applications and discuss how we can decide what makes a good business application.

Wordprocessing

This is the most common applications program widely used in homes and businesses. Wordprocessing programs have revolutionized the way we write, store and retrieve personal and business documents. Before the days of computers we either wrote by hand or used a typewriter. Mistakes could not be corrected without rewriting and a document could be re-used only by making a carbon copy or photocopying (when this became available) the original. Wordprocessing packages changed all this by allowing us to enter, format and manipulate text, use print enhancement features to make it look presentable, and make amendments on screen. We can store documents and retrieve them when required, thus enabling us to use the same document more than once and update it as necessary. The following is an overview of the features available in a typical wordprocessing package.

Entering and formatting text

Until recently wordprocessing programs were mainly an automated version of typewriters with added facilities for stylizing and editing. Users were presented with a blank screen for entering text and pull-down menus (a list of options revealed when certain keys are pressed), and keystrokes were available for accessing other features.

Wordprocessors have moved on a great deal in the past four or five years. Nowadays a wordprocessing screen contains a menu bar with options for different operations, and tool bars for easy access to some of them (Figure 5.1).

Additional choices can be made by using set keystrokes and menus can be revealed by the click of the right-hand mouse button. There are other tools on the screen such as scroll bars for moving up, down and sideways in the document, rulers for setting tabs and margins and a status bar which displays information on the current stage of processing.

We can create a new document to enter text or open (retrieve) a previously saved one. A document can be saved at intermediate stages (to ensure its safety in case something goes wrong with the system) as well as at the end before closing it. A number of documents can be opened and worked on at the same time. Using various options we can format a document to indent text, set margins, choose the spacing between lines, set columns, use headers, footers and page numbering and so on. We can also choose from a large selection of font styles and sizes and a number of print enhancement features such as bold, underline, italics, subscript, and superscript. Modern wordprocessors also allow us to choose a document style as a template, for example for a letter or a business report, and enter our own specifications to create professional effects.

Another way to improve the presentation of a document is to use a word-processor's desktop publishing (DTP) features. Only a few years ago separate

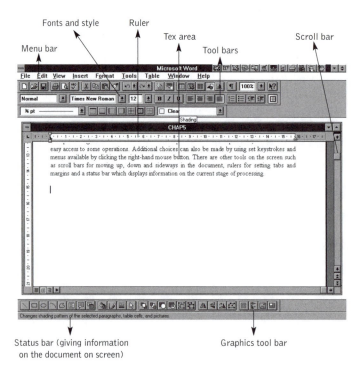

Figure 5.1: The screen display of a common wordprocessing program

DTP packages had to be used to stylize a document; now most wordprocessors incorporate a large number of DTP features and separate packages are only needed for very special effects.

Editing a document

In addition to adding and deleting text we can perform a number of other very useful tasks. Using *Find and Replace*, we can search for a particular string of text and replace it with something else. For example, we can ask the program to find every occurrence of the term 'word processor' and replace it with 'wordprocessor'. We can use *Cut and Paste* to move selected blocks of text from one place to another as well as in-between documents; blocks can also be moved by dragging them from one position to another; and they can be copied with equal ease. One very useful feature of most modern applications is *Undo* which enables a user to undo the last few changes made. Thus if you move a chunk of text from one place in a document to another and then change your mind, you can choose the Undo feature to cancel the change. The choice of options available is enormous and the settings chosen can be changed as many times as you wish.

Printing a document

A whole document or a section of it can be printed. A *Print preview* feature allows us to display the document in its print-ready format on the screen thus enabling us to make any final alterations necessary before the document is printed. Most wordprocessors allow both portrait (longer side of the page up) or landscape (the shorter side up) alignment as well as a choice of page set-up such as size of paper, selection of margins, and so on.

Additional tools

A number of special features designed to improve the quality of the text are also available in most modern wordprocessors. Amongst these are a spell checker which finds spelling errors and offers suggested corrections to choose from, a thesaurus program to suggest alternative words, a grammar checker which checks grammatical errors and writing style, a program for sorting lists of information, mail-merge which allows a user to insert information in predetermined locations of a standard document thus turning it into a personal one (such as putting individual names in a circular letter), and many more.

One tool which deserves a special mention here is the use of macros. A macro is the name given to a set of tasks, normally performed separately in sequence, saved as a block. For example, imagine we want to change the size and type of the font of a paragraph of text. Normally we would select the paragraph, choose the font-type necessary and click to change, and then choose the font-size and change that as well. These operations will need a number of actions. A macro enables us to save the sequence of actions as a set with a name, for example, FontChange. From then on, we can select any paragraph and run FontChange to perform the same actions on the chosen paragraph. The concept of a macro is similar to that of a stored program which, when run, follows the instructions in the program. Initially only systems software included this facility but now most common applications programs are equipped with it.

What actions would you need to record in a macro which would move a paragraph of a document to another document? What would be an appropriate name for it?

Drawing tools

A few years ago, introducing even simple diagrams needed special graphics programs. Most of today's wordprocessors allow us to draw diagrams, import pictures from a library of images stored as a part of the package, edit the pictures and use colour from a large selection available.

Integrating information

Joining documents created in different types of programs involved complicated operations in the past. Using modern software, a chart created in a spreadsheet program or a picture scanned by a scanning program, or a list of names and addresses from a database can easily be brought into a wordprocessed document and vice versa. This can be done by *Cut and Paste* or by importing files from one package into another both of which are easy operations offered by Microsoft Windows-type programs.

The role played by Microsoft Windows

Most Windows based packages have facilities for importing and exporting files between each other thus providing us with the flexible working environment that today's business world needs. Another way Windows offers flexibility is by creating a common look for all applications. Thus, many of the menu items and toolbars available in a wordprocessor, for example, file operations, editing, page formatting and print enhancements are also offered by other applications. This makes it possible for users to adapt to new applications easily.

Windows also allows users to open a number of applications, for example a wordprocessor and a spreadsheet at the same time and move between the applications as necessary. This is called multi-tasking and is useful for object linking and editing (OLE) which involves inserting an object (a selected part of a document), such as a chart from a spreadsheet, into another application, such as a wordprocessed document as a linked or embedded object. If linked, the object can be updated in the parent document and the result is reflected in the destination document. If the object is embedded, it is inserted in the receiving document with all its features but cannot be altered from the parent document. For example, if the object embedded is a chart from a wordprocessor into a spreadsheet application, then it retains all its formatting features such as fonts and style and can be altered in the wordprocessing application, but changes made in its parent (spreadsheet) document are not passed on to the destination. OLE works with all Microsoft Windows applications and is the basis of the interoperability between the applications for its Microsoft Office packages. Another very helpful feature offered by all Windows programs is the on-line *Help* menu which gives context-sensitive help and demonstrations on all aspects of the programs.

Can you think of some examples when you might need to link objects from different programs?

One important point one must remember is that not all applications are compatible with all computers. We mentioned Microsoft's Windows here because they are the most commonly used programs, but there are other players in the market such as Apple who have their own range of successful business applications and their unique brand of graphical user interfaces. Software written for Apple has its own common look and follows the same trend in interoperability between applications as do other brands of microcomputers sometimes with their specialist markets and applications. Additionally, modern software also offers facilities for reading files created in foreign formats. For example, Word for Windows, one of the leading wordprocessing packages available, can open documents created in other software such as WordPerfect, another popular wordprocessing package. At the end of processing, such packages also allow users to save the document in formats other than their own, for example, a document created in Word can be saved as a WordPerfect file. This enables users to work in variable environments such as home and office.

Desktop publishing

Desktop publishing is the electronic equivalent of a traditional printer's task: it allows us to design and print documents to a standard only achievable by professional printers in the past. The main use of a DTP package is to create a stylized template into which text from a wordprocessor and documents such as pictures, charts, tables, and so on from other applications are combined. We can use sophisticated page formatting features and our own choice of typefaces (size and style of fonts) which we can save as a template file called a *style sheet* and use as often as necessary. Separate styles can be saved for separate purposes, for example, headings, subheadings and the main text can be allocated different styles and saved under different names. Each page of a document is given a rectangular frame with which a style-sheet file is attached. Normally for a large and uniform document such as a book, each page is given the same style sheet whereas a business presentation may integrate a number of different style sheets. A page frame may include other frames into which files containing pictures, charts, and so on can be inserted to create a complete look such as the ones used in a magazine article or a newsletter (Figure 5.2). One advantage of creating separate frames for pictures is that the text in the documents aligns itself without overlapping with the pictures. Thus, a DTP package allows us to perform all of the traditional typesetting and cut and paste operations electronically with the added advantage of being able to edit as much as we wish before we produce a final printed version.

As explained, most of these facilities are available from most modern wordprocessing packages and for the majority of us a separate DTP package is not necessary. However, DTP has two advantages over a wordprocessor: first, it allows us to produce some advanced effects in document layout which are not yet available in a wordprocessor, and secondly, it is still easier to create and save our own style sheets on a DTP program than a wordprocessing program. It is only a matter of time before wordprocessing packages catch up in these areas and leave the use of DTP to professional publishers for special effects.

Compare the effort needed to create the following newsletter using a wordprocessing and a DTP package.

Lunchtime learning seminars look at widening access and participation

THE Centre for Access, Advice and Continuing Education (CAACE) at UEL is offering a series of lunchtime seminars examining the practical and theoretical aspects of the work of the Centre in relation to a series of projects externally funded by bodies such as the DfEE, HEFCE, Socrates and the European Social Fund.

All UEL staff are welcome to attend these seminars, which take place on Wednesdays starting at 1pm at CAACE, Artillery House, Stratford Campus. Coming seminars are as follows:

Socrates Adult Education Project: Widening Participation for Women from Ethnic Minorities (Wednesday 28 April): Jasbir Panesar and Sabhia Amin.

An AP(E)L Guidance Toolkit for Small and Medium Enterprises (Wednesday 26 May): Tony Wailey and Robert Simpson.

From Education Action Zone to Higher Education (Wednesday 23 June): Lynne Chiswick and Stephanie Clark.

In the next edition of *Lifelong Learning Lines*

LIFELONG LEARNING GOES GLOBAL: BULLETIN FROM THE EAST LONDON BUSINESS SCHOOL

MARTYN LARCOCK YEARS BUSINESS AS A LIFELONG LEARNER

CHRISTINE HODGSON REPORTS ON HER LEARNING LIFE

Have you got a lifelong learning story to tell? Contributions to LLL are welcome. Please contact Nod Miller via n.e.miller@uel.ac.uk

Business plans for business in the Thames Gateway Technology Centre

Lifelong learning for business and industry will play a key role in the Thames Gateway Technology Centre, which is to be housed in UEL's Docklands campus (above). DAVID HALL, director of the Centre, gives details.

THE Thames Gateway Technology Centre's long-term goals are increasing employer competitiveness and efficiency, developing employability and supporting business start-ups. The ends are commercial success and economic growth; the means are technology transfer and lifelong learning.

The Centre has been established to promote the interchange between higher education and employers across the region.

It acts as a catalyst and facilitator and aims to overcome the natural barriers that exist between the two, born out of differences in culture and language and a general (and mutual) lack of understanding.

Fundamental to its success will be the effective packaging of academic activity into a

form that is readily accepted and welcomed by employers.

Employers and universities work on different timescales and to different agendas. The TGTC starts with this recognition. It will work between small and large employers and the universities of East London, translating the two cultures and finding appropriate solutions.

Its expert project management will operate on behalf of the employer within the university and vice versa. Strong interpersonal skills and chameleon-like behaviour are at the top of the person specifications for TGTC staff.

As well over 95% of employers have fewer than 50 staff, the major audience for the TGTC will undoubtedly be small and medium-sized enterprises. For an SME, the point of outside

assistance is to help address today's problem today. The TGTC's services are being designed with this in mind.

Lifelong learning is a core theme driving this strategy. As universities continue to develop their knowledge and expertise, they also develop their facilities and resources. There is a continuous process of renewal, to which employers can gain access as their own needs and capabilities evolve over time.

The TGTC therefore represents a way of tapping into a resource that can help organisations to:
- reduce costs
- improve efficiency
- improve design
- increase sales

Key to its success will be the elimination of the invisible barriers to learning.

Figure 5.2: A newsletter (printed with permission from Professor N. Miller, University of East London)

Spreadsheets

Spreadsheets have always been used manually for business and personal data management. Daily transactions recorded by a shop owner as rows and columns of figures, or students' marks and grades kept by university departments are common examples. Without computers, the calculations have to be done manually and any corrections required cause the usual problems associated with any manual record keeping. Also, when items of data or a formula changes, results have to be recalculated and records amended accordingly.

A spreadsheet program is the electronic version of the above. For example, imagine a lecturer's marks sheet for a group of students: the sheet may contain students' names and marks for a number of tasks, each weighted differently, and the lecturer may want to display each student's overall percentage mark. Using a spreadsheet package, the marks can be entered and edited as necessary; the formula that calculates the overall marks needs to be entered only once and the spreadsheet performs the calculation automatically; when any mark is changed the result of the calculation changes automatically. In addition to this, if the weightings are changed the formula has to be changed only once and recalculations are performed by the program.

There are many other advantages of an electronic spreadsheet: for example a 'what if' facility which allows us to display the effect of predicted changes in the figures; charts of many different types to display the results of calculations graphically; statistical summary of data, and so on. Below, we will discuss some of the features in more detail.

Creating a spreadsheet

Figure 5.3 shows a typical spreadsheet. The example of the package used is from a program working under a Microsoft Windows environment and has the same common look of Windows programs.

When first opened, a spreadsheet program presents us with a screen divided into rows and columns. Columns are marked by the letters of the alphabet and the rows by numbers. The intersection of a row and a column is called a cell and has the address indicated by the intersection. (Thus in Figure 5.3 L7 is the address of the cell containing 44). There are hundreds of columns and thousands of cells in a spreadsheet, giving us the scope for entering as much data as we need.

Data is entered in addressed cells in the form of text (called labels), numbers and formulae. A formula, when entered using cell addresses, calculates the value

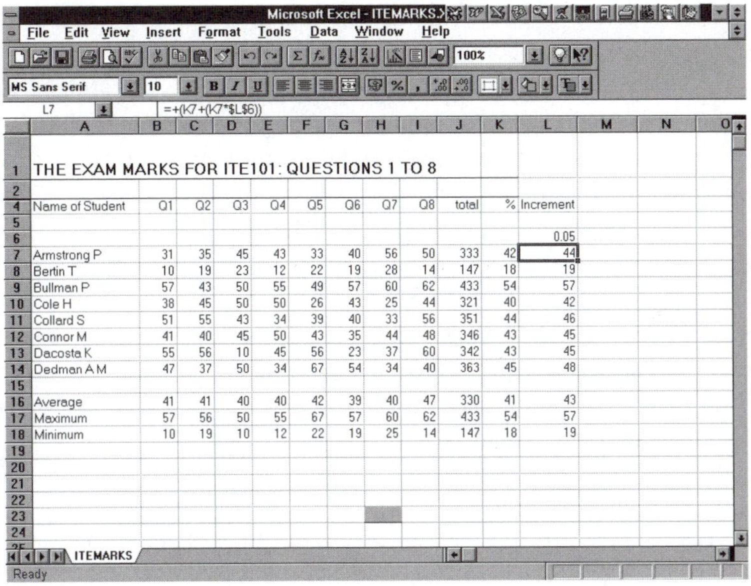

Microsoft Excel - ITEMARKS.X

File Edit View Insert Format Tools Data Window Help

MS Sans Serif   10   B I U   100%

L7   =+(K7+(K7*L6))

Name of Student	Q1	Q2	Q3	Q4	Q5	Q6	Q7	Q8	total	%	Increment
											0.05
Armstrong P	31	35	45	43	33	40	56	50	333	42	44
Bertin T	10	19	23	12	22	19	28	14	147	18	19
Bullman P	57	43	50	55	49	57	60	62	433	54	57
Cole H	38	45	50	50	26	43	25	44	321	40	42
Collard S	51	55	43	34	39	40	33	56	351	44	46
Connor M	41	40	45	50	43	35	44	48	346	43	45
Dacosta K	55	56	10	45	56	23	37	60	342	43	45
Dedman A M	47	37	50	34	67	54	34	40	363	45	48
Average	41	41	40	40	42	39	40	47	330	41	43
Maximum	57	56	50	55	67	57	60	62	433	54	57
Minimum	10	19	10	12	22	19	25	14	147	18	19

THE EXAM MARKS FOR ITE101: QUESTIONS 1 TO 8

ITEMARKS

Ready

Figure 5.3: Example of a spreadsheet

of the result using the data in those cells. Thus if cell J7 is to hold the sum of all the numbers between B7 and I7, the formula 'SUM(B7:I7)' entered in J7 will perform the operation. In addition, if the same operation has to be performed above or below row 7, the formula does not have to be entered in each row; copying the same formula by using the 'copy' feature will put the formula in subsequent rows with the row numbers adjusted appropriately. Thus, the formula in row 8 will be 'SUM(B8:I8)', that in row 9 will be 'SUM(B9:I9)' and so on. This is called *relative addressing*, because following a copy operation the cell addresses copied are changed automatically according to their positions relative to the cell copied. On the other hand, if for some reason we want to copy a formula but keep one or more cell numbers unchanged, we can do this by using a facility called *absolute addressing* which will be explained later.

There are a large number of predefined functions available which enable us to perform operations without having to enter a formula. For example, 'AVERAGE(B7:B14)' is a function that calculates the average of the cells in the range B7 to B14; 'MIN(B7:B14)' displays the minimum number in that range, and so on.

One very important feature an electronic spreadsheet offers is the facility for 'what if' analysis. By entering a figure in one cell and using this cell address in absolute addressing format (usually achieved by putting a '$' before the column and the row numbers) in a formula we can see the effect of the figure on the resulting spreadsheet. Absolute addressing stops the cell reference from being changed when a formula is copied. We can then alter the figure in the chosen cell to see its effect on the rest of the spreadsheet. This allows us to make forecasts for predicted changes in data. An example will make it clearer. Suppose we want to add 5% to the total marks for each candidate in the spreadsheet in Figure 5.3. We should put 0.05 (because 5 divided by 100 is 0.05) in a single cell, for example L6; we can then put the formula '(K7 * L6)+K7 in L7' which multiplies the initial total (in K7) by 0.05 to calculate the increase and adds it to K7. We then copy this formula to the cells K8 to K14; the $ signs used in the formula stops the cell reference L6 from changing as the row numbers change. However, K7 changes to K8, K9 etc. as the formula is copied. Thus 0.05 is multiplied to the total in each row. Using this method, the percentage added can be changed by simply changing the figure in L6.

Can you think of other examples of the use of 'what if' analysis for this spreadsheet?

Drawing graphs and charts from manually kept data is a laborious task. This is another area where the use of an electronic spreadsheet has made an enormous difference. Simply by indicating the range of values to be included we can create charts of many different types (line graph, bar chart, pie chart, and so on) in two and three dimensions. They can be labelled and many other features can be used to produce visual presentation of data to professional standards. Also, different types of charts can be drawn from the same set of data, for example, the same range of values can be seen on a bar chart or a pie chart to highlight different aspects of the same data.

Editing a spreadsheet

Common editing features available in any modern Windows programs (as described for a wordprocessing program) are also available in a spreadsheet, for example cut, paste, copy, move, delete, find, replace and so on. We can also insert new columns and rows, change their width and height, alter alignments of cell contents, and change old settings as necessary with little effort. Simple changes can be made by using the toolbar displayed on the screen, and items from the menu bar can be used for other changes. Many additional options can be made available by pressing the right-hand button of the mouse.

Formatting

The presentation and readability of a spreadsheet can be improved by using various options offered by a package. This includes print enhancement features such as bold, italics and underline, font styles and sizes, use of colour to highlight sections, alignment of data to left, right or centre, setting the number of decimal points for numeric data, sorting data and even displaying data as percentage figures rather than as absolute values. We can also use a template for the layout, either by choosing one from a range of different types offered by the program, or by creating our own and saving it as a style sheet. In fact, by using the advanced software tools available in a spreadsheet package, screen displays and menus can be built to provide end-users with an easy to use interface for entering data and producing reports of high quality. This allows one person to create a spreadsheet and others, often with little technical background, to use it.

Today's spreadsheet programs also offer some database facilities by allowing us to create tables of data and extract selective information to produce reports. It is often easier to use a spreadsheet rather than a database package when reports on financial data are required. We can also import documents from other programs such as text from a wordprocessor or graphics from another package thus making a spreadsheet package a very useful tool for creating business presentations, advertising leaflets containing summaries of financial information and other such documents. There are many other features we have not mentioned here, for example the use of macros, statistical analysis, creating a database and so on. Read some books specializing on spreadsheets for further details.

Databases

Before we can discuss database applications we need to understand what constitutes a database. Information systems are often built on a collection of data which is organized in a hierarchical order of fields, records and files. The concept is the same for computerized as well as manual systems, for example, a students' file with student IDs, names, major subject taken and so on, as shown in Figure 5.4.

Each column in the file represents a field which describes the type of data in the column: the column heading (for example, Student ID) representing the name of the field. The full set of fields in one row constitutes a record. Each record holds data on one item, in this case a student. A set of records is fields

Student ID	Last Name	First Name	Major	Date joined	Over 21
94067767	Agbasi	Gregory	Law	01/09/94	Yes
93446123	Akhter	Idris	Sociology	01/09/93	No
94001934	Enning	Paula	Bus St	01/09/94	Yes
93898456	Folorunso	Daly	Info Tech	01/09/94	Yes
94214524	Harrison	Graham	Info Tech	01/09/94	No
93539987	Hocking	Samantha	Info Tech	01/09/93	Yes
95642201	Kaur	Raj	Info Tech	01/0195	No
95343321	Parmar	Sabina	Law	01/01/94	No
94322178	Smith	Irene	Sociology	01/09/94	Yes

records

Figure 5.4: A typical student file

a repetition of the same pattern of data on different items, in this case on different students; together they form a file. Thus Figure 5.4 shows a file which is a collection of records on a number of students and each record is a collection of fields on one student.

In traditional computer systems a number of independent files were created and programs were designed to address these files to produce information. Any changes in the design of the files required changing the programs and vice versa because the files were tied to individual programs. Also, since files were not linked with each other, the same field often had to appear in more than one file. This led to duplication of data and increased the risk of discrepancy between files. An example will make this clear.

Let us consider the scenario of a traditional library system with a Members file which holds members' personal data such as membership number, name, address, date of birth and so on, and a Borrowers file which holds the membership numbers of those who borrowed books, the catalogue number of these books, the date borrowed, the due date for return and so on. A program uses these two files to find out which members have overdue books and their addresses in order to send reminders. The library may be a part of a central computer system for the borough which keeps a record of the names and addresses of the members in all its libraries because they can borrow books from any library in the borough. Thus members' details are held once in the central computer system and again, in the Members file in the library they are directly registered with. The following are the problems with such a system:

- Members' personal data is duplicated. This is unnecessary and wasteful and could be avoided if the two files were linked. Such duplication is called *redundancy* in database terminology.
- If a member moves and informs his or her local library, the change is not automatically passed on to the central filing system. This may give rise to incompatibility between two files making data unreliable.
- If a new item of data, for example, a member's occupation, is added to the Members' file, then the programs that read this file have to be changed.
- Often each file has to hold a large number of facts on one subject because files do not relate to each other. For example, the Borrowers file may have to hold the names and authors of the books borrowed because this information could not be extracted from another file.

Databases were introduced to eliminate such problems and to enable users of a computer system to centralize the information in order to improve efficiency. A database is a filing system in which files are linked with each other; using these links information can be obtained from a number of files and consolidated into one report. A set of programs called a database management system (DBMS) allows users to create, link and maintain a database. A database (the files) and the DBMS are independent of each other: normally the DBMS is purchased as a package (or developed by in-house IT professionals) and the database is created by users according to their own needs. Thus a DBMS provides a user with an environment within which he or she can create and operate a database but as they are not tied to each other, the structure and content of the database can be changed whenever necessary. Users can also extract information from the database on an ad hoc basis, that is, the questions a user can ask the database can be determined in-house. Thus, in the library system, a user may decide to ask the system to produce a list of all members who are over 70 years of age or those who have not borrowed any books in the past six months. These are called queries. In a well designed database such queries can be set without any need to interfere with the DBMS programs. In a traditional system this would not be possible unless programs were specifically written to produce such information. Also, because the files in a database are linked, each file holds data on one aspect of the system, with minimum duplication. Each file is given an identification field, called the *primary key*, which has a unique value for each record, such as membership number in the Members file. There may be a secondary key in a file if the primary key does not completely identify a record; in such a case the two keys are used together to find records. For example, if the surname field (which may be the same for two people) is used as the primary key then it may be necessary to use firstname as the secondary key. However, it is more convenient and efficient to give each record a unique code and use this as the only (primary) key.

The primary key is used to link one file to another which holds the same data as one of its fields. For example, the Books file in the library may be linked to the Borrowers file by the catalogue number of the book, which is the primary key in the Books file and appears as a field (called the foreign key) in the Borrowers file. Using this link all details of a book borrowed by a member can be obtained. Because files are linked in this way, each file can be quite narrow (containing a small number of fields), only holding the data directly relevant to the aspect concerned.

Can you think of the files required for a database which keeps students' personal records as well as academic details for a university department? What would be the primary key for each of the files?

Thus a database system attempts to eliminate the problems associated with traditional computer systems in the following ways:

● DBMS software is used to create and manage database applications. A DBMS is independent of the applications and therefore changes to the database made by users do not affect the software.

● Files are linked (integrated) with each other. Thus any change in data is automatically propagated through to other related files.

● The integration of files reduces the duplication (redundancy) of data and improves integrity (reliability) throughout the database.

● Individual files are kept narrow and manageable.

● Organizations using such a system would normally centralize their database systems. This allows all users in an organization access to the same data and offers IT managers better control over security and the management of data.

● The centralization of data improves the reliability of the information provided by an organization.

● Users can obtain answers to ad hoc queries and generate reports on any aspect of the database without any restrictions presented by the programs.

Disadvantages of a database over traditional computer systems

There are a few disadvantages of a database over traditional systems. Since in most organizations a database is used over a network as part of a multi-user system, security is a major concern. We have stated that a centralized database can enable managers to incorporate security features and control procedures, but on the other hand, the centralization gives individuals access to data from a desktop and thus the scope to abuse it. This will be discussed in more detail in Chapter 11.

Maintaining and updating a database can be major job and, if done badly, can affect an organization in a serious way. Normally a database administrator (DBA) is appointed who designs, creates and maintains the database. The quality of a database depends on the ability of the administrator to develop a system that offers maximum efficiency with minimum amount of redundancy. This should be addressed as a process of systems development, and is discussed in Chapter 9.

Using database applications

Let us now discuss the nature of database software and how it can be used to create and run a database. As with wordprocessing and spreadsheets, most of today's database software works within the Windows environment. Although the packages sold by different companies are very different from each other, they all present users with on-screen menus and icons which offer a host of features to choose from. However, because of the complicated nature of database applications, using a database program requires users to follow a set of specific steps:

1. To create a database by defining the structure of the files.
2. To set up the relationship (links) between these files.
3. To enter data.
4. To set up queries.
5. To create reports.
6. To implement the database.

Creating a database

The first step in creating a database is to give it a name under which all files created subsequently are kept. Each commercial database package has its own convention for naming a database and the files within it, although modern packages are very flexible and often do a number of things automatically to help users.

Next, the files (called tables in database terminology) are to be set up. This involves defining the structures of the files by identifying the fields in each file and their characteristics. We have to specify the following: the name of each field; the type, that is, alphanumeric (alphabetic characters and numbers), numeric, date, logical (true/false or yes/no), descriptive (to enter long text) and so on; width of the field, that is, how many characters are allowed; and any validation requirement which stops users from entering data that does not conform to the stated format, for example an improbable date of birth, and so on. Each package offers a set of options for field types and formats to choose from. At this stage the primary key in each file is also identified.

Setting up links

The links between files are set up by identifying the fields by which a pair of files are related and the nature of the relationship. There can be different types of relationships between files: for example, for each publisher in the Publishers file there may be a number of Books in the books file but for each book there may only be one publisher (usually). This is referred to as a one-to-many relationship between Publishers and Books. There may be other types of relationship but we will not go into the details here.

How would the tables in the students database you considered above (in the previous question) be linked?

Great care needs to be taken in setting up the structure of the files and their relationships: if mistakes are made at this stage information cannot be obtained correctly from the database. Careful planning in advance saves a lot of time at the implementation stage. Today's database packages offer help in a number of ways, for example, by displaying the links graphically in the form of arrows from one file to another, displaying error messages and showing useful hints on the screen.

Entering data

Entering data means putting records into the files. At this stage the software presents the user with an empty table rather like a manual file with columns and headings but no data. The columns are automatically adjusted according to the widths set and field names are displayed as column headings. Formats and validation rules set at the design stage ensure that inappropriate data cannot be entered. There is also an option to use a form looking very similar to the input forms often used in businesses for manual data entry to make the job easier for non-specialist users. When records in all files are entered, the database is fully set up.

Setting up queries

This operation can be performed at the stage when the database is set up or it can be left to individual users. Either way, this is the stage when a user asks for information based on queries which fulfil certain conditions. For example, we may want to list all those library members who live in a certain area and are under 16 years of age. We can set up a query by stating these conditions; business packages present screen formats which allow us to do this easily. A query can be set on single files or on a combination of files which are linked. Advanced users can set queries using more complicated conditions by using a fourth generation programming language (4GL) associated with each DBMS. This is called structured query language (SQL) and will be discussed briefly in Chapter 6.

Think of some useful queries for the students database.

Creating reports

Reports in databases are basically formatted listings of information. They can be created from the set of records in a file by adding headings, margins and other page formatting features, or they can be based on queries involving one or more files. Many database packages offer templates to help users to create well laid out reports for management information and presentation purposes. Reports can be saved as separate files and retrieved as necessary.

Implementing a database

Before a database is fully ready to be used, steps need to be followed to test it in the same way a program would be tested before it goes live. The database should be run with all possible kinds of data and queries and reports of all possible types should be produced. This normally reveals problems in the design of the database not previously anticipated, and has to be followed by a period of editing. This may involve amending the existing structure, adding, deleting or amending data, changing or adding queries and reports, changing font, style and layout to alter the presentation of tables and reports, using colour for highlighting sections, and so on. Before the database is implemented, that is, passed on to its users, it should go through the same stages of trial runs, pilot schemes and progressive testing as those followed by any new computer system; this is discussed in Chapter 9.

A database as the basis of an information system

Using modern database management systems and programming tools, database applications can be created with menus, icons, on-screen prompts and messages, screen layouts and so on to produce a custom-built system (an information system) suitable for the specific needs of an organization and its users. In many organizations, such an application is implemented as a multi-user system with different degrees of access given to users of different categories. For example, in a university, a student management database could be used by the lecturers to access lists of students in their courses, by the departmental administrators for retrieving information on student performance and by the heads of departments to request reports on capital expenditure.

Integrated packages

Some people prefer to use individual programs for wordprocessing and spreadsheets, and if necessary import files into each other to achieve integration of applications. Others find it easier to use an integrated package which contains a number of different applications under one umbrella thus providing a simple way of moving between applications and incorporating different types of documents into one. An integrated package can be very useful in an office because it creates an integrated work environment for different applications. For example, the Office 97 package introduced by Microsoft in 1996 is a complete office management system with wordprocessing, spreadsheet, database, publishing, personal organization and email programs. Using such software users link documents created in different applications using the principle of object linking and editing (OLE). However, individual programs often offer a wider choice of features than an integrated package. One well known integrated package is Lotus Smartsuite which currently offers a wide range of applications between wordprocessing and multimedia presentation.

How would you make use of an integrated package if you were the manager of the office of a university department looking after student administration?

Graphics

Modern wordprocessing packages often hold a library of graphics images which can be inserted into a document. They also offer tools for drawing lines and simple geometric figures. Graphics created this way can be edited, coloured and annotated. A number of applications enable users to create graphs and charts which can be imported, if necessary, into other applications to produce business presentations and demonstration material.

When more specialized work involving sophisticated images and animation is required we need graphics software which offers anything from simple drawings to computer-aided design (CAD) tools. Pictures can be created either by freehand drawing on screen or by using various geometric shapes available as drawing tools. Scanned pictures can be imported into a graphics program and then edited to customize them; animation can be produced using programming language tools; CAD software allows users to design objects in fine detail, edit and view pictures from different angles and perspectives, and use colour imaginatively to produce realistic images. Car manufacturers, architects, town planners and industrial designers are amongst those who use CAD. Virtual reality programs and multimedia applications have recently added a new dimension to the usefulness of graphics software.

There are two basic ways in which a graphic image is represented on a screen: *vector graphics* and *bit-mapped graphics*. Vector graphics is similar to the way we write and draw, by drawing lines. This is handled by a computer by identifying the positions of the two ends of a line relative to a fixed point on the monitor. The images are also stored in memory by recording the positions of the two end-points of each line. Bit-mapped images are created by treating the monitor as a grid, each cell is called a pixel and is identified by a number determined by its position relative to a fixed point in the grid. A picture is formed in the same way that dot-matrix printers represent characters on paper and, similarly, the quality of a picture improves with the number of pixels (called the resolution) on a monitor. An image is created by identifying the number of each pixel used and the colour or shade associated with it. A bit-mapped image is displayed and continuously refreshed, one line at a time, in the same way that pictures are displayed on a television screen. Usually scanning software, digital cameras and paint programs use bit-mapped images while vector images are used by drawing and computer-aided design programs.

Graphics images take up a large amount of disk space for storage and need a large amount of memory to be displayed because of the quantity of information that is associated with a picture. Bit-mapped images take considerably more space than vector images because information on each pixel in a bit-mapped image has to be stored. Vector images on the other hand, are identified by lines each of which covers a number of pixels. Graphics software tries to reduce the amount of disk space required by saving them as lossy images, that is, by compacting (squashing) the information together during storage and un-compacting it during display. The details of how this is done are outside the scope of this book but you can look at some books mentioned in the list of Further reading for more information.

Other applications

There are many other applications programs, some for general use and some dedicated to specialist areas. One which has become very common and quite popular is a personal organizer which enables a user to keep an electronic diary. Organizers come with most Windows packages as well as in a diary-sized dedicated computer format (a computer dedicated to one task only). Another common application is an electronic mail system (commonly known as email), which we will discuss briefly in Chapter 7.

One application which has taken an important role in certain organizations is the expert system. This is an artificial intelligence application used to program a computer to make expert-type decisions. It works by using a stored database (called a knowledge base) of an expert's knowledge in a particular field (such as medicine) and the rules about how that knowledge can be used. Using logic based program coding, answers to queries can be obtained by searching the knowledge base. Expert systems are often used in the medical field for preliminary diagnosis of illness. The system stores medical facts (a doctor's knowledge) and the rules on how those facts relate to each other; a user is then taken through a hierarchy of questions and diagnosis is made by relating the answer to the stored knowledge base. In such a system, the knowledge base may store rules such as:

IF   the patient exhibits symptom X and
      the patient exhibits symptom Y
THEN   the patient is likely to be suffering from disease A

The knowledge base contains many such rules and by connecting (or 'chaining') these rules, a diagnosis can be found. Other areas which use expert systems are geological prediction, chemical analysis and engineering fault detection. Read the books mentioned under Further reading at the end of the chapter for more information on expert systems.

Two other fields in which specialist applications programs are used are the health service, where an integrated health information system, used by GPs as well as hospitals and the NHS, allows medical practitioners to provide patient care and maintain communication with each other; and airline reservation systems, which allow flight booking to be performed on-line and with up to the minute accurate information.

There are many other fields where applications programs are used by individuals as well as organizations and every day new ones are being developed. A recent addition to this field is the use of hypertext programs. These are created on the same principle as databases but instead of linked tables, hypertext software uses linked documents. Once linked this way, a search facility can be used to find documents of a particular type, or links in one document can be used to access other linked documents. For example, a library can use hypertext to link its index of books and articles, as well as electronic copies of particular material such as abstracts of articles. A user can use key words to search the index for publications on a certain subject and access a number of relevant documents on that subject. One prominent user of hypertext is the World Wide Web (www), the interface which enables users to access the Internet by linking documents of all kinds, text, graphics and images, held in databases worldwide. When a document is opened, it displays links to other documents related to it. The linked documents, in turn, link to more documents, thus giving users access to a large source of valuable information. Thus, hypertext links allow a user to do a non-linear search by moving from one document to other related documents rather than having to browse through a predetermined list. We will discuss the Internet in more detail in Chapter 8.

 Can you think of some new areas where applications programs could be useful?

Most of the common commercially available software is easy to use and experienced users can get used to new packages quickly. However, most of them require some knowledge of the application area and it is important that users are given initial training before a new system is introduced. For example, you cannot use a spreadsheet or a database program effectively unless you understand the basic concept behind it. Formal training is essential to equip users to do this and to appreciate the potential of a program, although once trained in one area it is relatively easy to adapt to an update or a new program in the same area, or even in other areas, once the user gains enough confidence.

Evaluating software

The choice of packaged business software is large and often confusing. Software can only be evaluated properly after users have the experience of using it in-depth. Choosing one piece of software from a selection of unknown packages is difficult and risky. The reputation of a software company is sometimes used as an indicator of quality, but can be misleading. Many magazines print buyers' guides to software and these may provide a reasonable indication of quality. Some software companies allow users to test a package before a sale is agreed. Although these can influence the choice of the packages to be considered, the final selection must be based on a formal set of criteria rather than allowing ad hoc experimentation and decision making by individuals. The following is a suggested list of such criteria:

- **Functionality**: This is the measure of the extent to which the software meets the requirements of its users. It can only be judged fully if the suppliers allow a test period during which the software is put through a full run. If this is not possible then it may be necessary to rely on published material.

- **Ease of use**: Normally, after a system is set up users with little technical background have to use it. It is therefore of vital importance that packaged software is easy to use. The usability of a program is determined by a number of features such as: a realistic graphical user interface, on-line help facilities, helpful messages displayed on-screen to indicate what is happening at any stage, facilities available to adjust the screen display to a user's own level, an on-line tutorial, and so on.

- **Adaptability**: A package should be adaptable to the needs of its users. Unless vendors sell the program code as well (this is unusual for common business applications), changing a program is not possible: however, it may have modules offering different facilities from which different users can choose the suitable ones.

- **Compatibility**: Software needs to be compatible with the existing hardware and operating systems. For example, if an organization mostly uses PCs with Microsoft operating systems, software developed for Apple machines may not run on their systems. Network compatibility is another factor to consider.

- **Cost**: The price of new software and the cost of updates dominate the choice for most organizations. Some vendors offer special licensing arrangements for the rights to install a package on several machines and some also attach specific services such as on-line technical assistance within the cost. Generally speaking, the criterion used should be good value for money rather than savings at any cost.

- **After sales service**: On-line technical help, after sales training and support, arrangements for providing updates and so on, are very important services sometimes overlooked by vendors and customers. Assurance of these services is an indication of the reliability of the software and its vendors.
- **Documentation**: The quality of manuals and user guides greatly affects the usability of software and should therefore be checked before a choice is made.

An organization should give a group of people consisting of technical experts and non-technical users the responsibility to evaluate a package. They should follow a systematic procedure, such as using a table to mark the performance of a program against each criterion. This would give them the basis for comparison on which an objective choice can be made.

Most organizations now use commercial packages and small businesses often run their entire systems on them. The choice of software is an important part of the systems development process and one of the major responsibilities of project managers: this is discussed in Chapter 9. No packaged solution can fit an organization's needs as closely as a tailor-made program, but careful consideration of the important factors ensures that the best possible choice is made.

Summary

A large number of pre-packaged applications software are currently available for use both by organizations as well as individuals. Designed mainly for use on microcomputers, most of them are suitable for IBM-compatible machines, although other manufacturers, mainly Apple, have their own range of programs. The most common areas of application are wordprocessing, spreadsheets, databases, graphics, desktop publishing and integrated packages. The majority of modern software works under Windows and offers a common environment for all applications by providing a similar set of screen displays, toolbars and icons, file handling, editing and formatting features, help facilities and so on. Most of these programs are easy to use although some training is required before they can be used effectively.

The areas covered by pre-packaged software are large enough to enable most organizations to use such software for common applications thus leaving their programmers to devote time only to special purpose programs. However, choosing software is an important part of systems development and great care needs to be taken to ensure that the software chosen is functional, adaptable and usable. A set of criteria should be used to evaluate commercially available packages before they are introduced to the users.

Further reading

Read *Using Computers and Information: Tools for Knowledge Workers* by Jack B. Rochester, Que Education & Training, 1996 for more details on applications software.

Read *Using Graphics* by Malcolm Richardson, Blueprint, 1995 for information on the fundamental concepts in graphics.

Read *Artificial Intelligence* by Elaine Rich, McGraw-Hill, 1983 for information on artificial intelligence and expert systems.

There are many books on the market which cover details of commercial applications software. There are also a large number of books on how to use specific applications packages.

Revision questions

1. Describe the main purpose of the following programs:

   wordprocessing
   spreadsheets
   databases
   desktop publishing
   graphics
   hypertext.

2. List the main features offered by the leading software packages in each of the above areas.

3. Imagine that you work for or run a small advertising company. Describe a typical application (if any) for each of the above programs in your company.

4. Explain why a database approach is better than the traditional file-based computer systems.

5. List the criteria for the evaluation of a software package. You may like to add your own criteria to this list with explanations.

6. Describe any one package you have experience of and evaluate it on the basis of the above criteria.

7. There are many pieces of applications software that we have not mentioned in this chapter. Make a list of those that you have some knowledge of and write a brief description of their main functions.

Food for thought

Information Week, 2 October 1995, no.547, p.136
CMP Publications Inc.

Packages: one size fits all? (Off-the-shelf versus custom-built integrated business packages)
Michael Scofield

Software packages' shine may fade if they don't match your company's architecture

The spread of integrated client-server business packages such as SAP AG's R/3 suite of applications is adding a new twist to an old dilemma:
 Whether to buy off-the-shelf software or build your own.
 Integrated business software packages have many advantages. They provide a lot of functionality, plus support for multiple currencies and languages, more quickly and cheaply than you would writing it from scratch.
 However, there are disadvantages to using these packages, too. The one that concerns me most is that users must make their company's business model fit the package.
 I am not opposed to packaged software. I would never dream of writing my own spreadsheet software or my own computer-aided software engineering tool. But a business package is quite different. Your relationships with your customers, vendors, and employees are probably the most important ones in your organization. An application that automates those relationships is highly complex, because the relationships are also complex.
 This complexity is increasing, partly because companies seek to compete by providing more services or tailoring services to each customer. Technology is an enabler but is seldom the cause of business complexity. Indeed, legacy applications inhibit change if they cannot be updated quickly enough.
 When these applications fail to meet business needs, information systems managers and executives look for packaged software to provide a speedy solution. However, they often fail to fully understand the consequences.
 Every business software package is written with a company structure in mind – no matter how much flexibility the package is claimed to have. That structure is reflected in the data architecture of the package, from the number of layers it allows in your organization chart to the number of digits in the customer number. ▶

Your company also has a data architecture that reflects its structure. What if the two architectures are incompatible? It's possible to change a number of minor aspects of a package to fit your organization. But it's hardly ever possible to change the package's underlying architecture, unless you start modifying source code – a dangerous approach.

The other option is to change your business to fit the package. This approach may also have short-term appeal, since reengineering allows you to examine all aspects of your operations to see if they still make sense. But the long-term effect is that you relinquish ownership of your data architecture to the package designer.

If that designer knows more about your business than you do, then this may be a safe approach. But you're betting that, besides meeting your immediate needs, the package will be flexible enough to allow your business practices to evolve and become more complex to meet ongoing competitive pressures. When I buy a spreadsheet and adapt my view of the world to its tabular format, I haven't given up much. It's a far greater risk to accept a package's view of your relationships with important customers.

Silver bullet?

The current popularity of packages such as R/3 may be related to an American cultural fixation with short-term profit. Many companies, especially those that desperately need to expand into international markets, see this software as a silver bullet that will quickly give them the functionality they need.

I believe, however, that the most successful companies will take a longer-term approach and recognize that few packages are flexible enough to allow them to continually adapt. These companies will take ownership of their architecture and craft it to meet business objectives. This will not be easy; it will once again present businesses with the challenge of developing their own software fast enough to meet changing needs.

But an organization that doesn't change its architecture is either a monopoly in a noncompetitive market or a company that's ready to die. The future belongs to businesses that own their architecture and can manage their evolution.

Michael Scofield is a data administrator at a large manufacturing company in California.

Discussion questions

1. The article expresses some doubts about the suitability of a packaged program for a company's needs. Write an essay giving the opposite view by discussing the role today's business software packages play that has allowed their widespread use in large as well as small organizations.

2. Most small to medium sized companies cannot afford to employ their own programmers and have to depend on packaged software. Discuss, in the light of the comments made in the article, what they should do in order to extract the most possible benefits from them.

CHAPTER 6

Computer programs

Objectives

After reading this chapter you should have some understanding of:

▶ the concept of a computer program;
▶ the steps involved in the development and running of a program;
▶ the nature of programming languages and their roles.

Introduction

In the last chapter we discussed applications software. But how is this software created? How do we make a program perform the tasks we want it to perform? What steps do we follow? What techniques are available for us to achieve this? What makes good software? These are some of the questions we want to address in this chapter.

In spite of all the advancement in computer technology two things have not changed: computers as such do not have any intelligence, they are simply machines that must be driven by programs; and computers only understand one language which has two characters in its alphabet, '0' and '1' corresponding to an electronic switch 'off' and 'on' respectively. The quality of a computer system depends on the quality of the program. In this chapter we are going to get an overview of how a computer program is developed step by step, the tools available for designing and writing a program, the languages used to write programming code and the steps involved in turning a high level program into executable machine code.

The concept of a program

A computer program is a set of precise and step-by-step instructions which tell a computer exactly how to perform a task. To understand what this means, let us consider the example of the steps involved in making a telephone call (Figure 6.1). This is a task most of us perform automatically, but if you were asked to teach someone who has never used a telephone before how to do this you would have to give clear instructions explaining everything about dialling tones, when to dial, what to do if it rings or if no one answers, and so on. You could produce a guide to making a telephone call by writing the instructions as in Figure 6.1 next to the telephone.[1]

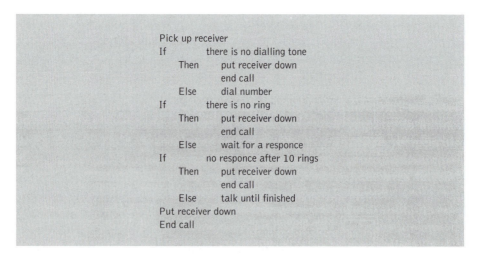

```
Pick up receiver
If            there is no dialling tone
      Then      put receiver down
                end call
      Else      dial number
If            there is no ring
      Then      put receiver down
                end call
      Else      wait for a responce
If            no responce after 10 rings
      Then      put receiver down
                end call
      Else      talk until finished
Put receiver down
End call
```

Figure 6.1: Making a telephone call

---

1   The example used in the Figure is skeletal and does not go into details such as engaged tones or a wrong number.

There are a few points to note about these instructions. Although most human beings who have some knowledge of a telephone will be able to make a call using the instructions, they do not, in any way, represent the clarity and detail a computer would need to be given to perform any task. Also, they contain repetitious details that a human being probably do not require, for example when they describe what to do if the call cannot continue either because there is no ring or no response. These points help to demonstrate the basic concept of a program: it is a thorough, step-by-step, logical and unambiguous set of instructions telling a computer what to do, covering all eventualities from the beginning to the end. In this chapter we are going to discuss the processes involved in developing a program and also take a brief look at different programming languages and their characteristics.

Can you revise the instructions in Figure 6.1 to cover more eventualities so a robot can follow it to make a phone call?

An example program

Before we discuss programming, let us examine a small program. Unless you write a program yourself it is hard to conceptualize the process involved. However, using an example of a program written in an English-like language, it may be possible to give you some idea of the task it performs and the data it processes.

Figure 6.2 shows a program called AverageMark which takes four marks and finds the average. It has four variables 'Mark 1', 'Mark 2', 'Mark 3' and 'Mark 4' which are names given to the items of data the program has to deal with. They are called variables because their values can change. The first four variables in this program are of type integer, meaning they are whole numbers. 'Average' is the name of the variable in which the result of the calculation (the average mark) is held. This is of type real, that is, it may contain decimal numbers.

The part of the program marked 1 contains the names of the variables it needs. Part 2 is for the program statements, that is the instructions the program has to execute. This part is enclosed in a block marked with BEGIN and END. In this block, the program first asks the user to type in four numbers. It reads those numbers and calculates the average. The result is then displayed with the necessary message. The text enclosed within { } are comments for other programmers; the computer does not read them. Because of the high level language used here the instructions are reasonably comprehensible without much explanation. Obviously real life programs can be very complex. Often programs are written by one person

```
PROGRAM AverageMark

   {This program averages a set of 4 marks}
1  VAR Mark 1, Mark 2, Mark 3, Mark 4: integer;
   Average: real;


   BEGIN
         WriteIn      ('Type 4 marks');        {Display instruction for user to
                                                type the numbers}

         ReadIn       (Mark1, Mark2,           {Reader types the marks}
                      Mark3, Mark4);
2
         Average:=    (Mark1 + Mark2 +         (program calculates the average)
                      Mark3 + Mark4)/4;

         WriteIn      ('Average of 4 marks     {Display message and the result}
                      is', Average)
   END
```

Figure 6.2: A computer program

and looked after by others. Therefore, it is essential that they are designed, coded and documented in a way that maintains their clarity. There are recommended good practices for programming which will be discussed later on in the chapter.

Writing a program

It is unusual for professional programmers to write a program as a stand-alone task. Normally, it is done as a part of the development of a complete information system. This is performed by a team of people who start with an initial requisition from users and follow a series of steps to arrive at a completed system. Programming is one of those steps which starts when the systems design team has produced a plan of the programs required to support the system, the tasks to be performed by each program, the files to be handled, the data to be input and the output to be produced. The team also specifies the procedures to follow in order to test the programs individually and then as parts of a complete suite of programs which link with each other to constitute the whole application. Systems development is described in some detail in Chapter 9. In this chapter we are concentrating on the stages involved in writing a program which begin when program specifications are obtained from the systems development team.

Broadly speaking, writing a program involves the following steps:

1. Design
2. Coding
3. Testing
4. Maintenance.

For small and uncomplicated projects these stages can be performed in sequence. In reality, most systems are larger and involve a number of programs linking with each other. In such cases there have to be overlaps between stages and often the need to go back to a stage in order to revise some actions taken previously. Each stage is accompanied by supporting documentation which details the characteristic of the stage and the information required to proceed to the next stage.

Designing a program

During systems design (the process of developing a computer system, to be covered in Chapter 9) a program specification is produced which defines *what* a program needs to do; at the program design stage the programmer has to determine *how* it is done. In other words, a programmer receives a problem from the systems development team and finds a solution at this stage. Thus, designing a program is similar to transforming a problem such as making a telephone call into the algorithm (step-by-step procedure) of Figure 6.1. The logic of the program is determined at this stage in a language-independent way so that at the next stage the design can be transferred into program statements in the chosen language relatively easily.

There are a number of tools a programmer can use to design a program, including pseudocodes, flowcharts, structure diagrams, data flow diagrams, Nassi-Schneiderman diagrams, HIPO diagrams and decision tables. We have already seen an example of pseudocode which consists of program statements written in structured English in a format that expresses the programming logic step by step as used in Figure 6.1; we will come back to pseudocodes in the next section. Flowcharts were widely used in the 1960s, 1970s and early 1980's. They give a clear, visual and detailed representation of a program's logic. Using a set of standard symbols[2] a programmer represents the flow of actions necessary to

---

2 Flowchart symbols are not described here because it is expected that the annotations used are adequate for the readers to understand the purpose of a symbol.

arrive at the solution. Figure 6.3 illustrates a flowchart for the telephone call program. Although flowcharts allow a detailed representation of program logic they are rarely used these days because the use of branching to transfer control to another part of a program (as explained below) makes it difficult to structure a program efficiently. Structured flowcharts can be used to alleviate the problem to a certain extent. We will discuss structured programming in the next section and will also introduce you to structure diagrams. A discussion of the other tools[3] mentioned above is outside the scope of this book but you can get more information by reading the books mentioned under Further reading.

Structured programming

For a complicated program, the design can continue for a number of pages. There may be a large number of conditions and branches following yes/no decisions thus making the design complex, resulting in a program which is difficult to write and maintain. Often programs are written by one person but looked after and modified by others. Clarity in program design is one of the most important aspects of good programming otherwise when problems occur it becomes almost impossible to find the errors or correct them; this has given rise to the concept of structured programming.

Structured programming is the term used to describe a program designed as a collection of modules (sections) each tackling one or a small number of tasks. The modules are written independently and the main program calls these modules as and when necessary. Each module can be built with a number of other modules in the same way, thus creating a hierarchy. This is called step-wise refinement.

Advantages of this design method are several. It is easy to understand: the first step in the series, called the main program, gives a clear outline of the overall design, showing the main modules in the program; each subsequent section does the same for the modules and submodules it covers. For large and complicated programs, each module can be written independently as a separate program and then joined together in the main program. When problems occur each module can be tested separately which makes error detection and correction, and consequently, the maintenance of programs easier. Structured programming also reduces unnecessary repetition of coding by using the same module as many times as necessary. Finally, modules can be saved as separate programs and used by other programs when appropriate.

---

3 Data flow diagrams are more commonly used for systems design than program design.

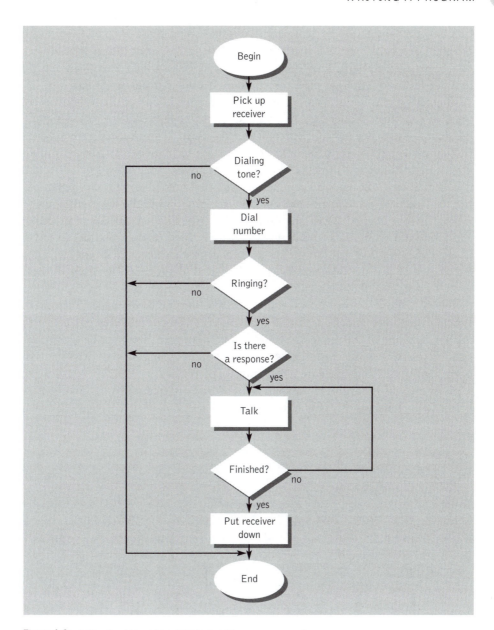

Figure 6.3: A flowchart to make a telephone call

The concept of structured programming was introduced by academics such as Professor Edsger Dijkstra towards the end of the 1960s. Soon afterwards the concept was translated into practical techniques by practitioners such as Ed Yourdon, Tom De Marco, Gerry Weinberg and Michael Jackson by the introduction and popularization of structure diagrams. Using these diagrams, an entire program can be drawn as a hierarchical tree of boxes, each box representing a set of operations. Higher level boxes represent modules which are further refined in lower levels to represent progressively finer details of program design.

There are a number of forms of structure diagrams but all of them follow three types of construct: sequence, selection and iteration. Different forms use slightly different notations to indicate different constructs. In Jackson's structure diagram (JSD) used as part of his structured programming technique, a sequence of modules or instructions is represented by a series of boxes at the same level; selection is indicated by a ° in the top right-hand corner of a box, and iteration (repetition) by a *. Modules in a sequence are called by the program in the order from left to right. Thus the telephone call program can be represented as a series of modules: check-dial-tone, ring, talk and exit, each consisting of further modules in lower levels (Figure 6.4). Control of the program goes first to 'check-dial-tone' which is a sequence of two modules: 'pick-up-receiver' and 'dialtone?'. The latter of these is a selection module in which different actions are taken according to whether there is a dialtone or not. This is indicated by a ° in the boxes under 'dialtone?'. When all modules under check-dial tone are completed, control is passed on to the next module in the sequence: 'ring'. As in 'dialtone?', the module 'ring' consists of selection based on whether the telephone is ringing or not. When all operations under 'ring' are completed, 'talk' is performed.

As shown in Figure 6.4, 'talk' is an iteration (indicated by a * in the box below), which means this part of the program carries on until a certain condition

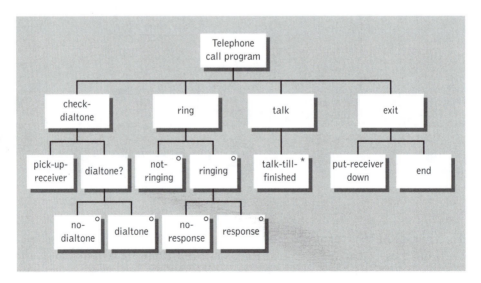

Figure 6.4: Structure diagram for the telephone call program

is fulfilled. Here the condition is 'if talking is finished'. At the end of 'talk', 'exit' is executed. This is the module which ends the program by following the sequence 'put-receiver-down' and 'end'.

As shown in the figure, structure diagrams allow you to design large modules such as 'ring' or small blocks of code as in 'dialtone' which involve only one operation of dialling a number. Details of programming operations are not normally expressed in JSDs; their main purpose is to represent the overall structure of a program. Pseudocodes are used to express the exact contents of each module. This can be done by writing the pseudocode for each module and then joining them together to construct a whole program, thus making designing and coding easier for a programmer. Figure 6.5 shows the pseudocode equivalent to the structure diagram of Figure 6.4.

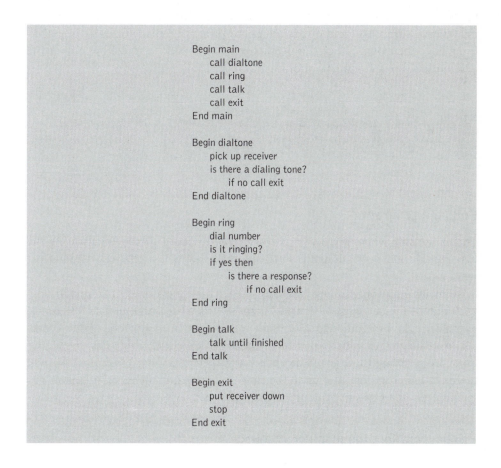

```
Begin main
        call dialtone
        call ring
        call talk
        call exit
End main

Begin dialtone
        pick up receiver
        is there a dialing tone?
            if no call exit
End dialtone

Begin ring
        dial number
        is it ringing?
        if yes then
                is there a response?
                    if no call exit
End ring

Begin talk
        talk until finished
End talk

Begin exit
        put receiver down
        stop
End exit
```

Figure 6.5: Pseudocode for the telephone call program

There can be more than one solution to a programming problem, and each may have its strengths and weaknesses. There are two immediately noticeable advantages of pseudocode. First, one can tell how the logic flows by reading the code; secondly, at this stage the entire program has been written without any consideration for the rules of the language to be used. Thus the problem is solved independently of the language, all that remains to be done is to translate this into program statements. The benefit of the indentations can also be seen: they give you a visual representation of the program blocks thus helping you to keep track of the flow. Some would say, however, that pseudocodes are too close to program statement and therefore time consuming and unnecessary.

In the 1980s new tools appeared to help programmers design and keep track of the flow of data through a program or to re-engineer (recode) old programs. These are called computer-aided software engineering (CASE) tools and are normally used for large and complicated software development. Experts argue over the relative advantages and disadvantages of different tools. Normally, organizations have their own policies and practices which may be to follow one of the design tools, use a combination of them or use CASE tools.

Try to find out which design tools are used by programmers in the corporate world. A Web search may reveal some information.

Coding a program

This is the step where the design is transferred to program statements using the language chosen. If the design is thorough then coding is a relatively straightforward job.

So, what is a programming language? As we have mentioned, a computer only understands the language of 0s and 1s, and this is what programmers had to use in the early days of computers. To make it easier for programmers, higher generations of languages which resembled English more closely were developed and these are translated into machine code using special systems programs. We will discuss these programs later on in the chapter. Let us first take a brief look at different levels and types of programming languages.

First generation: the machine language

First generation language has only two characters in the alphabet, 0 and 1 (called bits) and all instructions are written as strings of bits called bit patterns.

This is the language closest to the machine because it needs no translation and a programmer is able to address the hardware directly by using it. This gives the programmer total control of the machine and allows him or her to perform any task within the power of the hardware without the constraint of the rules which higher levels of languages are bound by. For this reason it is used to write microcodes, the set of instructions stored in ROM and required for starting the computer when switched on. We saw an example of a first generation program in Chapter 2.

However, a first generation language is difficult to use. It is machine dependent which means that each make of a processor has its own language, that is, its own version of bit patterns it understands. It takes too long to learn the language and use it correctly. Thus the control a first generation language gives to the programmer is counterbalanced by the time and expense of writing the programs. Nowadays very few programs are written using machine language.

Second generation: the low level language

In this generation, machine level instructions in bit patterns are replaced with mnemonics, which are words resembling the operation. For example, the mnemonic LDA is used to mean 'load the accumulator' (written as a bit pattern in machine language). Thus the low level language is a mnemonic version of the machine language and has the same benefits and drawbacks, except that it is a little easier to remember. These are also called assembly languages because a translating program called an assembler translates a low level program into bit patterns. Many systems programs are written in low level languages because they need to address the hardware more closely than is possible using higher level languages.

Third generation: the high level language

Although second generation languages made life slightly easier for programmers, the constraint of machine dependence meant that programmers needed to have thorough knowledge of machine architecture. This made programming a difficult and time consuming task. Third generation languages introduced the concept of machine independent programs written using English words. Thus the programmers benefited in two ways. First, learning a language required less intricate knowledge of the hardware. Secondly, writing a program became easier because a high level language allowed them to write codes in a manner similar to pseudocodes. However, the rules (called the syntax) of the languages had to be learnt and applied correctly to the design. Programming still remained a specialized job but became less tedious and a more satisfying task.

The first high level language was introduced in 1954 and was called FOR-TRAN (FORmula TRANslation). As the name suggests it was meant to handle mathematical formulae and was used mainly for scientific data processing.

Since the introduction of the first high level language many have been developed, some of them general purpose and others for specific applications. COBOL (COmmon Business Oriented Language) was introduced in 1959 mainly for business data processing because it could handle large amounts of data and had an English-like structure. It was very popular in the commercial world in the 1960s and 1970s and many old systems are still running on COBOL programs. There are other business languages such as PL/1 (Programming Language 1) and RPG (Report Program Generator). Some languages were developed using the concept of algorithms (pseudocodes) such as Algol (ALGOrithmic Language), Pascal (named after the French scientist) and C. These languages are often used to teach programming techniques because of their inherent structure. Introduced in 1972, C has the ability to address machine level features of a computer's architecture and even allows some assembly level codes to be mixed in with high level programs. Thus C can be used for systems programs as well as commercial applications. However, its low level nature and limited error checking facilities make a C program prone to human errors.

As computers became increasingly widespread and started finding their place in homes and schools, the need for an easy programming language suitable for non-professionals was felt. As a result BASIC (Beginners All-purpose Symbolic Instruction Code) was introduced. Although developed in 1965, it became popular in the mid 1970s mainly amongst hobbyists because of its simple rules and easy to understand structure. It also took its position in education and, to a certain extent, in business, especially following the introduction of structured BASIC.

There are many other programming languages in existence, some special purpose designed to handle specific types of data and instructions and others general purpose meant for a wider variety. The programming languages mentioned above are said to be *procedural*, because the instructions are written in the sequence they are to be executed. Many new languages have been developed since non-procedural programming was introduced, and this will be mentioned later.

Translating high level programs into machine language

High level languages made programmers' lives easier by moving away from the level of the machine, but the fact that a machine only understands machine language remained. Programs written in high level languages have to be translated by a translator program in the same way that a low level program is translated by an assembler. A program written in a high level language is called the source program which, after translation, becomes the object program. Normally, each statement in the source code gives rise to a number of statements in object code thus making the object program much longer than the source but much simpler. A translation program performs some other important tasks as well: it identifies any syntax errors (errors caused by the failure of the programmer to follow rules correctly) in the program code and produces error messages, in some cases it also attempts to correct some common errors. A translator also attempts to optimize the efficiency of a program by manipulating the object code to reduce execution time. Such tasks invariably increase the complexity and size of a translating program thus affecting the speed of translation.

As mentioned earlier, an *assembler* is a translating program for low level programs. There are two types of translator for high level programs: *compilers* and *interpreters*. A compiler analyzes and translates a whole source program (or a complete module of a source program) in a high level language into an object program in machine language. The process is performed in two stages: in stage one the syntax is checked and if errors are found, the compiler produces error messages and stops at the end of this stage. The second stage is entered into if no syntax errors are found and the rest of the tasks (translation, optimization and so on) of compilation are performed. A program can be run, that is, it becomes executable, only when the compilation process has been completed successfully following the correction of all syntax errors. Once translated into an executable program, it can be run as many times as necessary without any more translation unless any changes are made. However, a compiler does not check for semantic (logic) errors; thus a program may run but fail to perform the required tasks correctly. Most high level languages are compiled.

An interpreter runs a source program one statement at a time. It does not produce an object code; it analyzes each source program statement, checks for errors and then executes it. At any stage when it finds an error, the process stops. Since an interpreter does not produce a whole executable object program the translation has to be performed statement by statement every time the program is to be executed. Optimization is not possible and error messages are sometimes unclear because the interpreter has no overall view of the whole program. Logo, BASIC and Prolog are examples of interpreted high level languages.

Some other tasks may have to be performed before a program becomes fit to run. Sometimes a program has separate modules, compiled separately, which have to be linked to each other. A linkage program performs this task. It may also have to link an object program with modules kept in a 'library' in the backing store. Detailed discussion of a linkage program is outside the scope of this book.

Non-procedural (declarative) languages

The examples used so far have been of procedural languages. Although there is controversy over the distinction, broadly speaking a procedural language tells a computer exactly how things are to be done whereas a non-procedural (also called declarative) language specifies the problem and leaves it to the machine to decide how to solve it. Using the example of the telephone call program, a procedural language will state how to make the call, a non-procedural will just say 'Make a telephone call': how the job has to be done is left to a lower level translation program. Thus non-procedural languages are further removed from the machine. They fall into three main categories: functional, logic programming and object oriented.

Functional programming Each task in this category is declared as a function. A program is built up with a number of such functions which are called by the main program as and when necessary. Thus, we can write a function to sort some numbers, give it a name and call it whenever we need to. Sasl and Miranda are two examples of functional languages. LISP, used widely in the artificial intelligence field, works on the same principle.

Logic programming Logic programming involves writing rules for proving relationships between objects, and a program consists of a set of these relations. The program works by the interpreter trying to find the truth of each relationship. Thus, logic programs are rather like a set of theorems which are proved when the programs are run. PROLOG (PROgramming LOGic), used often in the artificial intelligence field, is a well known example of logic programming.[4]

Object oriented programming First introduced in the 1980s, object oriented programming (OOP) has become widespread and has taken us one step closer to user developed programs. In procedural languages if we want to perform a function, such as open a file, we would write a series of instructions on how to do it. We would include the name of the file to be opened, the program it has to be opened into and so on. This is a top down design. In OOP, we put such a function in a packet called an 'object' for general use without the name of the file, or the program. We attach the necessary code (the instructions) as well as the data it requires to the object. Such an object can then be used by anyone for any program. One way of understanding the concept would be to think about the buttons in windows based programs. The same buttons are used in all windows applications; when you click on one, it performs the actions within the context

---

4   However, PROLOG can have both procedural and declarative statements.

of the application being used because the necessary codes and data are already encapsulated into it. Each object is self-contained, that is, it contains all that it needs to run as an independent entity.

Objects on an OOP are put into classes (types) and new classes can be created by starting with an existing class and defining how it differs from that class. Thus a rectangle or a parallelogram belong to the class 'quadrilateral' (a shape with four sides) which, in turn, belongs to the class 'shape'. Using the windows analogy again, there may be a class called 'Format' under which there may be objects called 'Borders', 'Columns' and so on. Thus, a class (such as 'Format' or 'Shape') has a hierarchy of objects under it which, in turn, may have hierarchies below them. An object is created by starting with the properties of the parent class and then making changes to it, thus allowing objects under each class to inherit the properties of those above them. Thus we can create an object for a rectangle by using properties from quadrilateral and changing them as necessary.

An object oriented program is built up by putting objects together in the right sequence. Thus, we can write a program to create a document by first using an object which opens up a page with a predetermined style, then other objects to create a header, insert page numbers, put a logo at a certain position, and so on. It makes programming easier by using three basic principles: making an object re-usable by making it self-sufficient (called encapsulation in OOP terminology); allowing objects in the same class to inherit properties from each other (called inheritance); allowing an action to apply to any object in a class, for example, an operation to find the area of a quadrilateral can be applied equally to a rectangle (called polymorphism). This avoids the necessity for long and complicated program procedures (sometimes called spaghetti code) thus making the processes of program writing and maintainance easier than before. It also enables end-users to build a program without much formal training in programming.

Many procedural languages are now adopting the concept of OOP; C++ is such a language derived from C with improved error checking facilities. It is the most widely used object oriented language and many commercial programs written in C or an assembly language are being translated into C++. Smalltalk, Delphi and Modula-2 are other examples of object-oriented languages.

A programming language that deserves a special mention here is Java. Developed by Sun Microsystems this is the language which was initially introduced to create pages on the Internet. But now Java has established its position as an object oriented language and has attracted a widespread reputation for its portability and ease of use. Java is similar to C and C++ but less complicated to use. Java code is first compiled into machine code by a Java compiler and this can then be executed using a Java interpreter called a Java virtual machine (JVM). Thus any system installed with a JVM can run Java, making it highly portable. Additionally, because Java was originally created for the

Internet, today's database applications which are increasingly dependent on Internet technologies can utilize Java's special qualities very effectively. Java 1.2 is the most up to date GUI based version of Java and incorporates improved interfaces for graphics and imaging. Java Beans is the visual version of Java, that is, it enables end-users to create applications by using predefined objects with little need for coding. Small Java programs (called applets) are used by many websites (Internet pages).

Fourth generation (4GL): the very high level languages

The higher the level of a language, the more removed it is from a machine, and the more work goes on behind the scenes to convert it to the language of a computer. In a 4GL the programmer writes, in almost natural English, 'what' he or she wants to achieve. This is translated by the systems programs into program code. Query languages often used with database programs, report generators and applications generators are some examples of 4GL programming. This level of programming allows a non-expert user to customize applications by using very high level instructions with little knowledge of the theories of programming.

Look at the jobs pages of a publication such as *Computer Weekly* and conduct a survey of the extent of the use of different programming languages.

Query languages can be used to extract information from database files by using an almost natural language-like construction. The set of query language statements, as in Figure 6.6, will list the results of the students in an information technology department in the specified format. SQL and FOCUS are two common languages used in the commercial world.

```
FILE IS STUDENTS
LIST BY SURNAME, FIRSTNAME, ID, GRADE
SELECT DEPT=INFO-TECH
TITLE "End of year result"
COLUMN HEADINGS: "SURNAME","FIRST NAMES","REGISTRATION
NUMBER","RESULT"
```

Figure 6.6: A sample SQL program segment

Report generators are used to extract data from files and databases to create customized reports. *Applications generators* store modules of program codes. A user can state using simple statements what needs to be done and the applications generator will call the appropriate modules to perform the task. Computer-aided software engineering (CASE) is a progression from applications generators. It is used to automate analysis, design, implementation and maintenance of information systems.

As you can imagine, 4GLs are designed for end-users with a minimum of technical knowledge to develop systems. In this level of programming, the end-user simply identifies the tasks to be performed using a set format; the interpreter (or compiler) goes behind the scenes and translates these instructions into conventional program codes which are written by expert software developers and stored in computer memory. 4GLs also play an important role as productivity tools for professional programmers as they save time by allowing a relatively small number of instructions to be used to create large information systems.

Fifth generation: the natural language

So far more of a concept than a reality, this generation seeks to enable a computer to understand natural language without the constraints of logic or syntax. Attempts are being made to write programs that will convert human language with all its ambiguities, context sensitive use of the same word in different ways, incorrect use of grammar, and so on into machine codes. Fifth generation languages face the same difficulty as that faced by fifth generation computers: how to imitate the way a human brain works. Although some progress has been made, the concept of a computer understanding natural language is a long way away. So far, some applications software has been developed, mainly in the form of expert systems, which allow users to enter simple sentence instructions which are interpreted by the software in the context of the application. No doubt hand-in-hand with the work on neural networks, work on natural language development will go on. There is a sizeable number of people on both sides of the argument over whether or not this will become a reality.

Find out the current situation in the development of natural language recognition by looking at some articles in magazines and on the Web.

Testing a program

Since a computer is only a machine, it can follow the instructions in a program only if they are written exactly in the way it has been taught to understand. Like the grammar of a natural language each programming language has a set of rules called the syntax of the language. A computer can follow a language only when the syntax used is absolutely correct. Additionally, a program will not work if the logic (semantic) is incorrect. Thus testing a program has two dimensions: first, when the program is compiled the syntax is checked and the program is not translated until all errors are corrected; second, the programmer runs the program with data at which stage the semantic of the program is tested and if there are any errors, the program fails to perform the tasks intended. If this happens, corrections have to be made and the program recompiled. It is the programmer's job to run the program with as varied data as possible to test the program under all situations. Many of us have some experience of errors in commercially packaged programs and the problems they can cause. It is difficult and expensive to correct errors once a program is live (running as part of a system). Therefore, major attention should be paid to eliminating all errors before implementing a system. A well designed modular (structured) program lends itself easily to this stage for reasons we have described.

We are addressing the question of testing a program after design and coding for the sake of the organization of the text, but in practice testing should be associated with each stage of program development. A program should be checked at different levels using a test plan, produced while designing the program, which details the test steps to be taken and produces a list of test data and the expected results. First, the program design should be checked with different types of data by running them through the proposed algorithm to see if they produce the correct results. For example, if you write the pseudocode for a program to find the highest of a set of numbers, you can use a set of test data and go through the pseudocode like a machine to check if you get the correct result. The process is called dry running and if done thoroughly and methodically, can trap many errors at the design stage. At the coding stage validation checks can be incorporated. In this method, any data input to the program is checked against a given range before it is accepted as being of the correct format. An efficient program does not only process data correctly, it also knows how to handle incorrect data without bringing the system to a halt. For example, when you are asked to enter your pin code at a bank cashpoint which only accepts four numeric digits, the program includes checks which reject anything other than a four digit number. Thus, the program first checks that your entry is of the correct format before checking whether your pin is the correct one for your card and gives a suitable error message telling you what to do if you entered an invalid number. Different methods and techniques of validation checks are available to programmers, but we will not go into the details of these. Finally, at the completion of coding, the program must be verified against all possible types of data following the test plan mentioned above and the output checked against the expected results. The test plan should include correct as well as incorrect data of as many types as possible to verify that the program can cope under all circumstances.

Many real life systems are built with a number of programs working together, often one program accepting as input the data produced as output by another. In such cases each program is tested individually first and then all participating programs are tested together to check that they relate to each other correctly. This is systems testing which should also follow a carefully produced test plan with test data. In case of failure the 'offending' programs are tested and modified as necessary. When this stage is completed, the system should be tested with real data before allowing the implemention of the system for users. Thorough testing of programs is extremely important as any errors identified when the system is 'live' are a lot more damaging in terms of performance and cost than some extra time spent at the time of testing. Sometimes selected groups of users are allowed to test a system under actual working conditions before releasing it for general use. This is sometimes referred to as beta-testing, as opposed to alpha-testing, a term used to mean testing a system with imaginary test data as a part of program development.

Documentation

Although mentioned here separately for clarity, documentation is an essential part of each stage of programming. Programs are frequently specified by one person or a team, designed and written by different people and then finally looked after and updated by a third team. It is of vital importance that clear documentation is kept at every step to enable anyone involved in the maintenance to have a clear understanding of the programs. Often organizations have their own styles and standards of writing documentation to aid clarity. Records of the design tools used such as structure diagrams and pseudocodes, comments with program statements, self-explanatory data names and so on are aspects of good documentation together with descriptions of the purpose of programs, method of solutions, test plan and program printouts. We will revisit this subject in our discussion on systems development in Chapter 9.

Maintenance

Program maintenance is necessary for three different reasons. First, in spite of thorough testing, errors are often found in programs after they go live. The sources of such errors have to be found and corrected. Secondly, a correct program does not necessarily mean an efficient one; regular evaluation of programs must be carried out and necessary amendments made to improve their quality. This may follow comments from users or recommendations from a maintenance team following a quality assurance testing. Thirdly, changing circumstances sometimes necessitate changes in programs. For example, for a program producing payslips for company employees, any changes in the tax regulations may require recoding of certain parts.

A computer system is said to have a short lifespan of between five to 10 years (although some systems survive much longer than this) because of changing user needs and hardware and software environments. Therefore, systems should be evaluated at regular intervals which may result in major upgrading of programs. This should be treated as a new system development and follow the procedure required for this purpose. Programming is part of a systems development process and upgrading programs is also a part of upgrading a system. Systems development is discussed in detail in Chapter 9.

What could software developers do at the stage of writing programs to avoid problems such as the 'Millennium bug'? What lessons should we learn from this?

Summary

A computer program is a set of step-by-step instructions telling a computer exactly what needs to be done. A programmer plans, designs the logic of the program using a number of tools available, writes the code in a suitable programming language and tests the program using various methods and techniques before it goes live. There are a number of levels of programming languages between machine level, written using 0s and 1s, and very high level, which is almost like natural language. A vast number of programming languages are available, some general purpose and some meant for specific applications. The current trend in programming is towards making it as high level as possible, thus allowing end-users and non-technical applications programmers to develop systems. At every stage of the process documentation is kept because programs are often maintained by people who are not the original authors. Regular maintenance and periodic evaluation are important parts in the life of a program which may result in a major upgrading project sometimes involving a complete redevelopment of the system.

Further reading

Managing a Programming Project by Philip W. Metzger, Prentice Hall, 1973 describes very well the stages involved and the tools used in traditional programming techniques.

Read *Computer Program Design* by Elizabeth Dickson, McGraw-Hill, 1997 to understand the concept of program design.

Software Engineering Concept by Richard Fairley, McGraw-Hill, 1985 gives a good account of some of the common software design tools.

Revision questions

1. Write algorithms for the following tasks:
   (a) making a cup of tea;
   (b) crossing the road at a junction;
   (c) separating some marbles into groups by colour (red, green or blue) and counting the total in each group.

2. Explain the concept of structured programming and discuss the main benefits of it.

3. Examine your pseudocodes for question 1 and alter them if necessary to follow the concepts of structured programming.

4. Summarize the differences between the concepts and use of the generations of programming languages.

5. Summarize the importance of thoroughness in program testing and briefly describe the ways in which a program can be tested.

6. Produce a test plan for one of the programs above and test your design.

7. Discuss why program documentation is important, keeping in mind the various stages involved in program development and maintenance.

Food for thought

BYTE, August 1995

The end of programming
David S. Linthicum

Rapid application development promises applications without programming. Does it deliver?

RAD (rapid application development) tools are the microwave ovens of the programming world – they're new, they're fast, and they'll probably make a lot of people's lives easier. However, as anyone who has put aluminium foil into a microwave knows, you'll see benefits only if you use the tools properly.

When all the hype has settled, RAD tools promise two advantages over traditional programming. The first advantage is a shorter, more flexible development cycle, enabling you to leap directly from prototype to finished application. The second advantage is that a reasonably sophisticated end user can develop applications.

Sound too good to be true? Sometimes it is. RAD tools often require you to write code. But if you use them properly, you can reduce many programming tasks to drag-and-drop simplicity.

RAD's history

The roots of RAD lie in the prototyping tools of yore. With such tools, developers could quickly mock up an application so the end user could see and experience it before the design was finalised. Prototypes were the ultimate design tool, because they virtually eliminated misunderstandings about an application's look, feel, and capabilities. Once the developer and end user agreed on a prototype, the developer simply created an application that looked and acted like the prototype.

But these prototyping tools usually provided only 'smoke and mirrors' for the developer. Prototypes rarely became final applications. After finishing a prototype, the developer might actually build the application in a language such as COBOL or C.

If this seems wasteful, that's because it is. Developers were building the application twice. To solve this problem, RAD tools extend the capabilities of prototyping tools by providing developers with everything they need to build a prototype as well as turn it into a fully functional application.

It's a fairly elegant solution. Developers build applications with RAD tools primarily by designing the interface. They assemble components such as buttons, menus, data windows, and combo boxes. Developers are more concerned with what the program does than they are with how it does it. They show the application to users, get feedback, and make modifications to the application. This process continues until the user is happy.

Speed over design

Some traditional systems developers criticise this type of spiral development as a process of getting it wrong many times before getting it right once. Forgoing the design stage may cost more in the long run, they say, arguing that poorly designed applications are difficult to maintain, upgrade, and port.

The 'design-on-the-fly' method of development that RAD promotes does create applications quickly, but you then have to live with the application after deployment. Many RAD applications require a lot of fixing and redeployment cycles after delivery to get them right. This is known as the prototyping death spiral, and it could lead to user dissatisfaction, wasted money, and a short life span for the application.

From a design viewpoint, the key to good RAD development is to keep an eye on the big picture. When using RAD, organisations should not neglect the business objectives of the application. Developers need to design applications that take the greatest advantage of the object-oriented-like features that most tools provide, and that requires planning the application's implementation. Without careful planning, an application could fail to take advantage of reusable application components – worse, the application could become an unmaintainable mess.

Even if you save time when you're designing an application with a RAD tool, you may lose that time when you execute it or port it to another platform. RAD tools typically use interpreters and not compilers, and most interpreters execute about half as fast as compiled code. There can be a noticeable performance difference compared with a compiled language. Tools such as Borland's Delphi and Gupta's SQLWindows make strides by improving execution speed, but it will be some time before RAD matches the speed and performance of traditional compilers.

If you choose RAD, you could also be locking yourself into a platform. Most RAD tools don't provide much cross-platform portability. Delphi and Microsoft Visual Basic, for example, support only Windows. Some RAD tools support multiple platforms (e.g., Unify and Compuware's Uniface).

Get with the programmer

Programming without programmers is the way some vendors sell RAD tools. The idea is that by using visual programming, anyone can assemble applications without writing a single line of code.

Here's an example. IBM's VisualAge (a visual-programming tool that's based on Smalltalk) lets developers assemble an application from a palette of components – buttons, windows, menus, and so on. After placing all the necessary components on the application window, the developer links such nonvisual events as print commands to the components. When the user clicks on the print button, it invokes the connected nonvisual print event. But VisualAge, like other 'no-code' visual-programming tools such as Powersoft's PowerBuilder and Visual Basic, does not let developers create all applications visually.

With the exception of the simplest applications (e.g., order-entry systems and client databases), most developers will probably have to learn to program using the underlying programming language. Applications that require low-level API calls or have special calculation or display requirements will often need good old-fashioned

▶

programming. For example, if an application uses real-time data or array processing, it will require extra code beyond the initial visual construction.

Still, the time gained from using a RAD tool can be immense. Most VisualAge programmers report the ability to create up to 80 percent of an application visually, with the last 20 percent consisting of specialised functions.

RAD and reuse

Most RAD tools provide facilities for component reuse, but fast development often means developers don't take time to design their applications to make reuse a reality. For instance, when creating an application using PowerBuilder, developers will probably select as many components as possible from a library. They can use the components as is or modify them using PowerBuilder's inheritance features. But that's only if they have the time to browse the libraries to find the prebuilt objects.

The trick to making the most of reuse in the RAD world is to construct from the generic to the specific. Build simple components first and reuse them throughout the application, making modifications as needed through inheritance. Good candidates for reuse include data windows, pop-up windows, and printer dialogue boxes. Code reuse enables developers to modify an application in a single location and to have the changes propagate throughout the application, saving time in the process.

Many third parties have taken advantage of the reuse capabilities in RAD tools to build plug-in libraries. A developer can extend Visual Basic, for example, with VBXes (Visual Basic custom controls) and OCXes (OLE custom controls) from hundreds of vendors. These extensions add functions ranging from development project management to sophisticated database access, often at prices under $100. The power of VBXes and OCXes is so great that tools such as Delphi and Oracle's PowerObjects have designed in the capability to use them as well.

Reuse does not happen by accident. Developers need to put the time into the initial design and properly plan to set up the application to maximise reuse. The tragedy is that most RAD projects promote development speed, not reuse. Dozens of object-oriented analysis and design methodologies and CASE tools assist developers in this process. In most RAD projects, if you think through the application before you get lost in the RAD tool, you can create an application that maximises the use of recycled code.

Applications development managers need to encourage reuse among RAD development teams. RAD tools should include mechanisms that let developers locate and use existing objects, such as shared object browsers that provide a searchable database of objects for RAD tools that are shareable among developers.

Avoiding bad RAD

So, is it time to trade in our RAD tools for more traditional development tools, such as COBOL and C? Or is it time for programmers to find a new line of work as RAD takes over? The answer is a loud 'neither.' RAD has tremendous powers, but it is not without its limits. Although it is an important part of the enterprise applications development process, it doesn't eliminate the need for a good understanding of business requirements, a sound design, and skillful programming.

The process of building the application with the end user provides common ground, where the developer and the end user can reach an understanding as to how the application will appear and behave. But the developer is ultimately responsible for the long-term health of the application, and not just its rapid delivery. With RAD, developers can easily overlook critical issues during development, including structure, consistency, design, maintainability, and good use of reuse mechanisms. RAD-developed applications may appear healthy on the surface, but after a short time, developers and users begin to discover their shortcomings. After an application enters production, it's extremely difficult to correct problems that are normally corrected during development.

Most IS organisations will come in contact with RAD before the end of the century. Now is the time to look beyond the hype to see what it can do for you. More important, understand what RAD can't do. For all you programmers out there, your job is safer now.

Discussion questions

1. Using the information given in the article as well as some other sources, explain the basic principles behind rapid program development (RAD).

2. RAD was introduced mainly with a view to end-user development (EUD). Discuss the advantages and disadvantages of EUD. What factors need to be taken care of in order to make EUD a success?

3. Summarize the advantages of RAD as discussed in the article. Discuss the best ways possible to make the most of these advantages.

4. As the article demonstrates, there is a lot of misunderstanding about the nature and power of RAD. Discuss the discrepancies between the true nature of RAD and the common beliefs.

5. Find some alternative views on the subject by searching for other recent articles.

6. Where do you stand on the subject of 'programming without programmers' and why?

CHAPTER 7

Communicating data

Objectives

After reading this chapter you should have some understanding of:

▶ the need for electronic data communication;
▶ the components of a computer network;
▶ the different types of network and the way they are used;
▶ the methods and protocols used for the transmission of data;
▶ the applications of wide area networks.

Introduction

One aspect omitted from the description of a computer system in Chapter 2 was the possibility of there being more than one computer in the system. In today's world of work, people depend on fast communication, up to the minute accurate information and round the clock connectivity with their organizations. Data has to be passed over long distances, 24 hours a day and users need access to the data via desktop computers. Such demands in terms of speed and accessibility are at the root of what is now called the second IT revolution (the first was when microprocessors became commonplace).

In this chapter we will discuss how information technology provides the means for effective data communication and how it affects the way we communicate in the modern world.

The nature of data communication

Communication may involve just two computers linked together to share programs and information, or a large number of users covering a wide geographical area. When one computer is connected to another for the straightforward transmission of data all we need is a cable connecting the two and the software required for data transfer. If the computers are compatible with each other (that is, they both accept data in the same format) or data is converted appropriately when they are not, this constitutes the simplest kind of network possible. However, purists will not accept this view: the formal definition of a network could be given as *a number of interconnected devices capable of communicating and sharing each other's resources*. A network enables an organization to centralize its computer system and allows users to access the facilities of a large computer system via desktop computers. Today, networks are not only capable of containing a larger number of computers and peripherals, they can also connect fax machines, cameras, video and audio equipment in order to carry data in the form of text, speech, graphics, animation, and so on. Different networks can also be connected to each other to extend the range of communication.

Organizations need to communicate with each other – nationally and internationally – because competitive business advantage often depends on information from other organizations. For example, you may wish to withdraw cash from a machine in a Middle Eastern airport on your way from England to Singapore. Your card has to be validated and the financial transaction must take place for which the machine in the airport must be connected to a network which allows direct communication between the two countries. This necessitates a link between the two places. Multinational companies need to pass data between their offices in different countries and their branches within one country. This could involve anything from sending funds between offices, exchanging marketing information on their products, and distributing research findings to sending purchase orders and delivery notes.

Another facility which has benefited from the use of networks is the Internet, the international network of networks. The Internet allows a user to access information on almost anything, originating anywhere in the world. This has enabled users to keep in touch with each other, get information from a large number of databases maintained by various organizations, take part in debates on-line, acquire academic papers published by people in institutions all over the world and even conduct business globally. There are also some social debates surrounding the use of the Internet. With the enormous possibilities offered some have suggested that we will be able to create a 'global village' in which people all over the world are able to communicate with each other on an equal basis irrespective of geographical boundaries. There is great scepticism over this concept which we will discuss in Chapter 12.

As with all progressive ideas, networks have also given rise to some concerns. Data security and the right of individuals to maintain the privacy of personal information – which are serious issues of the day anyway – are more at stake with the widespread use of network communications. Additionally, some people unfortunately abuse the power of the Internet by promoting such things as obscenity, racial prejudice, religious fundamentalism and other forms of social ills. So far, there are no boundaries, ownership or sanctions (although some attempts are being made to introduce some control), thus giving users a free hand in the utilization of this enormous facility. As in any other medium of communication abuse is the price we pay for achieving the freedom we seek.

Basic components of a network

A network consists of a number of units: computers, terminals, communications channels, communications processors and above all, software to run the system.

Computers

A network uses computers mainly to process the data it transmits. This may be done by one central computer or a cluster of computers in which each has a slightly different role to play. For example, one computer may be designated the host processor for handling the processing of applications, programs and large databases. Another, often less powerful machine, may be used as the front-end processor to relieve the host of communications related tasks such as routing of messages (deciding which way data will be sent), error control and security checks as well as to facilitate communication between the host processor and the terminals. Thus the host performs the complicated task of processing the data and the front-end processor coordinates the communication between the sender and the receiver to reduce the load on the host. Figure 7.1 shows such an arrangement in which the front-end processor organizes its task by using a controller device to support a part of the network.

Find out if the computer centre in your university or the company you work for has a host and a front-end processor and which computer they use for each purpose.

The role a computer plays in a network also depends on the design (topology) of the network. For example, one network may contain a number of computers, all processing data at the same level. On the other hand, some networks have a hierarchical design in which the processing tasks are divided according to the position of a computer in the structure. We will discuss this under Topology later on in the chapter.

Terminals

Also called nodes, these are the end points of a network via which data is input and output. They are usually microcomputers (with or without processing power) for communicating with the network, and peripheral devices such as printers, video screens, cameras, fax machines and so on. PCs are often used in a

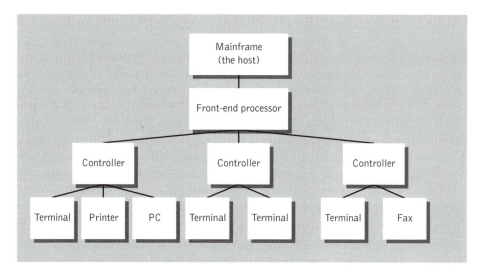

Figure 7.1: Use of a front-end processor

network as terminals as well as stand-alone computers, thus offering users the flexibility of a personal computer within the framework of a large network of hardware and software resources.

Communications channels

Data needs a channel to travel through. The technology used for this purpose has improved enormously in the past decade or so. A number of channel types are available now, each with their own strengths and weaknesses.

Twisted wire

Initially only telephone lines which consisted of strands of copper wire twisted in pairs were used to transmit computer data. This was largely to take advantage of the already existing telephone network, thus saving money. However, twisted wire channels are slow and suffer from interference in the lines.

Co-axial cables

Also used for cable television, a co-axial cable is an insulated copper wire sometimes laid under the ocean floor for international communications. Television aerials are made up of co-axial cables; they provide faster transmission with less interference. Co-axial cables are sometimes used for short distance communication between computers and terminals. However, they are more expensive than twisted wire and because of their thickness they are difficult to use.

Fibre optic cables

Both twisted wire and co-axial cables carry data in the form of electrical signals. By contrast, fibre optic cables, which are made of strands of transparent fibre bound together into cables, carry pulses of light generated by a laser source. They are cheaper to produce than their copper rivals and carry data much faster. They also provide better security of data against corruption or loss because there is less risk of interference from other signals. However, they are expensive and difficult to install and are often only used in the main, single channel parts of large (wide area) networks. Fibre optic cables offer enormous advantages in the quality and speed of data transmission both at corporate level and for domestic appliances, but at present the cost of installation obstructs widespread use. However, recently some small (local area) networks have been using optical fibre to transmit data between the server (a computer in a network which holds the main programs and files) and the terminals (computers which access programs and files from the server). This allows terminals to be further away (by about 10 times) from the server.

Microwaves

All the channels described so far carry data through continuous physical cables between the sender and the receiver. It is also possible to send data by wireless transmission. This is done by using high frequency microwave radio signals which travel in the earth's atmosphere. However, these waves carry data in straight lines and the earth's curvature stops them from going round the earth. This is overcome by placing antennae on microwave towers to reflect the radio waves to change their path (Figure 7.2a).

Nowadays satellites are placed in the earth's orbit to capture radio waves and relay them round the planet's surface (Figure 7.2b). Satellite transmission has made data communication between any two parts of the world possible.

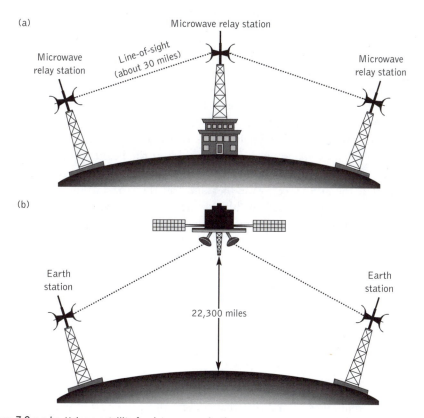

Figure 7.2 a + b: Using a satellite for data communication

Although building satellites is expensive, this mode of data transmission works out to be cheaper than laying continuous cables between communication centres.

There are other new techniques currently being developed for transmitting data, an example being laser or infra-red transmission between short distances. Most networks involving a large area use a combination of the channels available. For the first leg of the network, co-axial or fibre optic cables may be used; the second part may use the existing telephone network of twisted wire; and for the larger, intercontinental parts microwaves may be used in conjunction with satellites. The need for speed and economy are major deciding factors behind the choice of cables used. Other considerations include the security features available and interference on the lines.

 Look for some current articles to find out what new techniques are used for data transmission.

Transmission of data through a channel

There are two principal ways of transmitting data along a channel: parallel and serial. In parallel transmission messages are transmitted one byte, that is eight bits (normally one character), at a time. This requires eight channels running together. This can be expensive and is therefore used for short distance transmission. In serial transmission, data is sent a bit at a time. Usually this is used for long distance data communication.

Data transmission can be synchronous or asynchronous. In asynchronous transmission the message is sent with a start bit at the beginning and a stop bit at the end. The recipient of the message is not synchronized to the sender: the start bits alert the addressee to the message and the stop bit indicates the end. One message may even be sent in blocks each with its own start and stop bits and information on how these blocks link with each other because the blocks may not necessarily travel together. The blocks are put together at the receiving end by using the bits of information. In synchronous mode the sender and the receiver are synchronized so there is no need for start/stop bits.

Communications processors

Multiplexers

In a network data may be sent by a number of terminals via separate lines, at different speeds. A multiplexer is a device that collects all such data and sends it through one high speed line. At the other end, when data comes down one communications channel to be sent to different terminals, it is collected by the multiplexer which sorts out which item of data is for which terminal and sends it via appropriate lines (Figure 7.3). Thus, multiplexing is used to save time and cost by using one channel to transmit separate communications items for a major part of a network. This is applicable to channels of any type, co-axial cables to radio waves.

Modems

Channels designed to carry telephone conversations transmit analogue data, that is, data in the form of continuous electrical signals. Computer data is digital, a series of bits (0s and 1s), and therefore incompatible with speech which is a continuous flow of energy. When telephone channels are used for transmitting such data, a device called a modem (modulator/demodulator) is used which converts (modulates) the data sent by a computer to an analogue form before it passes it on to the common telephone channel. At the end of the channel, before the data is passed on to a computer, it is converted back (demodulated) to the digital form (Figure 7.4). Work is in progress to allow voice and data to transmit through the same channel simultaneously or alternately thus eliminating the need for a modem. When perfected, this will open many new doors in networking, for example for the transmission of voice over the Internet.

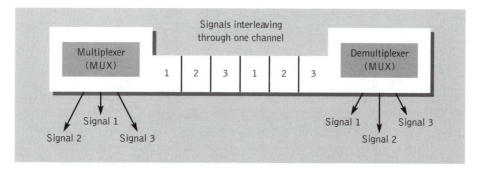

Figure 7.3: Data transmission via a multiplexer

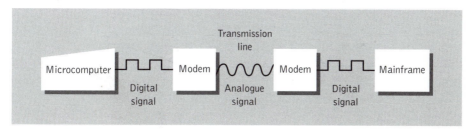

Figure 7.4: Use of modem

Types of network

Categorizing networks into types is difficult because of the variety of criteria by which different networks can be grouped together. One classification is done by the layout of the computers in a network, that is the topology; another is the way networks are built and used by organizations on the basis of the geographical areas covered; and a third could be the way computers in a network relate to each other, whether they are all equal or whether there is a central, more powerful, computer serving the terminals. We will discuss these classifications in the following section.

Network topology

This refers to the layout of computers in a network. There are three basic types of topology: star, ring and bus.

Star

In this layout there is a central host computer with smaller computers and terminals connected to it in the shape of a star (Figure 7.5).

The computers and terminals at the tips of the star are called nodes. Data from each of the nodes passes through the host which acts as the controller. The host holds all central data and programs. The nodes can access data and programs or

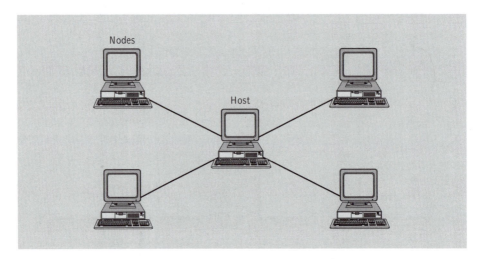

Figure 7.5: Star topology

communicate with each other only via the host. The benefit of this topology is derived from the centralization of major hardware and software resources. Also, attaching a new node is relatively easy since none of the others needs to be disturbed in the process. However, although the computers at the nodes can act as stand-alone systems to process data entirely local to them, they cannot communicate with other nodes if the central computer breaks down. The cost of cabling can also be high because each node needs a separate connection with the host.

Ring

In a ring network (Figure 7.6) the nodes are connected in a circular form. They have equal power, no computer serving any other.

A message from a computer is normally passed in one direction through each node until it reaches the destination(s). Thus each node acts as a repeater and boosts the signal. We will discuss repeaters in more detail later on. Ring topology is less expensive than star since there is no central controller. However, if one node fails the network comes to a halt although changing the direction to reach a computer is possible. Also, attaching a new node is cumbersome as it involves disconnecting the entire network.

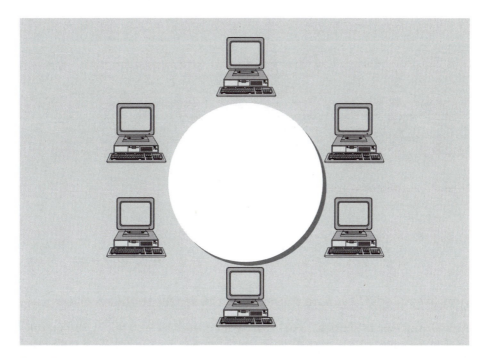

Figure 7.6: Ring topology

Bus

In a bus topology (Figure 7.7) the channel is laid out in a line as a backbone and nodes are connected to it with relatively short cables. A message sent by a node passes through the backbone with the address for the destination node attached to it. Each node examines the message travelling through the backbone and accepts it if it is meant for itself.

In this topology there is no central computer: a node can be a mainframe or a mini, a PC or a peripheral, all with the same importance. A bus topology easily allows the addition of new nodes because they can be attached to the bus without having to disturb any other nodes. Also, as the diagram indicates, if a node breaks down communication amongst the others is not affected. Because of the use of short cables, the cost of building a bus topology is relatively low.

There are other topologies which are basically a variation of the three just described. A tree topology (Figure 7.8) is a hierarchical star, and a fully connected network (Figure 7.9) is a variation of a ring in which any three nodes are connected by a ring. An organization may follow a combination of topologies: for example, a university may use a bus for its connections to different departments and a star for the computers within each department.

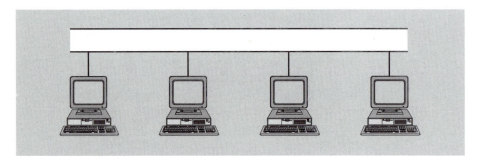

Figure 7.7 Bus topology

Which topology does your university or place of work have?

Access methods: how data moves from the sender to the receiver

As with any type of sharing, nodes sharing a network have to follow certain rules so that messages can be passed between them without the risk of interference. There are a number of ways in which messages can be sent, such as CSMA/CD,

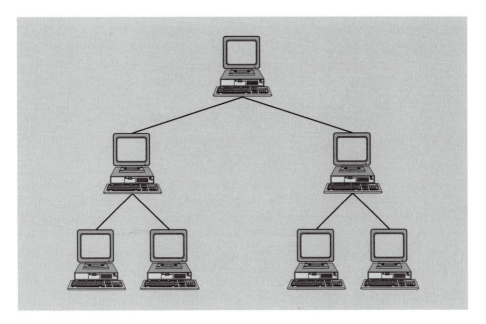

Figure 7.8: Tree topology

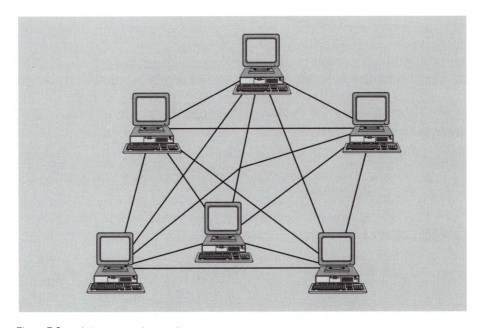

Figure 7.9: A fully connected network

token passing and polling. Which method is used depends mainly on the topology and the protocols (rules of communication) followed by the network.

CSMA/CD (carrier sense multiple access with collision detection) With this method every node sharing a network checks the channels and only sends a message when there is no other message being transmitted (that is, there is no risk of a collision). This may sound as if nodes have to wait for long periods for a gap in the traffic but in computing terms a message can be sent in a fraction of a second, thus waiting times are normally negligible.

Token passing With this method, a token (a specific electronic signal) passes through every node to check if a message is to be sent. When it finds such a node, the token collects the message and then goes straight to the addressee. After the message is delivered and the token is freed, it queries every node again to repeat the process. Thus a message can only be sent when a node is in possession of a free token, and while a token is carrying a message, all other nodes have to wait for it to be freed.

Polling Used mainly for centralized, main- or mini-computer based networks, polling works by the central computer querying (polling) each node in rotation. If a node has a message to send, it does so when polled. The centre collects the message and passes it on to the addressee before it polls the next node in sequence.

 Find out which access method is used in what type of organization and why.

Networks in organizations

There are different types of networks for different purposes, some are suitable for a single office, some for using within one building and some for national and international communications.

Private branch exchanges

Private branch exchanges (PBX) have been in existence since offices and office buildings first started using their own switchboards to operate internal telephone systems. The earlier PBXs had limited capacity with just the means to transfer telephone calls to the right extensions. Nowadays PBXs have a small processor inside them to support telephone lines, computers, printers, copying machines, fax machines and so on. A PBX is now able to handle analogue data through the telephone line as well as digital data from a computer, thus allowing communication between many different types of devices. For example, it is possible for a user to send a wordprocessed document directly to the printer, then send the printout to a photocopier or send a copy through the fax machine to someone on the other side of the world. No new lines have to be set up for a PBX network since the existing telephone lines are used. Although it can only handle a small amount of data it is highly cost effective for small offices which use simple computer applications and wish to gain connectivity cheaply.

Local area networks

A network spanning a limited area such as one office, a single building or a number of buildings within one boundary is called a local area network (LAN). They normally have their own communications channel using twisted wire or co-axial cable. A LAN also includes a network interface card inserted in each computer in the network and a cable interface unit, known technically as a hub. A hub is a hardware device which connects a number of nodes and sends signals from these nodes via a single channel to other parts of the LAN (Figure 7.10). A LAN is controlled entirely by the organization that owns it and is used mainly for sharing resources and information.

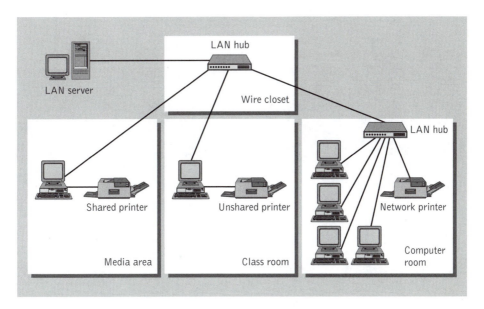

Figure 7.10: A typical LAN in a college

A LAN can only cover up to about 600m of cable distance, but it can incorporate computers and peripherals of any level of sophistication, from PCs and printers to minicomputers, mainframes and video-conferencing equipment. LANs can be connected to other LANs and to larger wide area networks to achieve widespread communication.

Find some examples of the use of small and large LANs. How are they organized?

Wide area networks

Wide area networks (WANs) are used to cover distances ranging from a few kilometres to countries worldwide (Figure 7.11). The channels used in WANs can be co-axial cable, fibre optic, satellite or a combination of all of these. The most common WAN is a country's telephone network. One can communicate with the rest of the world by connecting a modem to a PC which in turn is connected to the telephone line. Fax machines connected the same way allow users to transfer text and images through telephone lines to other fax machines on the network.

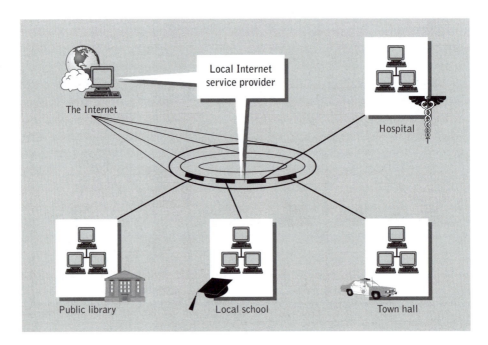

Figure 7.11: A simplified WAN of a town

Companies such as British Telecom offer the services of their national and international channels for voice and data communications. They provide two types of services: switched and dedicated line. *Switched* lines are similar to making a telephone call: the user makes a connection by dialling up and is charged according to the distance and time covered. There are several switching centres (exchanges) each covering a certain area. These are, in turn, connected to each other to cover larger distances. When a message is sent, it is collected by the switching centre in its area and sent to the addressee via the network of switching centres.

Switched services can be accessed by using circuit, message or packet switching methods. *Circuit switching* is similar to the service used by a telephone network. When a node wants to send a message to another, a temporary one-to-one connection is made by the switching centres between the two nodes. The connection remains until the transmission is completed. Since data between nodes travels only sporadically, circuit switching can be wasteful as no other nodes can access the two switched nodes until the connection is broken. *Message switched* services overcome this difficulty by attaching the address of the recipient as the header (the leading data) of a message. It is carried to the addressee by the switching centre. If the addressee node is busy, the message waits until the line is free. Thus, in this mode, a message can be sent at any time even though the addressee may not receive the message until later. *Packet switched* services break a message up into equal size packets and attach with each packet the address of the recipient, some data for protection against errors, and a link (an identifying piece of data) to the next packet of the message. The packets are sent separately and sometimes via separate routes. They are collected by the addressee computer as and when they arrive through the network and reassembled in the right order using the links. This method is the most efficient because best possible routes are found for packets and waiting times are normally very small. However, this is more expensive than the other methods.

Dedicated lines are permanently leased connections between two users. They are normally more expensive than switched lines but offer faster and easier connections between the two nodes thus making them suitable for large volume data transmission between two fixed locations, whereas switched lines are suitable when occasional connections are required to anywhere on a wide area network.

Find some examples of dedicated lines. What are the reasons companies have for using them?

Another alternative for organizations seeking wide area networking is to subscribe to an *integrated services digital network* (ISDN). This is a set of communication services offered by telecommunication companies which provides high speed data transfer. The service offers voice and data transmission via the same channel, thus eliminating the need for modems. ISDN uses two separate channels, one at high speed and one at a lower speed, and combines the use of the two to transmit data at a rate of 64 kbps (kilobits per second), much faster than the 14,000 bps using a modem. There are other technologies, such as satellite transmission which is fast but can only download information (load the receiver's computer with the information requested rather than being an interactive communication channel), digital subscriber lines (DSL) which offer fast data transfer but are expensive, and fibre-optic cable connection which provides high speed communication but is not available in all parts of the country. At the time of writing, researchers are working on the possibility of Internet connection via domestic electrical lines.

Find the current status of the technologies mentioned here.

Some large organizations maintain their own private WANs covering the countries and areas they want. Although this gives companies the maximum benefit in terms of access, it is a very expensive option. Recently value added networks (VAN) have become quite popular. These are networks set up and managed by private companies. Users can connect to them for a price and use the network without having to worry about data or channel management. VANs are normally data only networks, sometimes servicing a specialized user group and sometimes open to any user willing to pay for the service. VAN channels can be completely owned by private companies or can be a combination of private channels and national data networks. The providers of VAN also offer services such as email, error checking and so on, for which the subscribing companies do not have to take any responsibility.

Relationship between the computers in a network

When we talk about the relationship between computers in a network, we automatically refer to LANs since WANs do not connect computers; they are usually the result of interconnected LANs. On the basis of the topology and the status of each computer in relation to the others, LANs can be categorized in a number of ways.

Centralized networks

Traditionally, networks used a centralized computer system with terminals and peripherals connected to it in the form of a star. All data and programs in such a network were held by the centre which would contain the host as well as a front-end computer. The computer used for this purpose was a mainframe or a mini and the nodes were usually dumb terminals (computers without much processing power) serving only to access data from the central computer system. Modern centralized systems use PCs as intelligent terminals so users can input data via the nodes as well as use them as stand-alone computers for local applications. Printers and other peripheral devices are often located in user departments. Many large and dedicated computer systems such as those for airlines ticket reservation are centralized; users can enter new bookings, cancellations, payments and so on, via the nodes but all updating is done centrally. Figure 7.12 shows the structure of a centralized system where each terminal may be a PC, a printer, or just an input medium.

Distributed networks

With microcomputers becoming more and more powerful the focus in a network was shifted gradually from the large central systems to microcomputers located near end-users, giving rise to the term 'downsizing'. Distributed networks are a result of this shift.

In a distributed network the tasks to be performed are distributed amongst a number of small PC based computer systems, with a larger central computer coordinating the overall organization (Figure 7.13). The central computer, which can be a mini or a powerful PC (depending on the size of the organization), often holds copies of files and programs used by the smaller systems for security and supplies them to those systems when requested. For example, a university may

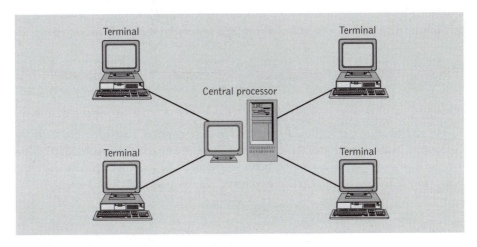

Figure 7.12: A centralized network

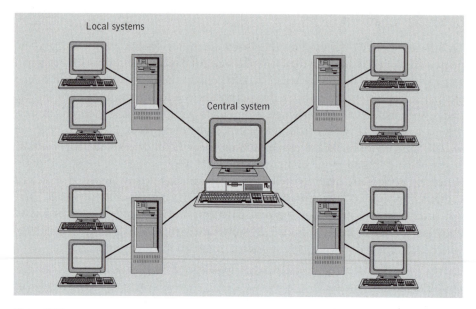

Figure 7.13: A distributed network

have a central computer system which runs the central services such as finance and student registration centrally while the departments run their own systems such as the courses database and timetables locally. When a department indicates that it wants to enter the details of a new student, the centre downloads the necessary files, that is, copies them from the central system to the local, and at the end of processing the files are updated centrally. The departments communicate with each other directly or via the central system depending on the way the system is set up.[1] This is in fact an example of a combination of centralized and distributed systems. There may be a main- or a minicomputer based centralized system for the administrative jobs and a PC based distributed system for staff and student to use.

What does your university or place of work use and how does it organize the jobs?

   The example of a distributed system used here raises a question: 'How do the computers in the centre and those within a department relate to each other? How are the files and operations shared between them?' The relationship between computers in a LAN can be classified in two ways: peer-to-peer and client/server.

---

1   In fact how the jobs are divided depends very much on the organizational structure: this example demonstrates the principle.

Peer-to-peer Normally used for small LANs, all PCs in a peer-to-peer network are equal in status to each other. The structure is that of a ring network where a message is passed from the sender through each PC until the addressee receives it. In a peer-to-peer network, each PC can share its resources with all other PCs, thus saving on resources. In fact, the software and peripheral devices can be situated anywhere on the network and their locations are transparent to users. This makes it suitable for a single office or a department in an organization.

Client/server network In many organizations downsizing led to client/server networks; the example used before for a distributed system is a typical one. In this structure the central computer is the main server with a large amount of memory serving the clients, which are the smaller networks in each department. The main server holds the programs and data used by the whole organization, for example, centralized databases and applications programs. Thus, in the university example, the central system is the server and the departments are the clients. The processing tasks are shared between the clients and the server, the exact division of responsibilities varying from organization to organization. For example, in some organizations when a user requests the use of an application, the application program and the necessary files are temporarily copied onto the user's PC and the processing is done by the PC itself. In other organizations all processing is done by the server, the client PCs only serving as the terminals for input and output. An organization may also use a combination of the two modes depending on the application being used. In large organizations (which a university often is), there may be a number of servers each dedicated to a specific system, for example, a server to handle all organizational jobs, one for use by the staff, one for students to log in, and so on. The main purpose of a client/server network is to share the load amongst computers and to organise access to users to achieve the most efficient network use.

Interconnecting networks

Sometimes organizations with business over a large area set up more than one LAN and connect the LANs to each other or even to WANs to achieve wider communication. Special devices have to be inserted in such networks in order to ensure that messages can be sent using the optimum route without sacrificing on quality. Repeaters, bridges, gateways and routers are some such devices.

A *repeater* (Figure 7.14) is used to connect different segments of a network to extend the area covered. Sometimes, due to cabling limitations, a signal loses its strength after travelling some distance. A repeater can be used at certain points in a

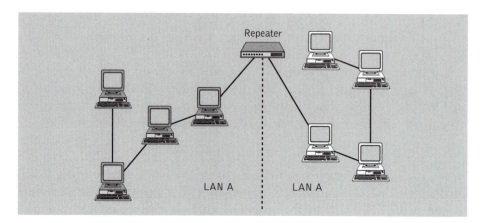

Figure 7.14: A repeater

cable to boost the strength of a signal before it is passed on. Thus, although repeaters are not used to interconnect LANs, they are useful for maintaining the strength of signals to enable them to be passed on to other LANs when they are connected.

Devices called bridges (Figure 7.15) and gateways (Figure 7.16) are used to connect one LAN to another. A *bridge* connects two LANs of the same type; a *gateway* connects LANs of different types. Using a combination of bridges and gateways LANs can be linked to each other and to WANs to achieve widespread connectivity.

Another component used to improve interconnectivity is a *router* (Figure 7.17). This is used to route a message from a node in one network to a node in another network. A number of routers are placed within interconnected LANs and paths are set up in-between any two of them. Routers choose the most suit-

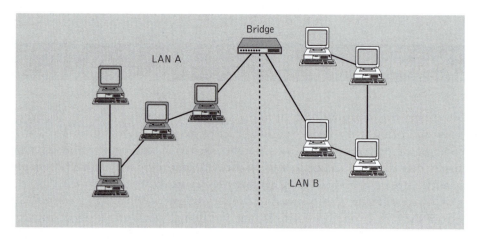

Figure 7.15: Use of a bridge

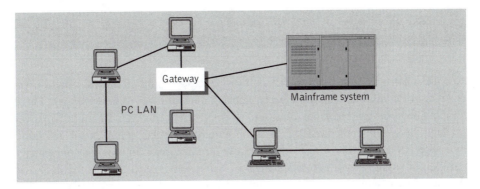

Figure 7.16 Use of a gateway

able paths between any two nodes to send messages. Thus, whereas a bridge simply passes a packet on to the next LAN, a router understands the destination of the packet and finds the most efficient route.

Sometimes a component called a *brouter* is used. This is a combination between a bridge and a router. It attempts to comprehend the destination of a packet; when it is successful it acts like a router and finds the most suitable route for the packet; otherwise it acts like a bridge and simply passes the packet on.

What are the roles of bridges, routers and gateways in the interconnection of smaller networks to the World Wide Web?

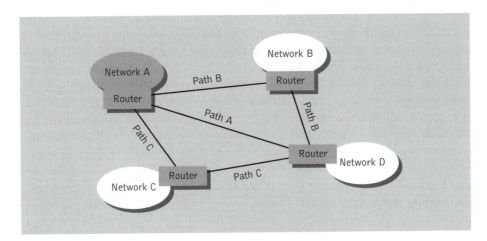

Figure 7.17 Use of router for a message from Network A to Network D

Communication standards and protocols

Networks often involve users in different organizations (and countries) using different types of components and methods, sending data of many different types. There have to be some agreed rules between all these users in order for data to travel through the systems otherwise the situation would be similar to two people speaking two different languages to each other without an interpreter. In the past connectivity between different networks was achieved by using software to convert the data sent through one network before it was transmitted to the other. This is similar to using an adapter every time you use a hair dryer that you bought in the USA to work in the UK. You can imagine how bad it would be if you travel regularly between many countries all of which have a different system. The solution would be for each country to agree on one standard system which works anywhere in the world. Network standards are agreed sets of rules which dictate the format and timing of messages to ensure internetwork compatibility. Organizations that send electronic data to others need to conform to a standard file format called the EDI (electronic data interchange)[2] standard which enables data of any type to be understood by the software on the receiving system. Before we can talk about standards, however, we need to understand the concept of protocols for electronic communications.

A protocol is a set of rules or conventions which govern the way a message is transmitted from the sender to the receiver passing through a number of steps and via a number of network elements. The process is similar to the way a letter written by you goes through a number of steps before it reaches the addressee: first you write the address and attach a stamp, then you put it in a letterbox, a postman collects it from the box and takes it to the sorting office and so on. At each stage there are rules to follow which are checked by some person (or a machine) before the letter can move on to the next stage. If at any stage something is found to be wrong the letter is sent back (ideally) to the previous stage for correction (if possible). Protocols for electronic communication are defined in terms of such stages (called layers), each layer being responsible for certain tasks associated with the communication of data. Thus one layer may oversee the formation of data to be transferred, another may check if it is correct, or the way it is transmitted and so on. Each layer can communicate only with those directly above and below itself. Thus when a node sends a message, it is checked at every stage of the preparation or communication of the message by the corresponding layer of protocol and control is passed over to the next layer if everything is satisfactory; this goes on until the message reaches the receiver node.[3]

---

2   The term EDI is also used to describe the electronic transfer of documents between organizations.
3   Hopefully this will become clearer later on when we describe a specific protocol.

Protocols have been created by a number of organizations, giving rise to a diverse set of conventions not fully compatible with each other. Leaders in this area are the Consultative Committee on International Telegraphy and Telephony (CCITT) and the International Standards Organization (ISO), both based in Geneva, Switzerland; and the Institute standards organizations in Switzerland; and the Institute of Electrical and Electronic Engineering (IEEE), based in the USA.

Most existing protocols are developed by individual manufacturers of the network technology and only work for their own products. In order to solve the resulting problem of incompatibility, the ISO has introduced open systems interconnection (OSI). This is a seven layer model (Figure 7.18) which attempts to agree on a common set of references to create an 'open' system. When a set of protocols is agreed upon by a number of users it becomes a standard. The OSI model has been accepted as the standard by many organizations and manufacturers, and networks are increasingly being built to comply with this model.

The seven layers in OSI are described as physical, datalink, network, transport, session, presentation and application. The physical layer is concerned with the transmission medium between two communicating machines. It checks that the sending and receiving nodes are properly set up. When satisfied, it passes the control on to the datalink layer which ensures that the message holds the necessary information for reliable transmission. The network layer is responsible for the correct routing of the data; the transport layer ensures that the data does not get corrupted during transmission; the session layer establishes synchronization of communications between users so the message can be received correctly; the pre-

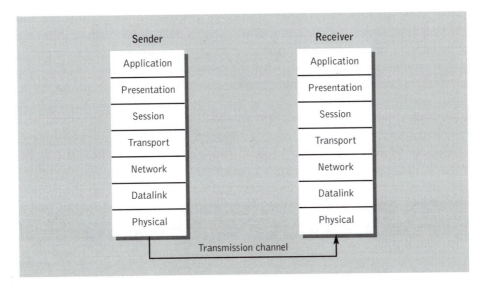

Figure 7.18: The OSI model

sentation layer is responsible for the presentation of the information in a meaningful way, and finally, the applications layer is the outermost layer responsible for providing user level access to information. Thus, each layer takes the responsibility for a small part of the transmission process. In order to do this, the layers need to follow a set of rules applicable to each layer. Consequently, a protocol is required for each layer. In a properly implemented network system, the application layer is the only stage that users have to be aware of, the others being transparent to them.

When a message is sent by a user from a node the application layer is activated; it checks the message and passes it on to the presentation layer. The presentation layer converts the message to the network code and passes it on to the session layer which establishes the session and passes it on to the transport layer, and the process goes on. Each layer attaches extra information (referred to as control information) to the message which enables the same layer of the receiving system to understand and process the message. When the message reaches the physical layer, it is transmitted through the communications channel. At the receiving end the same stages are gone through in the reverse direction from the physical to the application layer. Additionally, at each layer the control information attached to the message by the same layer of the sender system is acknowledged, processed and removed. The application layer passes the message in its original form to the user.

OSI is only a model – exact protocols for each layer, that is, the rules a message has to abide by to pass through each layer, are established separately. Some of this has already been done, others are in the process of development.

There are other protocols such as TCP/IP (transmission control protocol/Internet protocol) which is used for file transfer on the Internet and IBM's systems network architecture (SNA) which uses a model similar to the OSI. Each of these has its own set of rules and standards which have to be obeyed by participating networks. However, the trend is towards total standardization and most future protocols will no doubt attempt to follow the open systems route.

Find some information on the structure of TCP/IP and SNA.

Network software

As with any other aspect of computer technology, hardware on its own is powerless to do anything unless there is software to drive it. Even a very small network requires an operating system to run it. There are a number of LAN operating systems on the market. Netware by Novel was the dominant network for LANs in the 1970s and the 1980s. Since then Unix and Microsoft as well as computer manufacturer Digital Equipment Corporation (DEC), now owned by Compaq, have entered the market. Now there is strong competition between the software companies with Netware, Microsoft's Windows NT, and IBM's OS/2 taking the leading roles in the war over the operating systems market for PC based networks. They offer a combination of user friendly interfaces and support for a broad range of applications.

Currently the trend is towards open systems, allowing hardware and software from different manufacturers to work together. The Unix operating system, the vehicle for open systems, has created much interest among the larger organizations using LAN-to-LAN and LAN-to-WAN connectivity.

Find some information on the current situation with Windows NT and Unix.

Larger networks are served by network operating systems developed by computer manufacturers such as IBM and DEC. They follow the same layered approach as described above, each layer of the software controlling a limited number of functions to ensure that the complete process of transmission from when the signal is sent (the innermost layer) to the point when it is received by the addressee (the outermost layer) is performed satisfactorily. In addition to network operating systems, other items of software are required during intercomputer communications. Amongst these are: network BIOS, the basic programs which check that a network is properly connected with the necessary components and get it ready for use; web browsers (programs that allow us to search for data on the Internet) such as Netscape; and network applications software such as electronic mail.

A new category of software, called middleware, acts as the bridging software between a user and the Internet. It gives users an interface via which they can access selected services on the Internet, such as a website, an email service or a video-conferencing application. There are different kinds of middleware on the market for different types of services, for example, Netopia for a virtual office which connects a user to selected websites and network applications, and BusinessVue which automatically screens data on specific subjects from different websites.

Applications of a network

Organizations use networks for many reasons, from sharing resources to running video conferences around the world. The Internet has enabled individuals as well as businesses of all types and sizes to communicate with the rest of the world via their desktop PCs in a way not experienced before. Organizations with branches worldwide can share applications and data, banks can transfer funds, academics can exchange research findings and ordinary people can chat over the network. The following are some of the applications made possible by the existence of computer networks.

Electronic mail

Electronic mail (email) has revolutionized the way people in business and education communicate with each other. It has been widely used in universities since the mid 1980s, and is now becoming increasingly common amongst people at all levels.

A user connected to a network has an account in it which allows him or her to be allocated an email address. Using this address a user can send messages over the network to another user who also has an email address in the same way that we use postal addresses to send letters. The main advantage of the system is that the addressee does not have to be logged on at the time the message arrives. The message stays in an electronic mailbox (disk space reserved for emails) to be read when it is opened. Messages can be sent to groups of people at the same time, replies can be sent easily and messages can be saved, printed or deleted just like any computer file. There are a number of email software packages on the market to enable users to take advantage of the service within an organization as well as outside if they are connected to a WAN. Individuals using PCs at home and connected to the telephone network through a modem are also able to use the service. The Internet has increased the popularity of email enormously because most Internet service providers (companies offering Internet service to users) offer email as part of the service. Compuserve, America On-line (AOL), Freeserve are only a few of many such service providers.

A variation of email is 'chat' which allows users to send real time messages to others. Any message sent by one user in a group appears on the screen of all other users on the group connected at the time. This enables people to converse with each other interactively in the same way that they would if they were sharing a desk in an office or a coffee house.

Voice mail

This is the audio version of email, which works by connecting a telephone to the network. When a user rings a telephone number, if the person they are trying to reach is not available, they can dictate a message which is saved as a computer file on the recipient's mailbox disk. When the latter dials the mailbox using the phone, the awaiting message is read to the user over the phone. Voice mail is not yet as common as email but because of its simplicity it has the potential to become very popular when the technology is installed more widely. Cable & Wireless now offers this service to its customers as a part of the package with a telephone connection, and no doubt other telephone companies will follow suit in order to stay in competition.

Groupware

This is the software which allows members of a group to work on one project over a network. All members can access all relevant documents in the same way that they would be able to if they were gathered round a table with pen and paper. Groupware has revolutionized the way teams of people can work together without regard for location or the time of day. A relatively new initiative made possible by groupware is called computer supported cooperative work (CSCW). This refers to the collaboration amongst people, often widely dispersed, to work on one project and make decisions collectively. See the list of Further reading for more information on this subject.

Conferencing

This is run by conferencing software over a network, and allows all its users to 'talk' to each other. It is the electronic version of a face-to-face meeting; the partici-pants cannot see each other, but they can talk via their keyboards and VDUs. Video-conferencing – achieved by including video cameras in the network – also enables users to see each other on their screens. This is an expensive system and the technology has yet to be perfected, but it offers great advantages in the long run by saving users time and money on travelling long distances to attend meetings.

A number of conferencing products are in use in the corporate world, two of which are whiteboarding and applications sharing. Whiteboarding is an applica-tion which allows a number of users on a network to see the same set of documents on a screen in the same way that they would if they were looking at a board in a room. All participants can mark and annotate the documents on their own screens but only the user in control of the whiteboarding software has the power to change any documents which are then transmitted to all those connected. Applications sharing is similar, but it facilitates true teamwork by allowing all participants the right to alter the documents in use.

Bulletin boards

These are the electronic versions of public notice boards. Anyone with a phone, a modem and bulletin board software on their computer can access the service. It enables users to leave on-line messages, advertise goods and chat to each other. Unlike email, bulletin boards do not offer the facility for one-to-one message passing; they are intended as an open communication channel.

Surf the Internet for articles on the above applications.

Electronic fund transfer

Networks exist to enable people to transfer data electronically. A logical step from this is to enable financial transactions which include buying and selling over a network as well as making payments. This is called electronic fund transfer (EFT) and encompasses transactions of any scale: from large multinationals making billion pound deals to individuals taking advantage of home shopping and home banking or even using bank cashpoints to deposit or withdraw money. A variation of the latter is the recently introduced electronic cash (e-cash) facility: using a cashpoint-type machine, the holder of an e-cash card can load the card with a chosen amount of money from his or her bank account and spend this in shops instead of cash. Security is a major concern for such a system and features such as the electronic signature of the issuing bank (the same way that currency notes are signed) and a serial number with each amount loaded on a card are some of the ways used to deal with it. A pilot system called Mondex was launched by National Westminster Bank and Midland Bank in conjunction with British Telecom in Swindon (in the UK) and its surrounding area for the period July 1995 to July 1998. The implementation included the installion of telephone lines and the acceptance of Mondex by a large number of retailers and service industries. A survey revealed that over 80% of cardholders were very satisfied with the system (www.mondex.com). Students in some universities in the

UK can now use the card in university bars, shops, restaurants, vending machines and so on. The concept has been accepted by some other banks now, and smartcards have been introduced in many other countries.

There are other electronic transaction facilities such as Digicash – an electronic payment system licensed by Mastercard, and First Virtual – an electronic merchant bank which facilitates buying and selling information over the Internet. Such developments have given rise to a new phrase in the corporate world – electronic commerce – which means conducting commercial activities electronically. Electronic commerce, or e-commerce, has been described thus:

> electronic commerce enables businesses to innovate the whole processes from production to customer service, not in stages, but by integrating them in a seamless whole. Consumers can search and order products online, exchange product information, learn about product quality from other online users, and negotiate with sellers for lower prices and better quality. Governments are developing electronic commerce platforms to collect taxes, disseminate information, monitor market processes and interact with citizens via personalized, up-to-date communications network.
>
> (Choi et al., 1997)

Electronic commerce can be used for almost any product by any organization with the necesssary technical facilities. First Virtual acquires information from organizations (usually) and makes it available for sale to anyone who has an account with the company. A list of items for sale and their prices are circulated electronically to the users of the service and those interested can examine the information and pay for it over the network if they wish to buy. Clearly, there are advantages for the sellers because it cuts the overheads by a great deal but there is scepticism over the value of the service for the buyers for reasons of privacy, consumer rights, security, and so on. Using the Internet, companies can advertise, negotiate deals, arrange payments, in fact perform most business functions. This has increased the competition between companies and those without the facilities are going to lose out in today's virtual commercial world. Read the paper by Choi et al. (1997) (see the further reading section) to get an understanding of the implications of electronic commerce.

Find some articles on the Internet on e-commerce to study how they affect businesses, both large and small, and customers such as yourself.

The Internet

As mentioned at the beginning of this chapter, the Internet was the buzzword of the 1990s. It is the international telecommunications network that connects networks of all sizes and descriptions. No single organization runs or owns it and anyone can join it for a small fee. Since universities, libraries, government, private businesses and many other organizations joined the Internet it has become a potential source of an endless amount of information for computer users all over the world. Because of such importance it deserves discussion at some depth which we will undertake in the next chapter.

Telecommuting

As a direct result of the widespread use of networks many people are now able to work from home. They can be connected to their offices via their PCs and modems. This allows them to access information on-line, communicate with colleagues, perform tasks at home and transfer the results using the same system. Although there are many jobs which cannot be done from home because they need handling machinery or direct contact with people, the popularity of telecommuting is growing fast amongst professional and blue collar workers at all levels. Businesses are also seeing the benefits of time and money saved on travel, office space and so on. There is also the added benefit of working in one's home environment which has made telecommuting popular amongst women. On the other hand it has been blamed for contributing to isolation, the exploitation of women, and the destruction of business culture. We will discuss the social consequences of telecommuting in Chapter 12.

What facilities, in addition to connection to a national network, does a telecommuter need to be able to work effectively?

Networks in our personal lives

Personal computer users can now access some of the above services by connecting to the national telephone lines via a modem. This, with the right software, gives them access to all the services accessible by the Internet. Many people now use email services to keep in touch with friends and colleagues; home banking and shopping are now offered by a number of organizations; and many commercial services such as booking a theatre ticket or getting information on various commercial products are available from home. People can work, shop and entertain themselves without having to leave home. Whether this will be beneficial for society in general is, of course, a matter of debate. We will discusss the extent to which networks affect our lives in Chapter 12.

Summary

Computers can be connected together to form a network allowing electronic data to be passed from one place to another. This enables users in an organization to share hardware, software and information, and an individual to stay in touch with the rest of the world via a desktop computer. A network can consist of only a few computers within a small boundary (thus forming a LAN) or it can cover a much larger area to form a WAN. A network requires some basic components such as computers for sending, receiving and processing data, communications channels to carry the data and software to run the system. Different options in hardware and software are available; which ones are used and how the computers are laid out in relation to each other are decided on the basis of the requirements of an organization. Messages can travel in a network in a number of ways: these are called access methods and are designed to avoid collisions and bottlenecks.

Networks used nowadays range from a PBX telephone system used in an office to worldwide connections operated by large multinationals. Most organizations use the country's telephone network via a modem which transfers computer bits into analogue voice-type data. However, it is also possible to use dedicated lines and private digital networks which are more expensive but offer faster service. The recent introduction of ISDN connection has eliminated the need for a modem by offering the use of channels which can carry both analogue and digital data, thus increasing the speed of communication considerably. The organization of a network can range between being centralized where a large computer controls the activities between all communicating terminals, to peer-to-peer where every computer on the network is equal to the other. Since networks of different types can be connected together to form a larger network, they need special devices to route messages correctly; certain standards and protocols are also required to ensure that messages are passed round without loss of integrity. Although a number of different protocols exist at present, an attempt is being made to establish an open system of protocol to facilitate vendor independent communication. As with all computer applications, networks require an operating system to run them. In the past they were proprietary, but now PC networking software such as Windows NT supporting a broad range of applications and open systems such as Unix are becoming popular.

In addition to the use of networks in sharing resources, they are also essential for organizations to support email, bulletin boards, groupware, video-conferencing, electronic fund transfer, telecommuting, and so on. Individual PC users can also avail themselves of a number of these services by using a modem to connect to a public network. The growth of the Internet in the past five years has revolutionized the way computers are used. We can now have information from anywhere in the world on our desktops within a few seconds and stay in touch with the rest of the world at all times.

Further reading

Read Chapter 6 of *Managing Information Technology: What Managers Need to Know* by E. W. Martin, D. W. DeHayes, J. A. Hoffer and W. C. Perkins, second edition, Prentice Hall, 1994 for more information on some of the topics covered in this chapter.

Read *Local Area Networks: Including Internetworking and Interconnections with WANs* by Peter Hodson, DP Publications, 1992 for further details and an easy to understand description of the topics covered in this chapter including bridges, gateways and routers. Standards and protocols are also well covered.

For a more advanced description of the subject read *Internetworking LANs and WANs: Concepts, Techniques and Methods*, by Gilbert Held, John Wiley & Sons, 1994.

Groupware and Computer-Supported Cooperative Work: Assisting Human-Human Collaboration, written and edited by R. M. Baecker, Morgan Kaufmann Publishers Ltd, 1993 includes many articles, case studies and discussions on CSCW.

For a good discussion on electronic commerce read the article by Choi, Stahl and Whinston (1997) at http://cism.bus.utexas.edu/works/articles/cyberpayments.html. This is published by the Centre for Research in Electronic Commerce in the Graduate School of Business at the University of Texas at Austin. There may be more articles on this subject in their websites.

Look at the website www.netguru.net/course.htm for the home page of an organization called Netguru which gives free on-line courses on networks.

Revision questions

1. Explain the meaning of the following terms in relation to a network:

    nodes
    host
    communications channels
    modem
    multiplexer.

2. Describe the types of network topology available and their relative merits and demerits

3. Explain the meaning of the following groups of terms. Try to distinguish between the main characteristics of the items in each group:

    A   (i)   CSMA/CD
        (ii) token passing
        (iii) polling.

    B   (i)   packet switching
        (ii) message switching
        (iii) circuit switching.

    C   (i)   LAN
        (ii) WAN
        (iii) VAN.

    D   (i)   centralized network
        (ii) distributed network
        (iii) client/server network
        (iv) peer-to-peer network.

    E   (i)   repeater
        (ii) bridge
        (iii) router
        (iv) brouter
        (v)   gateway.

4. Discuss the need for network protocols.

5. Describe the main protocols used by networks in this country.

6. Discuss the role played by the Open Software Foundation (OSF) in the area of protocols.

7. Discuss the benefits and drawbacks for organizations of using networks (LAN and WAN).

8. What special software do we need for a networked computer system?

9. Describe the main commercial applications of a wide area network with critical comments on how they affect ordinary people.

Food for thought

BYTE, April 1997

European banks play their (smart) cards
Dan Amdur

Banks turn to smartcards to provide security and new services for on-line transactions

Tucked in a warehouse outside of Marseilles, France, lies a vision of the future: a 'smart village' where fees for parking meters, public transportation, movie tickets, and pay phone calls are digitally debited through chip cards. In other parts of this mock virtual city, smartcards act as the keys that unscramble a set-top box and unlock a corporate computer, while a medical smartcard records a patient's blood-pressure information from a home test for a doctor to scan during that patient's next office visit.

This smart city is actually a demonstration created by industry leader Gemplus two years ago to highlight the potential uses for smartcards. However, for banks in France and across Europe, this exhibit represents the finish line in the current race to offer the next generation of services to consumers and corporations alike in an increasingly wired world. While the Internet remains a top priority, many hopes are being placed on smartcards' ability to move Europe's financial system beyond that of the rest of the world – especially with the prospect of a unified currency becoming more likely with each passing month.

Setting standards

Since exploding on the scene in the U.S. three years ago, the Internet has largely remained an American institution. Although dozens of banks throughout Europe have also jumped on-line, most home-banking standards are being set within the U.S. by companies such as Intuit, MasterCard International, Microsoft, and Visa International. But while the near-term on-line future is being blazed in the U.S., banks and merchants in Europe are quietly pioneering the infrastructure for a secure transaction environment based on chip cards that bridge the gap between retail and virtual sales.

According to the market-research firm Dataquest (San Jose, CA), 90 percent of worldwide integrated-chip-card shipments went to Europe in 1995, while only 2 percent headed to the Americas. By the year 2001, Europe is expected to account for only 40 percent of these shipments, while Asia will command 25 percent and the Americas 20 percent.

Considering the lack of market penetration in the U.S. today, these figures can be interpreted as positive growth. But the reality of smartcard deployment in the Western Hemisphere is that many South American countries will be much more rapid adopters than the cautious banks of the U.S.

U.S. lags behind

A number of U.S. banks have thrown their support behind the electronic-purse systems pushed by MasterCard International and Visa International within the past year; the 1996 summer Olympics was heralded as the first step down the road to widespread consumer rollouts. However, squabbles over card formats, poor merchant outreach, and delayed commercial trials are all hampering the introduction of smartcards in North America. This situation is giving Europe the chance to command the lead in the growing market for card-based services.

'The U.S. market as we know it is not quite ready for smartcards,' says Paul Campbell, spokesperson for Schlumberger Industries' Electronic Transactions Division. 'We're all waiting for the U.S. market, but the market most likely to develop first by the year 2002 is the European one,' agrees French journalist Charles Copin, a longtime follower of the smartcard industry.

Although countries such as Belgium and the U.K. are currently experimenting with chip cards, the country with the widest penetration of cards in both its financial and social structure is France. This is where the first true chip card was developed in 1967 and where many of the major players in the chip-card industry originate. One of the core reasons that chip cards were adopted at such a steady pace in France was the pivotal role the government played in mandating their use.

In this environment, achieving significant penetration of chip cards was much simpler for banks, which pushed for chips to be installed on credit and debit cards. Now there are more than 25 million chip bank cards in France, with 85 percent of card payments made using a personal identification number (PIN) for security.

High start-up costs

For European banks, there are multiple benefits spurring the move toward smartcards. For example, the proliferation of electronic-purse schemes is creating a new source of revenue for banks, which are facing growing competition from outside firms that offer a wealth of new financial services, from investing to banking.

Under many of the stored-value card systems now under evaluation, digital currency resides in an account-holder's bank, as opposed to residing on the card itself. In turn, banks stand to profit from the 'float' that exists while consumers leave their digital cash idle on their cards. In France, for instance, about 3 percent of the value of prepaid phone cards is never used. This could translate to large unused sums of money in an electronic-purse system.

For merchants, however, the benefits of adopting a new payment type at the point of sale are less clear – especially in the current climate, where as many as four different standards (CLIP, Mondex, Proton, and VisaCash) are competing in the electronic-purse market and boosting the cost of terminals. High costs are also forcing banks to take a cautious look at the business benefit of issuing chip cards that cost between $2 and $8 each, depending on the application, versus magnetic-stripe cards, which can be produced for just 10 cents each.

In addition, banks are reluctant to commit to new technology and new payment types before consumers are prepared to embrace them. Jean-Pierre Camelot, director of Groupement des Cartes Bancaires, the French bank association that's charged with exploring new technologies, estimates that it will cost French banks as much as $1 billion to introduce a widespread electronic-purse method in that country. This figure could skyrocket for rollouts in other European countries.   ▶

Other competition

A key driving force behind chip-card use for bank cards in Europe is the idea of enabling off-line transactions by the use of PINs to reduce the fraud rate. With telecommunications costs at a premium in many regions of Europe, merchants have a strong incentive to move toward a chip-based approach that can support off-line transactions.

In addition to the reduction of fraud, two other main drivers for spurring smartcard adoption are the emergence of Internet commerce and the aforementioned possible competition from nonbank entities. 'Smartcards are a key element of the future of information technology,' affirms Tim Baker, head of technical communications for Gemplus.

Currently, the Secure Electronic Transaction (SET) specification is being rolled out by MasterCard and Visa to safeguard credit-card purchases conducted on the Web. SET is based on the use of a digital certificate residing on a user's hard drive. Visa and MasterCard, along with Europay International, are adapting the specification so that it operates with a smartcard, rather than a PC, as the secure token that holds the digital keys.

Bringing smartcards into the Internet market can improve security for transactions while also giving consumers portability, since they won't be tied to their PCs to use them, says Michel Roux, general manager of the Gemplus Multimedia Business Division. This portability comes in handy when working with access-control applications on intranets and other corporate networks, another very big potential market for the cards, he adds.

Gemplus is currently working with Visa to launch a pilot this year that combines SET with smartcards. In addition, a variety of terminal vendors, including Dassault Automatismes et Télécommunications and VeriFone, are developing inexpensive plug-in smartcard readers for PCs. Also, modem manufacturer Hayes has announced that it's building smartcard support into its line of modems.

While the virtual world represents a promising market for chip cards, more immediate room for expansion comes from applications promoted by nonbank industries. This has forced banks across Europe into partnerships to prevent cards issued in loyalty programs from shutting out traditional financial institutions.

One such focus of competition in France runs up and down the railway lines that crisscross the country. Cards are already becoming a popular tool for aiding the transportation industry through contactless initiatives, such as the Tunnel Prado-Carenage in Marseilles, where one-quarter of the 30,000 cars that now travel through the tunnel each day pay their tolls with wireless smartcards.

But in the next few years, local and national transportation authorities alike will be heavily promoting smartcard use for ticketing and retail applications. Groupement des Cartes Bancaires recently announced it was forming a working group to manage an electronic-purse project for transport and shopping services. The move was largely a defensive one, since the national French railway organization, Société Nationale des Chemins de Fer Français (SNCF), has been pursuing smartcards for ticketing applications for years. But instead of directly competing against SNCF, French banks are grudgingly agreeing to develop interoperable specifications that can be used for both transportation and retail applications.

Merchant support is critical

'All present electronic-purse pilots have proved unsuccessful because they have not had enough merchant support,' says SNCF treasurer Eugene Caffart. 'We provide a critical mass of users, and we expect these users to pressure shops to accept these cards later.'

The merging of transportation and retail applications presages an effort under way in France to create a universal electronic purse that incorporates other payment applications, such as public phones. Phone cards, bank/loyalty cards, and transportation cards will represent the three largest chip-card markets by 2000, according to internal estimates from Gemplus and Schlumberger. Merchants are already turning a wary eye toward these types of closed systems in anticipation of a wider potential market.

One early outside merchant to take an interest in the SNCF project was fast-food giant McDonald's, which became a member of the working group in 1991. Still, the prospects for a universal card and nonbank competition remain slight in several European countries, despite rollout promises in the U.K. and Germany.

To be successful, banks across Europe will need to wring more revenues out of chip-based stored-value applications than they do in the lower-cost debit environment, according to reports from Retail Banking Research. With merchant investments already extensive in their support of existing debit terminals, banks will need to help finance merchant migration toward this new payment standard over the next few years, the research firm adds. This will be a necessary step toward promoting consumer use, since many consumers are unlikely to adopt these new stored-value applications unless they are guaranteed widespread acceptance for low-value retail transactions, ranging from fast food to gas stations.

Discussion questions

1. The first paragraph of the article expresses a view of the future which is technically feasible. We are already experiencing the effects of a wired society to some extent. Do you think the model demonstrated in the 'smart village' is a promising view of the future world?

2. The article demonstrates how different countries are competing with each other in an attempt to be ahead in the race to adopt chip-cards. What are the advantages and disadvantages of this race from the users' point of view?

3. Discuss how a chip-card is expected to work and how it can change the way we handle money. Who benefits more from it, the banker or the user?

4. As usual with all electronic data, security is an important concern. What can go wrong with the use of chip-cards and how are organizations trying to deal with it?

5. Using some other sources, discuss where you see us in ten years from now in terms of electronic commerce.

CHAPTER 8

Information superhighway and the Internet

Objectives

After reading this chapter you should have some understanding of:

▶ the concept of the information superhighway;
▶ the nature of the Internet;
▶ the concept of the World Wide Web;
▶ how the World Wide Web can be used.

Introduction

The advances made in communications technology in recent years have added a number of new terms to the English vocabulary: cyberspace, the World Wide Web (WWW), the information superhighway, the Internet or simply the Net, and so on. Whilst those in touch with the technology may know what these terms mean, others have only a vague or no understanding of them. Yet, these are all important terms representing significant phenomena which affect our lives in various ways. Not only do businesses of all sizes now use computers connected to nationwide and international networks, increasingly home computer users are doing likewise. People are expecting to be able to access the vast amount of information made available by the WWW from home and from work. In this chapter we are going to examine what these terms mean, how they relate to the Internet, the origin of the Internet and the WWW, and above all, how we can use the facilities offered by such technology.

The information superhighway

According to the Oxford dictionary, a highway is a road, a main route (or the motorway) which connects different parts of a country. A superhighway can there-fore be taken as a major, high-speed transport system that provides connectivity between places, within a country and in-between countries. With the existence of a physical superhighway such as worldwide road, water and air links, we are now capable of accessing any goods from almost any country anywhere in the world. An information superhighway aims to do the same for information via electronic links. In other words, an information superhighway is a complete high-speed elec-tronic network system that connects countries, businesses and homes, enabling us to send and receive information from anywhere. Although the existence of the Internet has made this possible to a certain extent, we are still far away from an information superhighway for a number of reasons. First, we still need a computer to do this and people who have access to a computer are still in a minority; sec-ondly, large parts of the world are not connected to the Internet; and most importantly, an information superhighway is not simply a connection of networks, it needs an infrastructure to ensure that the concept of worldwide connectivity works. Using the example of a physical superhighway again, although theoretically speaking it is possible to transfer goods between any two places in the world, in reality, there are many places in the world which cannot use the system effectively, perhaps because the road links are not adequate or the government in one country does not have the necessary agreement with another or the transport system used in a country is not suitable for the type of goods that need to be carried. An infra-structure provides not only the physical links but also clearly stated rules and a carefully laid out structure which enable the system to function.

Attempts are being made in the USA to build a national information infra-structure (NII) which would provide connectivity to all homes and offices within the country. It could be similar to a country's telephone system which offers easy to access, inexpensive connectivity throughout the country. It is envisaged that private companies will build such an infrastructure and charge users for the service. However, two areas of concern immediately come to mind: the service providers may not consider all areas of the country equally suitable for investment, and whilst such an NII works within the country, on the international scale a large part of the world remains excluded.

What is the Internet?

As stated in Chapter 1, the Internet is a network of networks spanning a large part of the world. Thus, it can be seen as a step towards the information superhighway. The origin of the Internet is in the US based network called ARPANET (the Advanced Research Projects Agency) set up in 1969 to coordinate the research and development activities of different sections of the US Department of Defense (DoD). ARPANET provided the facility for the DoD to share research findings with academics working on their projects. At the beginning it included a number of universities who were commissioned by the DoD to carry out the R&D work. The popularity of the service amongst its users gave rise to the idea of sharing information with institutions worldwide by connecting the large networks in different countries to each other with a view to creating a superhighway for data communication. By the early 1990s much of this had been achieved and the rules were set up to enable users to access information from any part of this global network. This attracted an enormous amount of interest from academics and business organizations. Large databases on an unlimited range of subjects were made available on the network by all types of organizations all over the world. This enabled users to access documents from these databases via their desktop machines. Necessary protocols (TCP/IP) were established to allow users anywhere on the network to use the service effectively. They could access information on an endless variety of subjects, do business deals, make financial transactions and much more. Software developers also took advantage by introducing a large number of applications such as email, remote file transfer facilities and programs designed to search the large databases of information. This whole scene came to be known as the Internet.

Connecting to the Internet

Each of the networks (normally WANs) connected on the Internet has a host computer system and connection to the Internet can be made by linking to such a host, normally via a LAN. Additionally, there are a number of internet service providers (ISPs) which are large computer systems permanently connected to the Internet in order to provide access to their clients. ISPs vary from small local, or one-person-band services to global services run by companies such as British Telecom. Users can register directly with an ISP and connection to the Internet is provided when they dial-up using a telephone and a modem or an ISDN line. ISPs give full access to the Internet but do not always offer any extra facilities normally available via on-line service providers. On-line service providers such as CompuServe and America On Line (AOL), which individuals and businesses can join for a monthly or yearly fee (as well as, in some cases, a set-up fee), are commercial information systems which provide access to the Internet via an electronic gateway connected to their own computer systems. They also provide their own on-line services such as Usenet groups, email and bulletin boards. AOL, which is mainly consumer orientated, has now bought CompuServe, which is used by mainly businesses, to become a leading provider for both communities. Most ISPs these days offer most of the important services offered by an on-line service provider and they are cheaper. A good ISP offers free web space (usually 5 Mb), multiple email addresses, automatic screening of junk mail, and so on. Users have to pay the telephone charge incurred as a result of connection through the telephone while on-line. Dixons, the electrical goods chain, introduced the first free Internet service provider called Freeserve in 1998. The trend was soon followed by many other companies which in turn increased the number of Internet users rapidly. The cost is normally covered by the telephone companies and advertisers who are clearly expecting to get a return from the users and it is arguable whether users are really saving any money.

Some ISPs serve specific communities of users. The community is identified by a domain name such as 'ac' for academic institutions, 'com' for commercial sites and 'org' for private organizations. The email address of a user on the Internet includes the name of the domain together with other information such as username, institution, country and so on – in the same way that a postal address includes the name of the street, town and country. Thus someone called 'King' working for University of East London may have an email address king@uel.ac.uk, the '@' sign normally used to separate the user identification and the rest of the address.

Find the names of as many service providers as you can by looking at magazines, and by surfing the Internet.

The World Wide Web

The introduction in 1993 of the World Wide Web, a graphical user interface for the Internet, was one of the most important steps taken to popularize the service. Before this, users had to enter text based commands to gain access to the Internet. It was rather like using an application program, such as a wordprocessor, without Windows.[1] By using text, sound, graphics and animation, the WWW creates an environment which enables users to enter the address of a document required. Each document stored anywhere on the Internet has a unique site, normally referred to as its website, with an address, just like every email user has a unique address. These addresses are called uniform resource locators (URLs). The following are examples of some URLs:

http://bbc.co.uk/education	the address for the BBC's education site;
http://www.number.10.gov.uk	the website for 10 Downing Street;
http://athena.wednet.edu/index.html	the website for Athena, part of NASA's Learning Technologies Project for earth and space science.

As you can see, each URL starts with 'http' (hypertext transport protocol) which is the protocol designed to support hypertext links (see Chapter 5). This is followed by the rest of the URL (separated by ://) which includes the domain name ('co', 'gov', 'edu'), the country ('uk') and other parts to identify the document's exact position. Figure 8.1 illustrates a web page.

Many users, both individuals and organizations, create a *homepage* – a website used as a starting point. Homepages are often made to look attractive with the use of text, colour, graphics, animation and sound. They also provide hypertext links to other sites, internal and external. For example, your university may have a homepage containing a list of the services it offers and teaching departments. By clicking with the mouse on one of these you can get more details on your chosen area and further links to information on specific matters. You may also find links to external sites such as the local sports centre or the bookshop. Figure 8.2 is an example of the homepage for the University of East London.

A homepage can be created for the WWW by using very high level programming languages such as hypertext markup language (HTML) or Java. These languages enable us to enter text with print enhancement features similar to an advanced wordprocessor and incorporate graphics, animation and sound to create documents with attractive presentation qualities. They also provide easy means of using hypertext links. This is done by inserting the address of the document to link to at the appropriate point of the document to link from. When the

---

1 If you have any experience of using DOS based applications you will be able to imagine the situation.

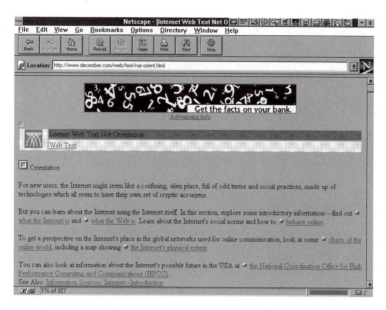

Figure 8.1: A web page

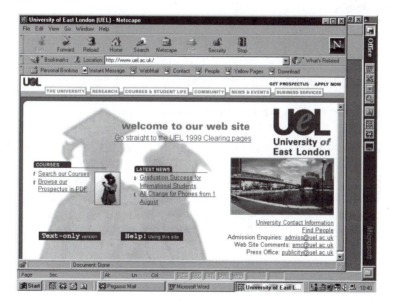

Figure 8.2: Example of a homepage (reprinted with permission of UEL web designer)

Compare the design of some homepages to find out what the designers are trying to achieve.

website is completed these links appear in a different colour and with an under-line(see Figure 8.1[2]) and show up as a hand when the mouse cursor is placed on them. Clicking at this point takes the user to the linked document. Linking can be done between different parts of one document, different documents within one page and between different websites. HTML is easy to use and capable of coping with text, audio, graphics and video data. It creates 'static' pages, that is, a user can access a page but cannot send any information back. Web pages created by Java can be interactive, that is, users can input commands and expect to get a response. This is useful for the use of computer games and on-line databases on the Internet.

The WWW offers many other features some of which are very similar to Windows programs, for example, File, Edit, View and Print. A useful feature is the *Bookmark* option, which enables a user to add the URL of any document to a list for future use. This means that the same document can be accessed later on by clicking on its entry on the list rather than having to enter the URL or use a search engine (see below).

To Bookmark a document you found on the Internet, click on the Bookmark option, then click on Add. Using this method add some of the documents you have found useful while reading this book to your Bookmark.

The process of search has been made easier by the introduction of browsing pro-grams (known as *browsers*). Mosaic was the first browser introduced in the early 1990s; the most well known these days are Netscape (developed by the creator of Mosaic) and Microsoft's Internet Explorer. A browser offers search engines and navigation tools to make browsing (or surfing) the Internet easier for its users. *Search engines* are programs that allow users to enter one or more key-words on the subject on which information is required. They search through large databases of keywords and present a list of matched documents together with an interface for easy navigation. Yahoo!, Alta Vista and Lycos are a few of the better known search engines. Their URLs are as follows:

http://www.yahoo.com   for Yahoo
http://www.lycos.co.uk   for Lycos
http://www.altavista.com   for Alta Vista

---

2   You can't see the colour changes in Fig 8.1 due to the black and white reproduction.

However, most browsers include a short-cut for accessing the search engines thus making it unnecessary to enter a URL.

Microsoft's Internet Explorer is a browsing program for PC users with the Windows operating systems. It is an integrated suite of applications that includes email, HTML creation tools, a conferencing program and other useful software.

Save a document you found on the Internet by using File/Save As. Then retrieve it in your wordprocessing program. This will show you the codes (HTML) used to create the website.

Other Internet services

In addition to using the Internet for retrieving information, all of the applications of a large network mentioned in the previous chapter are also available, such as email, chat, bulletin boards and so on. Other services offered by the Internet are Usenet, file transfer, Telnet and Gopher.

Usenet is a service provided for groups of people, called *newsgroups*, who want to share information and comments on specific topics. For example, there may be a newsgroup for amateur violinists or one for diabetics. By using newsreader software you can join a newsgroup and take part in discussions on your chosen topic, send articles, access and save articles in files for later use on your PC, and so on.

There are many computer systems worldwide which hold computer programs and other useful files in archives for public distribution through the Internet. A program called *Archie* gives a list of all archives and their addresses. These files can be downloaded (retrieved) by using a service called *file transfer* available on the Internet. Using a protocol known as the *file transfer protocol* (FTP) the service checks that no errors occur during transmission and transfers files of any format over the Internet.

Telnet is a service that allows a user to connect to a remote ISP and use it as his or her own. It works by transferring a user's files, using FTP, to the remote system. This is an easy way to access remote databases, libraries and so on.

Gopher is a multi-level index organized by the source of the information. Thus you can use Gopher to locate a document by searching through menus if you do not wish to browse the Internet. This was very useful before browsing programs such as Netscape were introduced because it was the only way to organize a search amongst the vast store of information available on the Internet. The wide area information server (*WAIS*) is a similar service offered by the Internet except that the index is organized by content rather than by source. WAIS organizes information into different databases, each on a specific subject and allows users to search through them and download any information they require.

Try to use some of these services and compare their utility with that of the World Wide Web.

Some problems with the Internet

One problem faced by many users of the Internet is the time it takes to access some documents. Often the documents are large because of the multimedia data format they use. Also the host computer systems for many of the documents are remote to the users and the files have to travel through a large number of gateways. Users in the UK can access information relatively easily in the early part of the day, but the system slows down considerably in the afternoon. This is because users in the USA are at work by that time and demands on the lines are much heavier. It is hoped that more widespread use of ISDN lines and cable networks will ease the problem to a certain extent. Recently IBM has reported a new technology called transcoding proxy which is designed to reduce the load on the Internet service. It uses a special (proxy) server for the so-called 'low bandwidth' users such as those connecting via a mobile phone or using a notebook computer. It is programmed to understand the type of device and simplifies the information supplied if necessary. For example, if a user with a hand held computer with a monochrome screen wants a document with graphics, the proxy server supplies it without colour. This reduces transmission time and speeds up Internet access for both remote as well as ordinary users.

Security is a serious problem for Internet users. There have been cases of vandals putting virus documents on the Internet which, when accessed, can affect the PC used. Also, with the increasing popularity of Internet shopping, banking and other financial transactions, it is relatively easy for a hacker to abuse the system. This could be via fraudulent businesses conducted by bogus companies; credit card numbers and other personal details being disclosed to criminals during an electronic transaction; sensitive information becoming available over the WWW, and so on. Methods used to safeguard data travelling over the Internet include encryption (a type of coding used to hide data) and the use of passwords for sensitive sites. We will discuss this in Chapter 11.

Other concerns have been raised at both individual and organizational levels over the utility of the Internet. Amongst these are the following.

● Although there is an addressing protocol governing the creation of URLs, the number of addresses available is inadequate for such a large system. Improvement of the situation involves investment in hardware and software resources. This requires guidance and leadership which is difficult to find for a system of such a varied and uncontrollable nature.

- Organizations have complained about employees who waste working time by browsing unnecessarily.

- The uncontrolled availability of the system can lead to information of poor quality and low integrity. Anyone with access to the Internet can put information on the web. Thus, although much of the information available is very useful, there is also a large body of documents and web pages that have little value. They not only serve as an irritation to serious users, they also add to the time it takes to find the right information.

- Many web pages only refer to sources of information rather than giving us the information themselves. Since there is often no indication in the title of the nature of the page, users have to look through a large number of unnecessary documents to find what they need.

- 'Firewalls' (see below) created for security by individual organizations can reduce the speed of communication.

- It may be difficult for home users (for example, users who do not connect via employers) to get full access to the Internet.

- Often, finding useful information of a specific nature is not possible simply by keyword search. Users need to know the exact URL, which may be difficult to acquire.

- The most alarming problem with the Internet arises from the anonymity of its users, which can lead to people taking improper advantage of it. The Internet was initially developed as a source of information for ordinary people but its inappropriate use by those who wish to pursue criminal or immoral activities such as planning terrorist attacks or running child pornography networks has given rise to serious concerns. There have been ongoing debates on whether or not some control should be imposed on the level of access to the system. We will discuss the ethics of the Internet in Chapter 12.

 List the problems you have faced as a user of the Internet.

Look at the list of Further reading for more information on the problems associated with the Internet.

Some organizations are now using a subset of the Internet within their own company networks. Worried by the lack of data security on the Internet and the time wasted in surfing it, they use commercially available software to build their own internal systems which enable their employees to create web pages, transfer files and send emails internally and even access remote systems via Telnet. Such a system is called an *intranet*. Intranet pages are created in exactly the same way as with the Internet and the protocol used is the same. However, users on the system are either blocked completely from the Internet or separated from it by a firewall, a security system which allows only authorized users to gain access. *Food for thought* at the end of this chapter attempts to give some insight into the use of an intranet and also raises some thought provoking questions which are equally applicable to the Internet.

Why do you think an organization would choose to use an intranet instead of the Internet?

Another recent innovation in data communications is the use of an *extranet* – that is, giving chosen companies access to an organization's information using Internet technology. Used like an Internet on a private wide area network between a number of organizations, an extranet enables companies to have easy access to their suppliers and business partners.

There is no doubt that the Internet has brought a vast amount of information to our doorsteps. Whether we benefit from this new world of information and whether our experience of using it is a pleasant one or not depends, to a large extent, on whether we follow the unwritten codes of behaviour. Debates on this subject have given rise to the new term *netiquette* which refers to the 'do's and dont's' of Internet use. Look at the list of Further reading for more discussion on this.

Summary

An information superhighway refers to a worldwide network of electronic links connecting computer systems with an established infrastructure to enable us to transfer data and information from any part of the world to any other. The data/information transferred can take a number of forms: text, graphics, video, music and so on. The Internet is a step in this direction. It uses national and international communications channels such as telephone lines and cable connection and TCP/IP protocol to enable us to communicate with other parts of the world electronically. Using the Internet we can access a vast amount of information made available by large databases maintained over the network, we can send electronic mails, transfer files, use electronic bulletin boards and much more. Connection to the Internet can be made by connecting to an internet service provider, a large computer system connected to the Internet permanently.

The World Wide Web is the graphical interface of the Internet. It uses text, sound, graphics and animation, to enable users to access the Internet easily. Browsers, such as Netscape and Internet Explorer offer facilities for navigating the WWW, creating documents with hypertext links, performing keyword searches via search engines and so on. However, there are also some problems in the use of the Internet, for example, it can be very slow at times, there can be problems of security and reliability of information and it can be used for improper purposes. Some organizations use an intranet and/or an extranet in order to utilize the benefits of the Internet but avoid some of its pitfalls.

Further reading

Read a magazine such as *.net* to find out more about the information available on the Internet. Such magazines will also give you information on how to connect to the Internet, how to use email, web addresses of useful documents and so on.

WAIS and Gopher Services – A Guide for Internet End-Users by E.L. Morgan, Mecklermedia, 1994 gives an account of the various services available on the Internet.

Read Chapter 8A of *Computers for Your Future 98* by Roberta Baber and Marilyn Meyer, Que Education & Training, 1998 for more information on some of the topics covered in this chapter.

For the problems and the policy issues on the Internet read *Civilizing Cyberspace: Policy, Power and the Information Superhighway* by Steven E. Miller, ACM Press, 1996.

Netiquette is covered well on the website: http://www.enid.org/enidschools/co/endihigh/TUTORIAL/index.htm.

Revision questions

1. Explain the concept of the information superhighway.

2. What is the Internet?

3. How does the Internet relate to the information superhighway?

4. How can you connect to the Internet?

5. Write a brief note on the following concepts:

    (a) a website
    (b) a homepage

(c) a URL
(d) a browser
(e) hypertext markup language
(f) hypertext links
(g) a search engine.

6. Write a brief note on the services available via the Internet.

7. What are the problems with the use of the Internet?

8. If you are an Internet user, discuss your own feelings about the above problems.

9. Discuss how you can utilize the Internet for your studies. What are the problems with it?

Food for thought

InfoWorld, 11 August 1997, vol.19, no.32, p.85(2)
InfoWorld Media Group

Intranet design: hack through the tangle of the corporate intranet
Cate T. Corcoran

Categorizing data and creating corporate templates are crucial to effective navigation. Like a rain forest that grows so densely it chokes itself to death or a city that springs up so fast its neighborhoods don't connect, corporate intranets are getting so big so fast that users can't find anything on them.

Intranets are turning into time wasters instead of timesavers. At Microsoft, for example, a recent user survey revealed that employees couldn't find what they were looking for 25 percent of the time on the company's intranet, which has hundreds of thousands of documents on more than 400 servers.

'Because the technology makes it so easy to post, there's a lot of information available on intranets but it's not organized very well, so it's unusable,' says Judith Fleenor, senior product manager for Silicon Reef, a San Francisco-based online communications-services company specializing in Internet content management and design.

At the same time, intranets are beginning to run more core business functions. Many corporations began by posting a few documents from human resources. Then every department started posting information. Now intranets are starting to become collaborative workspaces rivaling Lotus Notes in scope. The potential benefits include better and more efficient communication and faster decision making. In some cases, an intranet better integrates existing applications and eases the workload of IS.

Large companies are in a transition phase, moving from putting up the infrastructure and publishing departmental information to a more strategic approach of figuring out how that information can change how people work, says Mary Cronin, a consultant with Mainspring Communications, in Cambridge, Mass., and a Boston College business professor.

At Hewlett-Packard, for example, the global sales force has posted information about customers and what they're doing with HP products but other departments have also found it useful, Cronin says.

To realize an intranet's strategic potential, companies must have a vision of what they want to accomplish and a central plan to carry it out. Once they have an objective, companies can then decide how to logically organize information so users can find it efficiently. They can also choose an architecture that will be able to handle anticipated increases in traffic and new types of applications and data down the line.

The first step is deciding what to do. Cronin suggests asking what the critical functions of each department are and how people find the bits of information they use to do their jobs. Ask users what they need, says Paul Klouda, a consultant with HP's Professional Services Organization, in Palo Alto, Calif. Silicon Reef, which began life as a Web-site developer, has created a detailed method for helping companies streamline information exchange.

First, Fleenor says, figure out who is communicating and what information they're exchanging. Chances are this won't be reflected in the organizational chart, which does not mirror the flow of information in a company or a company's business processes. You can hold meetings and have each employee fill out an information-analysis worksheet for a month. As employees sit at their desks, they log the key people they speak to, what they get, and how long it takes.

Mirror the business

Once you have your objectives in mind, you are ready to design the intranet architecture. This includes templates and graphics standards, policies for creating and maintaining the information structure, and the organization of information, as well as technical platforms and tools.

Recognize that your goal is to facilitate communication (or integrate existing applications, build an easier-to-use analysis program, etc.), not promote a certain technology. So, for example, if Lotus Notes or some other program is already in place and being put to good use, it probably doesn't make sense to move those communications to an intranet, experts say.

Many companies organize their pages hierarchically beginning with a front door or home page that presents what is essentially a table of contents. Further choices are often categorized by department, but almost any kind of category is possible. One of the advantages of the electronic medium is that it lends itself to cross-referencing and multiple points of entry, says Srinija Srinivasan, who manages Yahoo's indexing process, in Santa Clara, Calif.

At Silicon Reef, information on the intranet is grouped according to what employees want to do, not by department. The first level is an out board, where everyone checks in and out to cut down on calls to the receptionist (there are no set work hours). The next section is 'keeping current,' where people can find out about Internet sites they should visit, new technology, and personal and company information. Another section contains all the company's projects, past and present, and a fourth level contains employee resources, such as forms, time tracking, project codes, and client information. Another section is about technology and contains a discussion board and applications that the company has developed for clients. ▶

Some Internet sites are abandoning the front-door hierarchical structure in favor of a wizard that guides you through the site like a presentation, but this third-generation approach is probably not suited to most intranets, says Mark Johnson, a consultant with database consulting company Context Integration, in South San Francisco, Calif.

Many intranets feature at least a simple search engine, which lets users go directly to a site using a keyword instead of clicking down through hierarchies of pages to find what they're looking for. There are many search engines available, but the best ones are easy to use, support a rich query language (such as natural language and Boolean operators) and let the user specify multiple constraints on a search, Srinivasan says.

Indexes that users can browse are also useful search tools, because they allow users to find things they don't know how to ask for. These, such as Yahoo and Excite, organize information according to category. This is a daunting task that someone has to be responsible for, but users can help cut the workload by suggesting how to categorize their information. To categorize information in a way that others find intuitive, it's helpful to imagine the top 10 reasons why someone might want such information, Srinivasan says.

Control vs. chaos

It's a good idea to create templates for pages and graphics standards in order to ease both document creation and use. You don't want to dictate too many rules that will stifle creativity and delay publication, but it's good to standardize on a few elements such as a navigation bar for every page and icons for e-mail and chatting, designers say. That way you establish basic 'grammar' for visual communication that everyone can understand.

Similar issues come into play when setting other policies. Every company is different and should set up rules and procedures that reflect its own corporate culture. Many technology companies, including Microsoft, Intuit, HP, and Silicon Graphics, have fairly relaxed corporate policies about who can post where. Generally, someone is responsible for and has exclusive access to the top few tiers, but the other levels are left up to individuals.

Other companies may require postings to go through an editing process or be approved by one or more Webmasters, who then push the content to the server, which only they have access to.

What can be posted will also vary. Intuit specifies that all pages should be business-related, whereas Microsoft has a special section called MS Community for social functions such as support groups and topic folders on pets and other interests. At Visa U.S.A., in San Mateo, Calif., a central group governs how to post and keeps the hierarchical structure in place, but it exercises little control over content, says Marc Perl, Visa business and service manager and member of InfoWorld's Corporate Advisory Board.

As companies move to make their intranets more useful, they should strive to balance control with freedom.

'Having a lot of control will slow things down,' Fleenor says. 'But by having no control, you will probably end up with a mass of information that's unusable by 90 percent of the population.'

The harder a piece of information is to find, the more time people will spend tinkering and finding other things to distract them, Fleenor says.

The payoff

Intranets have grown to the point where companies are beginning to formally evaluate their usefulness. At Visa, the intranet includes hundreds of servers and 5,000 users from Singapore to London. At HP there are probably a couple million pages or documents, says Bob Walker, who was until recently the company's CIO and now manages the HP Professional Services Organization.

Silicon Reef is beginning to track the time it spends maintaining its intranet and the time it saves. Microsoft has conducted user surveys and revamped its intranet four times. At Citibank, Webmasters can tell what countries visitors come from and how often they access what documents. And research companies such as International Data Corp., in Framingham, Mass., have concluded that intranets offer a quick return on investment.

But IS veterans such as Visa's Perl caution that companies should not forget that intranets cost money. Although it's true that intranets are relatively easy to put up, the more extensive they become, the more they cost to maintain.

'It costs to create, it costs to store, it costs to have people look at it,' Perl says. 'Is this really increasing productivity? I don't think we know yet.'

Cate T. Corcoran writes about how computers affect productivity. She is based in San Francisco.

Discussion questions

1. The article gives an idea of the nature and function of an intranet. It uses Internet terminology to explain how an intranet serves a company. Summarize what you understand an intranet to be from the article.

2. The author stated 'Intranets are turning into time wasters instead of timesavers'. Discuss the reasons behind the statement.

3. The author also gives examples of how an intranet can be used for the benefit of a company. Summarize the advantages offered by an intranet from these examples.

4. Discuss the appropriate strategies for avoiding the pitfalls of an intranet and making it a success.

5. Using the principles discussed in the article, suggest the structure and functions of an intranet for a company you know.

6. How can you apply the lessons you learnt from this article on an intranet in the use of the Internet for an organization and for individuals?

Developing a computer system

Introduction

In previous chapters we have discussed computer hardware and software, studying how their quality affects the performance of a computer system, how different types of software help to meet different user needs and how a number of computers and peripherals can be connected together to achieve optimum results. But how is such a system set up and how do we ensure that it serves its purpose fully?

A great deal of thought and planning is needed before a computer system is installed. When you buy a computer for personal use there are many factors to be considered such as what your specific needs in hardware and software are, the suitability of products available on the market, the maintenance of the system and so on. If you are the only user then you can make these decisions informally, and if you make a mistake you can correct it relatively easily even though you may have to pay a price. When the computer system under consideration belongs to an organization, mistakes may have far-reaching effects and very expensive consequences. It is therefore very important that established procedures are followed in the development of a computer system. This process is known as systems analysis and design since it involves the analysis of user requirements and the design and implementation of an appropriate computerized system. The system developed could be based on PCs and run on packaged software, or it could be a large network of computers supported by a powerful operating system and complicated programs. In either case very careful consideration must be given to the objectives of the system and the needs of its users. In this chapter we will discuss this process and study the alternative methods and models available for developing a successful computer system for an organization.

The need for a methodology

In the 1950s and 1960s very few companies followed a methodology – a set of formal steps – to develop their computer systems. Systems were usually developed by experienced programmers following an approach made by a user department. Programmers used their experience and knowledge to write programs to run the system; if anything went wrong with it, users came back to the programmers for the necessary amendment. These were one-off solutions and the success of the system depended on the knowledge and skill of the programmer. Systems took a long time to develop and frequently went over the schedule for time and budget. There was little documentation and almost no formal procedure. If the original programmers left, it became very difficult for others to maintain the system and it often had to be rewritten. Also, programmers did not always understand the user needs and therefore the systems developed were often unsuitable.

It was felt increasingly that there was a need for a proper analysis of the system to be developed. As organizations in the 1960s and 1970s required more complicated systems, one-off solutions were seen as inadequate and a more systematic approach was called for. As a result, a number of methodologies were introduced for computer systems development.

A methodology is a series of steps taken to arrive at the desired solution for a system. People in charge of a systems development process decide on the methodology on the basis of some assumptions and beliefs which govern the way they perceive a computer system. For example, they may think of the system as the domain of IT professionals who know what is best for a company and its employees, or they may hold the view that it belongs to those who have to use the system and who should therefore have a considerable input to the design process. Sometimes the steps taken are not recognized as belonging to an approved methodology because they do not follow a clearly defined set of procedures, but there is always an underlying philosophy which dictates the approach taken to the design of a computer system.

In the 1970s and early 1980s systems development methodologies were very structured with little flexibility or allowances for uncertainties – the so-called hard systems methodology. Later on soft systems methodology was introduced which took account of multiple perceptions of a problem by users with different needs. In the following sections we will take a brief look at some of the methodologies used by organizations.

Systems development life cycle

Developed in the late 1960s and introduced widely in the 1970s, the systems development life cycle (SDLC) model is the traditional model for systems development which consists of eight main stages:

1. User specification
2. Feasibility study
3. Information gathering and analysis
4. Systems design
5. Programming
6. Systems testing
7. Conversion and implementation
8. Maintenance and review.

Although authors differ in the way they classify these stages, there is general agreement on the sequence of activities involved in the process. The above model is referred to as traditional since further models have been developed based on more modern and flexible approaches. It describes a structured process in which the stages normally occur in sequential order. This is referred to as a life cycle because it has a beginning, a lifespan and a distinct end. When one stage is completed the next stage begins, until all the stages have been carried out in sequence. However, there are a number of loop-back points where progress to the next activity depends on the decision made at the current stage (Figure 9.1). A negative decision may involve either aborting the development process (as

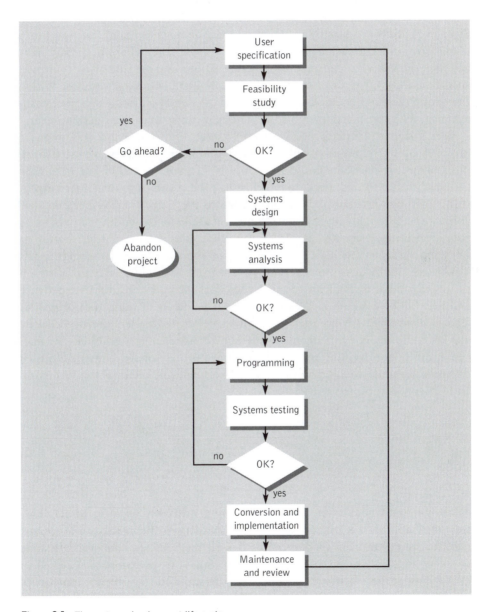

Figure 9.1: The systems development life cycle

after feasibility study in the figure) or going back to a previous stage (as after systems testing in the figure). Following the implementation the system developed is continually reviewed and maintained by making adjustments as required. At regular intervals a major review of the system is undertaken, possibly resulting in complete redevelopment.

The job of systems development is normally carried out by a team of IT professionals consisting of systems analysts, programmers and operations staff. Systems analysts are usually experienced programmers although they may also come from other areas such as business management, where they may have acquired the knowledge of organizational functions and the role of computers in such functions. Operations staff implement and run computer systems. Within this group there are people at all levels from data entry staff to operations management, the latter being the most likely to be involved in systems development.

Each system to be developed is called a project and is allocated a team and a project leader. Organizations follow one of a number of different ways of forming a project team: there could be a pool of IT professionals from which the people with appropriate backgrounds for the project can be drawn; alternatively, there could be set teams and a project given to the team which is free and suitable for the system in hand. The project leader could be drawn from a number of people with the designated status, or the role could be allocated in rotation to the senior systems analysts. Each of these methods has its own strengths and weaknesses. Permanent project teams benefit from an established team spirit; on the other hand, drawing teams from a pool gives members breadth of experience and the skill of working in different teams. The effects of the choice of project leaders have similar consequences: permanent project leaders are experienced and have knowledge of the team members; rotating team leadership has the benefit of on-the-job training for less experienced professionals. Organizations of different sizes and categories use different strategies in deciding the formation and leadership of project teams.

Get in touch with a company which uses computers for large applications such as payroll. Find out how it forms its systems development teams.

Although SDLC has come under increasing criticism because of its 'old-fashioned' approach to systems design, it still underpins the methods followed by many organizations. The modern, more flexible methods often incorporate some of the activities involved in SDLC adapted to a 'soft' philosophy. We need to take a look at these activities in order to understand the alternative approaches to systems development.

User specification

This stage begins when the IT management of an organization identifies an area for computerization or for replacing an existing computer system with a new one. This may be triggered by a request for investigation into a problem area from the user management in another part of the same organization or it may come from another organization looking for the services of a company with expertise in systems development. The purpose of this stage is to give formal terms of reference for the feasibility study for a new project. The user specification at this stage is treated only as the starting point. If the development of the system is agreed then formal user specification is created by the development team at the analysis stage following a proper investigation of the exact user requirements.

Feasibility study

Before management commits any resources to the project, a feasibility study is carried out. The purpose of the activity is to study the user specification and outline a number of probable designs for a proposed system. The study team then produces a cost-benefit analysis of each design and an outline plan for the systems development work. The stage ends with full documentation of the tasks performed and a report with recommendations. This information is used by management to make a decision on whether or not to continue with the project and, if the decision is positive, which one of the proposed outline designs to pursue. Thus, at the end of the feasibility study, there is a possible cut-off point (see Figure 9.1) beyond which many proposed systems do not go.

Information gathering and analysis

This stage commences when the go-ahead is received from the feasibility study and management has decided to resource a full systems development for a new project. It starts with a detailed investigation of the problem area, which involves collecting information on the current system through interviews, questionnaires and the survey of existing documentation. Information is collected from users in order to get a thorough understanding of how the current system works, the input to and output from the system, procedures followed for the processing of data, security measures, back-up facilities, and so on. This information is then analyzed and the problem areas of the current system identified. It is crucial at this stage to understand the strengths and weaknesses of the current system so the new one can build on the strengths and eliminate the weaknesses. There are tools available for aiding the analysis stage such as data flow diagrams, check-lists, process specification, data dictionary, and so on. We will discuss data flow diagrams briefly later in this chapter; descriptions of the other tools are obtainable from books on systems analysis and design (see the list of Further reading) but are outside the scope of this text.

Find out how your chosen company collects information.

Systems design

When the information gathering and analysis stage is completed, the project team has a clear picture of their perceived requirements for the proposed system. Using this information as the point of reference, the team can start the design process. Systems design produces a detailed plan of the new system showing how each activity involved in the system is to be performed. This includes written specifications for all aspects of a system such as input, output, storage, user interface, file design, processing, security measures, manual procedures, documentation, test plans, implementation plans, training criteria, organizational procedures, purchase of hardware and software and personnel matters.

Systems design is the most time consuming and also the most crucial activity in a systems development project. Precise and documented plans of how each of the above activities is to be performed and what is to be produced at the end of it are made so that the staff involved in putting the plans into practice have clear and unambiguous guidelines. For example, the design for input requirements must specify what data is input, the methods of data entry, the hardware medium/device used to input data, format of the data input, and so on. The design for processing gives precise details of what programs have to be written, the input, processing and output requirements of each program, the files used by each program, the formats of output, the test plans, and so on. Thus when the design is completed and programming starts, programmers have clear and precise instructions to follow. As Figure 9.1 shows, when the new system is tested and faults caused by design errors are detected, it goes back to the designers for amendment. Careful consideration at the design stage reduces the risk of a major disaster at testing.

In the 1970s and 1980s most large organizations had in-house programmers, and project teams produced program specifications for them to follow. Smaller organizations employed software companies to write programs to their specifications. Because of the existence of a wide range of general purpose applications packages, designers currently have the choice to opt for in-house program development or buy applications packages. Although most large organizations develop their own software for large systems, a project team may recommend general purpose applications for some parts of a new system. Small businesses often run PC based systems with off-the-shelf software. In such a case the project leader draws a detailed plan for what is required from the program on the basis of which an application package can be chosen. Development of PC based systems will be discussed later on in the chapter.

Find out if your chosen company uses its own programmers to write programs or uses packaged software, and why.

Systems design produces as its output a plan for the rest of the systems development process. Those involved in programming, testing, implementation and maintenance use the design specification in the same way that a builder follows an architect's plans.

Programming

Although some IT professionals designated as analyst/programmers are given responsibilities for some parts of the systems design process, for example writing program specification, designing files, and so on, they do not normally get heavily involved in systems development until the programming stage starts. A programmer's task is to use the specification to plan the structure, design the detailed logic for the program, document the structure and logic, code the program, test and debug (correct) it, and at the end of this process, pass the program and documentation to the systems development team. A number of programmers are normally allocated to a project and, depending on the size of the programs, each programmer is asked to write a number of programs. At this stage the testing is done individually by programmers using representative test data. Full testing with all programs and real data is done in the systems testing stage. Programming is discussed in detail in Chapter 6.

Systems testing

This stage begins when all programs have been written and tested individually and turned over to the systems team by individual programmers. Systems testing involves running all programs using at first test data and then real data. The test plan consisting of the method of testing and test data should already have been specified at the systems design stage. Tests at this stage reveal if programs are working together correctly. This is called linking and often involves the output from one program being used as the input for another. Often, errors which were left undetected at the programming stage are detected here; such programs are given back to programmers for correction. Errors caused by faults in program specification – often the result of inadequate information gathering and analysis – are also possible. The process goes back to the appropriate stage depending on the error found.

Systems testing must be extremely thorough and foolproof because this is the last opportunity to correct mistakes made in the development process before the system goes live. Many well publicized IT failures have been blamed on inadequate testing. Time and effort spent at this stage can save valuable resources later.

How does your chosen company test a new computer system?

Conversion and implementation

When the systems testing has been completed and all errors eliminated, the systems team is ready to convert the old system into the new one. The most important task in conversion involves creating new files from old ones. If the old system was manual then file conversion is a major task, sometimes involving programmers who may have to write file conversion programs, data entry staff who have to key in and store data, and operations staff to run the programs to create and update files. If the changeover is from an old computerized system to a new one the task may be a little simpler since the personnel involved in doing this may already have some experience in this area.

The conversion process has another important element besides file conversion. Users have to be converted from the old system to the new and training is required for this purpose. The extent of training required is assessed by the systems team at the design stage and a plan is drawn up. Organizations vary in their approach to training. Some have their own training facilities, others buy the services of training companies for this purpose. Whichever approach is used, thorough initial training as well as continual user support when the system is up and running are crucial for the success of a system. One of the major criticisms of many systems which followed traditional development methods has been inadequate user support. Traditionally users have been given training in only those parts of the computer systems that are directly relevant to them. Modern approaches have identified this as short-sighted and inadequate. According to current thinking, users must have an understanding of the whole system and an acceptance of its value. We will discuss the importance of user involvement in systems development in more detail later.

Implementation of the newly developed system can start next. This must be guided by careful planning because failure of the new system, once installed, can have a disastrous effect on an organization. The process of changeover from the old system to the new can be risky and most organizations cater for back-up procedures in case things go wrong.

Implementation can be done using one of four different modes: pilot, parallel, gradual and immediate.

Pilot implementation

This is only possible if the new system is to be installed in more than one site. In such an instance only one of the sites is initially converted to the new system; only when it proves efficient and error-free are the other sites converted. This way all resources can be concentrated to make the system work for the pilot site. At the same time the pilot site can, in the case of major problems, be quickly reverted to the old system, which is still being used by personnel in the other sites.

Parallel implementation

As the name suggests, in this mode the old and the new systems are run in parallel for a specified length of time. Full conversion takes place only when the new system proves successful. Its accuracy can be monitored by comparing the output from the two systems (although this may be difficult if the outputs are not identical). This allows the systems team to correct any errors and eliminate any problems in the newly developed system without running the risk of shutdown. However, this can be expensive since resources have to be used for staffing both systems.

Gradual implementation

The first two methods carry the lowest risk of complete standstill. If, for some reason, neither of these is possible, a gradual implementation of the new system may be a good compromise solution. In this method only certain parts of the new system are implemented, for example in a library the books catalogue may be converted to the new system while leaving the rest as they were. The maintenance and use of the catalogue is tested thoroughly and only when it is proven to be satisfactory is another part converted. This is the middle of the road solution where the cost is not very high because changes are made in small steps, but the risk of damaging failure is higher than the previous methods. This is because even after one part of a system is working, the remaining parts may have serious defects which may not be detected until much later.

Immediate implementation

This method involves the overnight substitution of the old system by the new one. Despite great risks of disastrous failure, it can be an economic way of conversion provided very thorough testing has been performed before implementation. Also, if this method is followed, the systems team must have clear contingency plans for possible failure. This may involve keeping copies of all data and printouts of all files and transactions until the system proves to be satisfactory.

How did your chosen company implement its last system?

As for most other activities, organizations usually have standard policies for implementation. However, factors related to the nature of the system developed can force them to change these from time to time.

Maintenance and review

The job of the systems design team does not finish with the implementation of a system. Regardless of how thoroughly a system has been tested before full implementation, errors may be detected long after a system is implemented: a planned maintenance procedure is essential to ensure continued efficiency. Errors are only one of many reasons for the need for maintenance. Changes in the circumstances of an organization often necessitate a review of existing systems, computerized and manual. This could be the initiatives taken to update hardware, the demand for extra features from software, changes in government regulations, changes in company policy, new ventures in business, the relationship between one system and others running in the organization, and so on.

Most organizations have established procedures for maintenance work. Some have maintenance teams whose main responsibility is to look after live systems; in other organizations the original development teams are also responsible for the maintenance of their systems; yet others give the job to any IT professionals who are free. Maintenance involves checking the output of existing systems and correcting any errors that occur. This may require altering programs or even amending elements of the design. If changing circumstances initiate amendments this may need more thorough development work. There are also occasions when a system fails to meet its objectives to the extent that more drastic steps, perhaps involving completely new systems development, become necessary.

In any case, computer systems should be reviewed thoroughly after every five or six years and usually no computer system can survive without an update or redevelopment for more than eight or nine years. Rapid innovations in technology, as well as business requirements for competitive advantage, soon make an existing system look out of date. These situations usually mean rejecting the current system and initiating a new project which would go through all the steps of a systems development starting with user specification.

Critique of the traditional systems development approach

The conventional life cycle approach has come under criticism for a number of reasons. First, the life cycle is long, often about two years. Within this time the technology, as well as users' needs, may change, thus making the system out of date before it starts. Secondly, following a number of prominent computer systems failures, doubts have been raised over the appropriateness of the traditional method. One factor identified as contributing to this is the lack of effective user involvement in the development process. A computer system can have a wide range of users. In a retail business, the people at the sales desk who take orders from customers, the warehouse staff who have to maintain an up to date stock, the clerical staff who keep track of the company's correspondence, or the management who need daily business reports are all users, each with unique requirements from the system. A system which does not meet these users' needs is of no value to the organization. Additionally, the traditional approach is expensive and highly dependent on the expertise of the development team. Because of its structured nature there is very little scope for correcting errors or making improvements once a stage is completed. Thus, if a system is found to have major faults, the effect on an organization's resources is enormous. Finally, with an increasing trend towards downsizing, many companies are building PC based systems and creating a drive towards a less structured, individualized approach. It has been suggested that the traditional life cycle method may be suitable for large, well defined systems of a complex and technical nature run by experts in technology, such as the payroll of an organization or an engineering system controlling the processes in a chemical plant, but more flexible methods are necessary for most other systems.

Find some articles from the Web which critically discuss the SDLC approach to systems design. What arguments are they making?

Other philosophies guiding systems development

Following concern over the traditional approach to systems development a number of alternative philosophies have been presented. These philosophies viewed the task from different perspectives and introduced themes that would approach the problem from a different level. We will discuss some of these themes below.

One of these themes took the systems approach which looked at the organization as a whole rather than as a collection of specific tasks that a computer system was expected to perform. It recognized that problems in an organization may not be straightforward or predictable. It also pointed out that an organization is not a closed system: its performance depends on its relationship with its environment – for example, its customers, suppliers, the government and so on. The next theme proposed to see a new computer system as a tool to improve the competitive advantage of an organization. Thus it took a strategic view of the role of an information system and concentrated on exploring different ways of using IT to enhance business activities. A third approach also took a strategic view of business problems by advocating business process re-engineering which concentrates on making fundamental changes to the way things are done in an organization. This approach is based on re-examining the present systems including the information system and if necessary, redesigning these systems in order to achieve efficiency. The philosophies behind the above approaches were utilized in a model called the planning model which is built on thorough planning of a whole information system rather than looking at individual applications and developing computer systems in a piecemeal fashion. It involves top management in the planning who may not be connected with the IT department, thus improving key management decision making.

Another theme, which has led to important new methodologies for systems development, uses the concept of modelling an information system on the basis of the data or processes used in it.[1] An information system is viewed as a hierarchy of processes or a collection of data (a database) and a number of tools and a structured approach are used to model and then build the system. In fact, SDLC uses the process model although it does not use the tools and techniques and does not take the structured design approach advocated by academics working on the modelling theme. In database approaches to systems design, data is seen as the building block of a system. More recently, an object model, the basic principle behind which was discussed in Chapter 6, is taken where real life objects are seen as the building blocks. We will not go into the details of the subject here but you can get more information on these approaches by reading the books mentioned under Further reading.

Other philosophies used in information systems development are the use of automated tools such as in code generators and CASE tools used in program development (see Chapter 6). These tools attempt to computerize all the processes involved in systems development, thus saving time and facilitating the involvement of non-technical users in the process.

Prototyping is another theme. Quite common in spheres such as the motor industry, it is now advocated for systems development by many experts in this area. Instead of doing a thorough analysis and design of a complete system this model produces a limited experimental system which fulfils only a part of the user requirements (Figure 9.2). This can be done in a fraction of the time and other resources required to develop the whole system. Further prototypes are released and refined in steps using feedback from the users. Thus prototyping is an iterative process which gives users the scope to use and understand a system gradually and allows a system team to utilize increasing user participation effectively.

An alternative model for systems design is to follow the philosophy of software engineering which uses engineering principles, mathematical tools and a disciplined approach to design and documentation to specify and design software. However, such an approach cannot always take into account the unpredictable nature of an information system and cannot cater for varying and sometimes imprecise user needs. This is taken care of in the participative approach which advocates end-user involvement in systems development and forms the basis of soft design methodologies. This approach recognizes that the success of a computer system depends on its acceptability to its users who may have expectations and perspectives which are vastly different from those in charge of technology. Thus end-user satisfaction should be at the core of a systems design philosophy and the best results are obtained when end-users are allowed to play an important role in systems development.

---

1 Modelling is the abstraction of a real world object or principle.

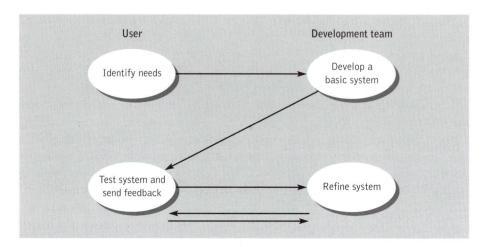

Figure 9.2: Prototyping

The above themes have led to much debate in systems development and have given rise to a number of alternative methodologies. Detailed discussion of all of these are beyond the scope of this book, but a brief look at some alternative models follows.

Some methodologies

Following the theme of process modelling, structured analysis and design of information systems (STRADIS) was introduced in 1979. This uses a number of diagrammatical tools such as data flow diagrams (DFDs) and decision tables to create a logical model of the system in progressively finer stages of detail and concentrates on the tasks at each stage in a very structured way. A data flow diagram enables a systems designer to use standardized symbols to represent the logical flow of information through a process without having to give any consideration to the hardware or the way things are done. Figure 9.3 shows a DFD for a hotel booking system. Detailed descriptions of the symbols used are outside the scope of this book but because of the self-explanatory nature of the technique, it should be possible to understand the flow of data in such a system. The diagram is normally drawn in stages concentrating on a small aspect of data flow at a time; this allows stepwise refinement.

Going along with the structured theme, structured systems analysis and design methodology (SSADM) was introduced in the UK in the early 1980s. This

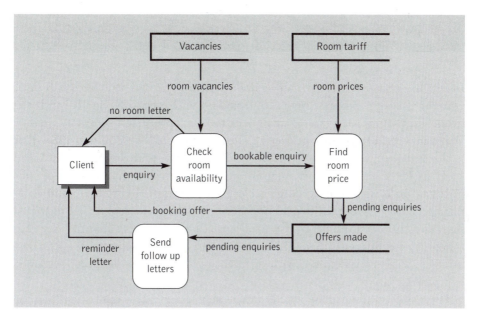

Figure 9.3: DFD for hotel booking
Source: adapted from Mason and Willcocks (1994)

divides systems development into two separate stages of analysis and design and using detailed rules and guidelines the two processes are defined as a series of tasks in a similar way to SDLC. Unlike SDLC, it uses DFDs and other tools to model the system and puts greater emphasis on the users of the system. Also, by separating systems analysis from design, it leaves less at stake on the ability of the analyst. Finally, because of the rigid structure and rules, documentation is normally of high quality.

There are other structured approaches to systems development, such as Jackson's systems development which incorporates Jackson's structured programming (see Chapter 6), and object oriented analysis. These are classed as hard methodologies because they put the greatest emphasis on the requirements for the functionalities of the system and try to find the best hardware and software combinations for it. Although user participation is encouraged by most of these methodologies, little importance is given to the 'human factors' of a computer system and there is little scope for adjustment based on experience or feedback. Soft systems methodologies attempt to do this.

Which method of systems development does your chosen company use? What are its reasons for choosing this method?

Soft systems philosophy

In real life very few systems can be defined within a rigid structure. It is difficult for users to express their requirements with absolute clarity, and it is often impossible for systems designers to conceptualize users' needs fully. There may be a mismatch between the perceptions of these two groups. This is the starting point of the so-called 'soft systems' philosophy presented in 1981 by Peter Checkland. It is based on the assumption that many problems in organizations cannot be defined clearly because of their 'fuzzy' and complicated nature. Most real world problems need stepwise refinement based on increasing understanding of the problem. Checkland also pointed out that there may be different stakeholders in an organization such as end-users, customers, suppliers and so on, with different needs which a computer system is expected to satisfy.

Hard systems philosophy assumes that each system has a stated goal and the purpose of systems development is to determine 'how' to achieve that goal. Soft systems start with the notion of a purpose rather than a fixed goal; the job of the systems designers is to decide 'what' needs to be done to serve the purpose and then 'how' to achieve it. To use an analogy, a hard system may start to solve the problem of a faulty air conditioning system whereas a soft system may start with the purpose of improving the comfort level of a building. Thus soft systems start with a problem situation and attempts to find a solution.

In the soft systems approach, a preliminary conceptual model of the system is developed on the basis of the initial understanding of the situation; the model is then developed increasingly as continual information gathering from users increases the level of understanding of the problems. Thus soft systems design places an emphasis on the perceptions of users at different positions and levels. It also provides scope for gradual improvement of the system by continuing discussion, debate and negotiation. The methodologies described below conform to the soft philosophy although some of them resulted from original work independent of Peter Checkland.

Surf the Internet for articles on the experience of the use of soft systems philosophy by some organizations. What do you conclude from these articles about the suitability of this philosophy?

Effective technical and human implementation of computer-based systems (ETHICS)

Carrying on with the participative approach of soft systems design, ETHICS addresses the development of a computer system not as a technical issue but as an organizational one and concerns itself with the process of change. Proposed by Enid Mumford in the early to middle 1980s, this methodology takes the ethical view that technology must serve to improve the level of job satisfaction of employees. It also believes that workers at different levels may have conflicting interests and therefore user participation and consultation should be major elements of systems design. The methodology designed with these objectives in mind has a number of versions. These vary in the number of steps recommended depending on how the social and technical factors have been separated but the underlying philosophy remains the same. Some critics have argued that user participation at such a large extent is not practical whilst some large companies such as DEC have used it for designing their computer systems. The concept of user participation has increased in popularity following the failure of a number of systems because of the lack of usability.

End-user development

An increasing number of organizations are subscribing to the school of thought that at the root of a system's success is the involvement of its users in the development stage. Some are going further than this: aided by the introduction of fourth generation languages and interface design tools, many organizations are getting their users to develop systems themselves. In this model technologists take an advisory role. End-users decide on a set of objectives based on their business needs, establish clear criteria for measuring the system's performance and then draw a development plan. They may choose to use prototyping or even a traditional model for developing the system themselves. The technical development is undertaken by the technologists. This model normally works for small, microcomputer based systems run by packaged applications programs, although the introduction of fourth generation languages has made it possible to develop customized software by users with a limited knowledge of programming.

Multiview

This methodology perceives an information system as a hybrid process with both technical and human aspects. It has been influenced by the work of Checkland and Mumford as well as some aspects of hard methodologies. It sets out to be flexible, based on the assumption that a particular technique, or aspect of one methodology, will work in certain situations but will not be suitable for others. It takes into account different (multiple) perspectives or views: organizational, technical, human-oriented and economic. In a number of stages it addresses both the social and technical aspects of a system in a semi-structured way. This methodology has been found to be successful for PC based systems.

Each of the above models has its strengths and weaknesses. Organizations may choose the ones most suitable to themselves or may even find a model based on a combination of these. One factor is common in all alternative approaches – users take an important role in the systems development process.

Outsourcing

Some organizations are opting to employ external vendors to develop and sometimes run a computer system. On the one hand, this strategy can provide a solution when resources in an organization are limited, on the other, outsourcing can cause loss of control and vendor dependency.

Setting up a PC based system

PCs are used by most organizations as desktop machines. Large organizations use them as part of a distributed network, as intelligent terminals. Used in this way PCs function as the means to connect to the network as well as independent machines capable of running programs themselves. This gives individual users and departments the choice to access the facilities provided by the network and at the same time use software of their own choosing. Smaller organizations, such as estate agents or libraries, may, on the other hand, run their entire computer systems on PCs. The systems development process, as described above, is not fully appropriate in such cases because usually they would not design the entire system themselves, or write the programs. They would either buy applications packages or employ a software company to write the programs. The process of acquiring a PC based system depends on the size of the system and the complexity of the applications. Organizations looking for networked PCs running tailor-made software for specific applications may choose to buy the services of consultants who will follow the steps described above. The time taken and the number of options investigated at each stage could be less than those for a full-scale development of a computer system for a large number of users. However, the objectives of the development process and the aims of each step remain the same, although the tasks performed could be a subset of those enumerated above.

Some organizations may decide to run their PC based systems on general purpose applications packages. A thorough analysis of what is needed and what the available packages offer is necessary in such cases. A team of people with a mixture of expertise in management, technology and the current system (which includes end-users) should be appointed to decide what the new system should comprise, and how it should be implemented. The following is an example of the steps a typical organization in this position would follow:

1. Identifying the objectives of the new system.

2. Setting up the budget.

3. Investigating user needs.

4. Undertaking a feasibility study based on a number of options in outline form. The options should include both hardware and software with cost-benefit analysis of each. Considerations for hardware are as follows: type of computers to use, the amount of memory required, storage capacity and devices, whether to use networked or stand-alone computers, the type of the network, number and situations of terminals, and so on. Software considerations involve choosing systems and applications programs.

5. Carrying out a detailed evaluation of one or two options chosen from the feasibility study. Any applications software recommended should be evaluated thoroughly at this stage to see how closely it meets the requirements. The evaluation criteria must be set clearly and all applications considered should be evaluated thoroughly. The subject of software evaluation is discussed in Chapter 5.

6. Investigating training needs.

7. Deciding on the location of the computers, cabling, layout, health and safety, security procedure, maintenance procedure, and so on.

8. Purchasing and implementing the new system. Outside technical help may be required at this stage. The implementation plan should incorporate back-up procedures for possible problems at the initial stage.

9. Day to day maintenance of the computer system. Most organizations running such a system would have a technician capable of looking after a PC based system. However, they should also have a maintenance contract with companies to cover major problems with hardware and software.

By opting for commercially available software, users subject themselves to the same strengths and weaknesses of a packaged solution. Many organizations use stand-alone PCs for individual use. In such cases computers and the software are often chosen on an ad hoc basis. Although the choice of brand names is large most leading PC software offers similar facilities. Enthusiasts would normally go for brands of hardware and software they are familiar with, for example an Apple or an IBM compatible PC together with its often well established software. Ideally, a selection of the available software should be evaluated systematically using clear criteria based on the requirements of the users. Evaluations of such packaged applications are published by many magazines and consumer groups. Thorough study of the reports produced by these bodies is one way of selecting software. A factor in choosing hardware and software systems, often overlooked by customers, is the quality of after sales support provided by the vendors.

Find an organization such as an insurance broker or an estate agent, that has set up a PC based system. Interview them to find out how they did it and how this compares with what you have learnt from this chapter.

The success of a computer system

In spite of spending large amounts of resources and employing experienced corporate high fliers to take charge of new projects, many computer systems fail. Following a number of embarrassing systems failures in the UK and elsewhere (such as the computer-aided despatch system of the London Ambulance Service and Taurus of the London stock exchange) much discussion and research has taken place into the reasons for such disasters. IT systems are unique in a number of ways. They affect everyone associated with an organization, from the top management to the postroom, as well as outsiders such as clients and customers. An IT system cannot be evaluated fully using predetermined criteria because its success or failure depends on how effectively it can be used after it is implemented; its long term success depends on the daily experiences of its users as well as its technical accuracy and speed of operation. Many organizations see an IT project as a technical task and employ technically skilled people to develop it. Increasing examples of failed systems developed by such people have led to the widely accepted conclusion that IT development is a business challenge and not a technical task: it needs business solutions. A new computer system demands many changes in the work habits of its users, therefore the introduction of a new system should be seen as the management of change and needs to be led by managers with business knowledge, vision and leadership skills. Over-focus on the technology and unwillingness to address the political and strategic issues within the organizations have been blamed for the lack of success of many computer systems.

In the days of centralized computer systems matters were slightly easier. Although the main goal of a system was also to improve business practices, the use of computers was confined to the data processing department. Systems were developed by technical staff to be operated by technically skilled personnel. The project team could concentrate on the technical problems and follow accepted systems design methodologies. A business could depend on the expertise and experience of the people in its data processing department for implementing and maintaining its computer systems. Downsizing, with distributed systems, has changed the culture in organizations. Computers are no longer within the boundaries of a data processing department. The introduction of a new computer system needs managers with the interpersonal skills necessary to motivate users, manage organizational politics and build a relationship with staff in order to lead an organizational change.

Computer systems failure is an important area of study. A full discussion of this topic is outside the scope of this book but the following are the main factors identified by academic researchers and business consultants as the reasons behind most failures:

- a communication gap between technical and non-technical staff. Often the job of information gathering is left to systems designers. They have a tendency to assume that users know exactly what they expect from the computer system and are able to express it clearly. The reality is that users have their own perceptions of how they want the system to behave. Translating this into functional requirements is the job of the development team. Information gathering should be seen as a management job to be done by people with an understanding of user perspectives;

- an eagerness to go for the most advanced technology rather than investigating the most suitable solution to the problem in hand;

- a lack of personnel with administrative skills. Computers cannot substitute the personal and interpersonal skills of people they often replace which, in many cases, include middle management;

- a lack of understanding of technology by some senior managers. This leads to oversimplification of problems and inadequate resource allocation;

- a lack of strategic thinking and the tendency to put fragmented efforts in different sections of a business;

- a lack of collaboration between managers, users and technical staff. A system not understood and accepted by users is a failed system. A new computer system has to be 'sold' to its users and requires close collaboration between the groups of personnel involved. Management must avoid creating too much hype or allowing users to expect that the new system will solve all problems;

● a lack of evaluation criteria. Although evaluating a computer system is less straightforward than evaluating other systems, such as a newly built bridge, there must be some established procedure for measuring the efficiency of the product;

● misallocation of responsibilities. Technical people are often used as document writers and trainers. Professional communicators are needed for these tasks;

● a mismatch between business strategy and IT strategy. It may be necessary to amend business practices to suit a promising IT strategy. Because of the subjective nature of an IT system, its introduction may have to challenge the current corporate culture. A flexible approach that can change and allow the business to grow is the key to success.

Computers allow businesses to use information for competitive advantage. New projects should concentrate on how they can utilize applications to improve the business process. A continuous roll-out of small manageable systems can be more flexible and adaptable than large expensive ones. Above all, a skilled and contented workforce is the driver of a successful computer system. Therefore management must spend resources on ongoing training and continual user support to ensure business advantage through information technology.

Find some articles on real life systems failure. What are the most common reasons behind these failures?

Summary

Traditionally, computer systems were developed by following the hard systems methodology, so-called because of its formal approach to development: a team of experts start with a formal request from users and go through a series of stages to design, develop, test and implement the system. Following a number of IT systems failures, researchers have presented us with a number of alternative methodologies based on the philosophy of 'soft' systems design. This has two main aspects: an iterative approach to design, and user involvement at all stages of development. In this approach, the systems team develops a basic model and improves it incrementally by collecting user feedback at each stage. Systems designed by end-users themselves are also becoming increasingly popular. All in all soft systems design has been collecting momentum although it has not been easy to persuade some technical staff to accept the new philosophy.

The concept of systems analysis and design applies equally to large systems supported by mainframes and minis and PC based systems used in small businesses, although the tasks to be performed at each stage of development may be different. The main objective of an IT system is to ensure that it is accepted by its users; a system which sits on the shelf is a failed one. Studies have identified a number of reasons for such failures, at the root of which is a lack of communication between technical experts and non-technical users. Soft systems methodologies have attempted to address this issue.

Further reading

Read Chapter 3 of *Information Systems Development: Methodologies, Techniques and Tools* by D. E. Avison and G. Fitzgerald, Second edition, McGraw-Hill, 1995 for more information on the themes in information systems development.

Read Chapter 4 of the above book for more information on the tools and techniques used in systems development.

Read *Systems Analysis, Systems Design* by David Mason and Leslie Wilcocks, Alfred Waller Ltd, 1994 for more information on different methods of systems development.

For more information on soft systems design read *Information systems Development: An Introduction to Information Systems* by Paul Beynon-Davis, Third edition, Macmillan Press, 1998.

Computerising the Corporation: The Intimate Link between People and the Machine, by V.C. McConell and W. Koch, Van Nostrand Reinhold, 1990 covers systems failure well.

Revision questions

1. List the steps involved in the traditional systems design life cycle with a brief description of the function of each step.

2. Discuss the strengths and weaknesses of the above methodology.

3. Distinguish between the hard and soft systems design philosophies.

4. Discuss briefly the themes which have guided the discussions and debates over systems design methodologies.

5. Describe briefly the 'alternative' methodologies used in developing an IT system. How do they compare with the traditional design?

6. What are the important criteria for the development of a PC based system?

7. In recent years we have heard about a number of systems failures. What are the main reasons for such failures and what can be done to minimize the risks?

Food for thought

Computer Weekly, 31 March, 1994
Reed Business Publishing Ltd (UK)

A lesson to be learnt from Indian culture
Alan Howard

The Naskapi Indians in Western Canada are successful hunters. Before venturing out they ask the question 'Where should we hunt today?' To answer this question they take the shoulder bone of a caribou and hold it over a fire until it cracks. They hunt in whichever direction the crack points.

An interesting story but what does this teach us about IT strategy? There are a number of lessons. The Naskapi strategy is successful for four reasons. First, they have a clear objective. Second, they believe in the strategy. Third, strategy formulation is so quick and simple that they spend little time on it and thus spend more time hunting. Fourth, if they don't find game that day no one person is to blame.

Compare that to IT strategy formulation in many organisations. A clear business plan does not exist. It is very rare to win total support for a strategy. Strategy is agonised over for months on end. If the strategy fails the consultants and/or IT manager are sacked and the process begins again under the auspices of a new leader.

Perhaps there are two aspects of western culture which mitigate against successful strategy formulation – individualism and formal-rational thinking. Excessive individualism makes it difficult for people to work in teams and to be philosophical about so-called 'failure'. Failure is taken personally and heads roll or careers are stunted.

Western training and culture focuses on rational views of the world. Eastern cultures view life as a continuous cyclic process rather than a series of sequential and discrete events. Change is evolutionary rather than revolutionary.

For western managers there is nothing quite as satisfying as doing a rigorous and wide-ranging diagnosis of a situation. The problem is that the diagnosis quickly gets out of phase with changing realities. The longer the diagnosis lasts the greater the chances that the goal posts have moved.

Lengthy analysis also raises expectations about outcomes. In strategic planning for IT and information systems, managers must accept that business, technological and organisational environments are changing so rapidly that strategy must be as much about awareness, intuition, learning common sense and sophisticated loss-cutting actions as about long-term planning. No plan by itself guarantees success.

An enterprise must instil confidence in its staff, get them moving in some general direction and make sure they learn from events. Just-in-time strategies will suffice. Trying to anticipate everything that will happen and all the resources needed is a futile task. Invest in general knowledge, wide-ranging skills and competent people.

Given the diversity of information technology and uncertainty about the future, many different strategies are possible. What we can learn from the Naskapi is that whatever the strategy people must have a clear mission. The strategy must not be too complex.

A critical mass of people, ideally everyone, must believe in the strategy. Finally, if the strategy does not work, maybe it isn't just the leader's fault!

Discussion questions

1. What are the strengths of the Indian hunting strategies?

2. How do the above strategies relate to IT development?

3. Do you agree with the author's view that these strategies can be applied to IT systems? Give reasons for your response.

4. A number of reasons for IT failure have been discussed in this chapter. Find some press reports of well publicized systems failure and try to relate these cases to the points made in the chapter and this article; then critically review those points.

CHAPTER 10

Computers and humans

Objectives

At the end of this chapter you should have some understanding of:

▶ how the use of computers can present health and safety hazards;
▶ what we can do to minimize the risks;
▶ the importance of people's personal reactions to computer hardware and software.

Introduction

About 10 years ago when computers started occupying a place on the desktops of the corporate and educational worlds, they were seen as machines designed to perform practical tasks; very little consideration was given to the effects they had on human beings. The Health and Safety at Work (HASAW) Act 1974, together with other supporting acts, focused only on common hazards at work such as fire, overcrowding, poor ventilation, extreme temperatures and so on. Employers' choices of computer hardware and software were based mainly on their budgets and the quality of the output required. Human factors, such as the look of a PC, the level of comfort and the effects of hardware and software design on users' health, were not important issues. However, as human beings became increasingly exposed to computers people began to realize that computers can bring specific health and safety hazards not covered by HASAW. Also, the relationship between the performance of a worker and his or her reaction to hardware and software design became an important issue. From such concerns and discussions came two important areas of study: health and safety in computing, and human computer interaction which we will discuss in this chapter.

Health and safety in computing

In recent years various debates have taken place on the subject of health hazards associated with the use of PCs. Common areas of concern, sometimes referred to as computer related disorders (CRDs), are repetitive strain injury (RSI), effects of VDU radiation, problems with vision and headaches, and the environmental pollution such as noise, heat and low humidity generated by computer hardware. There are other safety hazards such as the danger from cluttered cables on the floor and the risk of fire resulting from faulty electric components. Since 1992 work involving computers has been subject to European Community health and safety regulations concerning monitors, keyboards, desks, chairs and the work environment, that is, lighting, humidity, noise, glare, amongst other things. Ergonomics has now become an important term in computing: this is the study of the environment of work in relation with natural human conditions. In other words, an ergonomically designed office aims to fit human bodies and minds in their most comfortable state, thus minimizing the risk to their health and safety.

Before we can discuss office ergonomics let us consider the main areas of concern.

Risks associated with the use of computers

Repetitive strain injury (RSI)

As the name suggests this term is used to indicate injuries to tissues resulting from repeated small movements of any part of the body. RSI is not restricted to computer users. Manual workers, secretaries, workers in the clothing trade, sportsmen and women, have suffered from RSI for many years. Some sufferers have taken their employers to court claiming industrial injury although only a handful have been successful.

In computing, the most common complaints are RSI of the hands, wrists and forearms, known as carpal tunnel syndrome (CTS). Repeated use of these parts of the body causes the tendons (the tissues extending from the forearm into the hands running through wrist bones called the carpal tunnel) to swell. This puts pressure on the nerve through the middle of the tunnel causing pain and other symptoms. And, because this nerve originates from the spinal cord in the neck, CTS can eventually cause more severe damage.

Search the Internet and other sources of information to find out about cases of computer related RSI which have been taken to court by employees. What were the outcomes?

There are many aspects of computing that can cause RSI, keyboard design being the most common contributing factor. The layout of the keyboard, its height and slope, its weight which affects its stability and therefore how much strain it puts on a user's hands, the feedback when a key is pressed, the curvature of the keys – all of these determine the level of repetitive strain that a keyboard can cause. The layout of the workstation (the computer, the desk, the chair) is another important factor. Wrongly positioned computer components can force a user to twist and turn thus causing long term physical damage, and a badly designed chair that provides inadequate body support can be a major reason for RSI. With the increasing use of graphical user interfaces, users spend a lot of time operating a mouse. An unsuitable height and shape for the mouse can cause CTS, and frequent clicking and double-clicking can contribute to RSI.

Eye disorders

Prolonged staring at computer screens can give rise to common complaints such as eye strain, headaches and damage to eyesight. A poll conducted in the USA has shown that computer related eye strain is the most common office related health complaint (Seymour, J., *PC Magazine*, Oct., p.93 1995). Nowadays many employers offer free eye tests to those employees who spend a considerable amount of time in front of computers.

Conjunctivitis, an eye infection causing bloodshot, itchy and watering eyes, has been said to be a problem caused by VDUs. The electromagnetic radiation from a VDU produces negative ions near the screen and around a user's body. They attract positively charged dust particles which can cause irritation, clogging and infection in the eye. However, recent reports by the Health and Safety Executive (HSE) have stated that the radiation from modern VDUs is too low to cause such symptoms.

VDU radiation

The most controversial concern over computer use is the effect of VDU radiation on human bodies. In addition to eye irritation, more serious concerns have been expressed over the effect of electromagnetic radiation from screens on human cells and unborn babies. Research has been carried out in an attempt to establish whether there is any link between cancer or miscarriages and VDU radiation. The results so far have denied such risks although this has not resulted in fully eliminating public concern.

Other factors

Other less talked about hazards in computer rooms include photocopiers and laser printers that emit ozone, noisy printers and high temperatures due to over-heated machines.

A relatively new danger area has been identified by researchers in the University of Washington who have studied the effects of the head-mounted displays (HMDs) used for virtual reality applications. These are sensory devices designed to synchronize a user's eyes and ears with a screen display. If poorly designed or overused they can cause eye strain, nausea, simulator sickness (disorientation) and even flashbacks. Research carried out in the University of Edinburgh in 1993 concluded that poorly designed HMDs could cause permanent brain damage (Johnson, 1995 – see Further Reading section) and long term psychological effects. However, it has been proven that properly designed HMDs are perfectly safe and, correctly used for short lengths of time, should not pose any danger.

Find out what you can about the advances made in the design of an HMD to improve its ergonomic qualities.

Stress caused by software

So far we have talked about computer related disorders caused mainly by hardware and the environment. An area which has been in the public focus for some time is the stress caused by badly designed software. Poor program inter-faces (on-screen displays) with inadequate feedback and inappropriate error messages can cause a great deal of user frustration. We will look at the causes of such stress and the measures to be taken against it later on under human computer interaction.

In recent years scientists and computer manufacturers have been working towards making the use of computers safer. Ergonomic design of computers and careful layout of computer rooms are now essential parts of systems design procedure. Current Health and Safety regulations, together with the rise in expensive lawsuits and losses due to employee absences because of computer related illnesses, have prompted employers to take ergonomics seriously.

An ergonomic office

An ergonomic office is one in which a number of steps have been taken to minimize the risks to human health. This involves improving the design of hardware, software and the working environment as well as maintaining good standards in the way computers are used. In order to achieve the best possible results, specific attention needs to be given to the following areas.

The workstation

The key concept in workstation design is adjustability. Since computer users do not come in an average size, workstations should not be made to suit an average person. A user must be able to adjust the height of the desk, the height and angle of the monitor, and the level of the pullout keyboard stand (if any). The chair should swivel and have multiple adjustable points to give the user maximum leg, back and lumbar support. An adjustable foot rest and padded wrist rest are useful for user comfort, although using a wrist rest while typing is not recom-

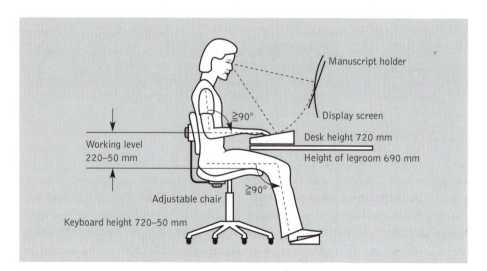

Figure 10.1: An ergonomically correct workstation

mended. Space is an extremely important factor: users need adequate clearance between the top of their thighs and the underside of the work surface. The amount of space on the work surface should accommodate the keyboard and the pointing device and still have enough room to work comfortably. Any other equipment such as telephones, document holders, stationery, manuals and so on, should be suitably placed to allow the user maximum space and flexibility without the need to stretch or twist to reach. Figure 10.1 illustrates many of the recommendations for good workstation design.

Look at some of the workstations in your university, place of work and other places. How do they compare with what has been said here about good design?

Input devices

The most commonly used input device is the keyboard. The layout of the keys as well as the height and slope of QWERTY keyboards have been criticized for failing to give users much hand and wrist support. A number of alternatives to the QWERTY design have been produced and some have proved to be more efficient and easier to use. However, they have not made much impact on the market, mostly because of the cost involved in mass retraining and widespread keyboard replacement.

Ideally, a keyboard should not be more than 2.5 cm thick at the near edge; most come with a tilt of about 1.25 cm but some designers have recommended a negative tilt (higher at the front). The weight of the keyboard is also important: light keyboards or those that slide on the work surface are uncomfortable to use. For adequate finger support there should be enough resistance in the keys to require a minimum force to be activated without being stiff. Auditory or tactile feedback from keys is important and curvature of the keys should fit the shape of human fingerpads. The use of function keys and scrolling (arrow) keys saves on mouse movements and is seen as beneficial. Some keyboards are made with numeric keypads that can be shifted to the left to suit left-handed users. It is now possible to buy ergonomically styled keyboards even though the layout of the keys has not changed much.

Although no input device can replace a keyboard for text input yet, many functional keypresses have been taken over by devices such as the mouse, the trackball and special purpose keypads. Mouse design has become an important issue in health and safety; areas being investigated by manufacturers include left-handed as well as right-handed mice, cordless or radio-signalled mice, and mice that fits into users' hands naturally. A mouse with a third button which can be programmed to perform certain functions (for example, one click to replace double-clicking) reduces stress on fingers. Increasing numbers of computer users are known to prefer other input devices such as the trackball or light pen: trackballs need less space to work and pens have obvious advantages in comfort and usability.

Find some examples of ergonomic keyboards. How widespread is their use?

VDU screens

There are two aspects of VDU screens that determine their ergonomic quality: viewing comfort and VDU radiation. The importance of the height and angle of the monitor has already been discussed. Other features that can improve viewing comfort are: high resolution, low flicker rate and large screens. Flicker rate can be reduced by using monitors in which every line is scanned rather than the usual alternate lines. Flat screens with etched or coated displays are said to be easier on the eye and antiglare screens can be fitted on monitors for increased comfort. Use of colour on the screen also affects usability: this can be achieved by using software with a display that is bright, clear and soothing to the eyes.

VDU radiation has caused much concern in recent years. While the debate goes on, many manufacturers are now making low emission monitors. Filters attached to the monitor reduce radiation and limit the build-up of static electricity near a screen, thus reducing the accumulation of dust particles around the user's face. However, filters are only partially effective since studies have shown that the highest emission comes from the sides and back of a monitor. The most effective way of reducing the risk of harm by radiation is to ensure that the screen is at least 60 cm away and that the back or the side of any other monitors in the room are at least 120 cm away from a user.

Environment

Improving the working environment is important for any type of work, but it is crucial for computer users because many of them spend long hours in the same position. The temperature, humidity and noise in a room can affect a user's stress levels considerably. A good ergonomically designed computer room should maintain a background temperature of around 20°C; and many computers are now built with quieter fan units. Clutter of cables on the floor is dangerous as well as unpleasant to the eye: cable lines can be built under the floor or through standing poles into the ceiling.

Lighting in the room is another important factor. Screens should not be too dim or too bright but should match the brightness of the ambient lighting. To avoid reflection from the screen, windows and other sources of light should be off to the side of the monitor rather than in front of or behind it. The emission of ozone from photocopiers and laser printers can be counteracted by improving ventilation. Most such equipment contains a charcoal filter to absorb ozone: this should be replaced after every 10,000 copies. Good ventilation, a smoke free environment, a clean room to reduce dust particles and static build-up on the screen, the use of an ion generator to neutralize static radiation, and a spacious and pleasant room design all go towards making computing a less hazardous occupation.

User habits

The most important factor in reducing risks involved in any job is good work practice. Taking frequent short breaks (one every hour) from looking at the screen and stretching the body, arms and legs at regular intervals can make a considerable difference. Users can take responsibility for their own welfare to a large extent although the contributions made by an overall organizational policy cannot be overemphasized. Managers have a duty to improve the ergonomic quality of an organization's work environment for all types of work. Thanks to recent regulations and increasing awareness amongst employees, many organizations are beginning to invest in this area.

Conduct a survey of the precautions users take in the use of computer equipment. What proportion of users follow the rules for safety?

The law

Health and safety in computing is covered by the 1992 EC regulations which include the following recommendations:

- Employers have a duty to identify any health risks in conjunction with their employees.
- Workstations must meet certain minimum requirements.
- Monitors should have brightness and contrast control.
- Employees must take frequent breaks.
- Health and safety training should be given to all employees.
- Employers must provide and pay for eye tests, lenses and spectacle frames for computer users.

However, there are no strict technical specifications, only objectives and recommendations. Also, some of the directives are vague and can be difficult to implement; for example, the law does not state how long breaks should be.

There are two main ways in which an employer can be prosecuted in this area: a civil prosecution can be brought on grounds of negligence, or the Health and Safety Executive can inspect an office and take action which can eventually lead to a prohibition notice forcing an employer to shut down until improvements are made. So far a number of people have taken their employers to court but have had limited success in proving negligence. It is difficult to prove that any injury or ill-health is directly related to computer use. However, continued debate on these issues together with stricter regulations have made employers aware of their responsibilities.

What do you think are the most effective ways to make employers take health and safety in computing seriously?

Human computer interaction

Ergonomically designed workstations and offices ensure the physical well-being of users. However, this on its own cannot be adequate because a person's physical condition is closely intertwined with his or her emotional state. As computers become an integral part of an office, the dividing line between them and other office equipment – telephones, fax machines, photocopiers – is getting thinner. Also, the concept of the term 'user' is changing: a few years ago a user was a member of the data processing staff whose main concern was the speed and power of the computer. These days many jobs involve computers, and workers at all levels and in all areas can be users. Additionally, people operating cash machines outside banks, playing video games or monitoring their own shopping record in supermarkets are also users of computers. Thus the interaction between humans and computers has spread from the technical level to the social level; consequently, the way humans relate to computers has provoked much academic debate.

The main concern of those involved in the study of human computer interaction (HCI) is the quality of the experience users gain as a result of their interaction with computers. A large part of this depends on the working environment which we have already discussed. Another factor which makes a considerable contribution to the user experience is the interface design. Laurel (1990 – see Further Reading section) has described an interface as the place where contact between two entities occurs. Thus the hardware and software devices through which we communicate with a computer are our interfaces.

Although a relatively new topic in the study of computers, interface design has now become a vast area of research and debate incorporating the expertise of people in subjects as varied as computer science, psychology, engineering, art and medicine. The importance of a software interface was first taken seriously by the Apple programmers. They introduced graphical user interfaces with their programs back in the 1980s. User friendliness was their main selling point. The trend they began was followed by other companies and has now become almost a standard for common business applications. Today's software comes with easy to use, intuitive interfaces designed for users who are not technical specialists. Nowadays, ordinary people buy personal computers and, in most cases, can use them without any expert help. Figure 10.2 shows an interface where a novice user can go through levels of options clearly displayed on the screen in order to enter into the required program.

A thorough discussion of all aspects of human computer interfaces is outside the scope of this book; in this chapter we are going to give an overview of the guiding principles behind good interface design, the concepts upon which interface design is modelled and the qualities of a well designed user interface.

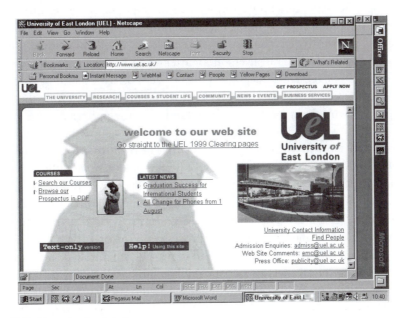

Figure 10.2: Example of an interface

The guiding principles

Before computers became commonplace, the goal of an interface designer was to produce a functional system with the main emphasis on speed and power. Now, the most important goals are usability, safety and perceived functionality, that is, the effectiveness of a system to its user. As computers become increasingly more integrated into everyday objects such as a microwave oven or a car, there is an urgent need to make the technology invisible to its user. This can only be achieved by enabling users to interact with the task in hand rather than the machine. Thus the ultimate goal is to empower users by making the machine respond to their needs rather than the other way round.

The underlying concepts

The above principles suggest that the focus of an interface design should be its users who these days come from a large spectrum of social and technical backgrounds with widely different needs. Some demand speed and are happy with technically complex systems whilst others may consider ease of use as the most important factor. To satisfy the needs of both these groups, interfaces have to reflect the way humans accept and process information. This requires an understanding of the way we acquire knowledge, memorize, perceive information, communicate and apply reasoning. The discipline that dominates the study of these issues is cognitive psychology which enables us to examine these processes and create a mental model of users in an attempt to conceptualize the strengths and weaknesses of human perception. This provides us with the tools we need to create effective user interfaces. For example, an appreciation of how the human visual system works enables us to understand how the patterns and colours of screen displays work for users. A study of how human memory functions for both long term and short term storage of information helps us to create the most suitable icons and menus. An understanding of how users learn, how they use verbal metaphors and so on enables us to develop applications which are intuitive and easy to use. In the current trend towards multimedia, virtual reality and increasingly intuitive graphical user interfaces, a good software designer models an application to reflect the actual thought processes of the user. User interfaces can vary between an elaborate display designed to provide a naturalistic representation useful for non-technical users to a command line interface which works mainly by typed instructions, special keystrokes and text based on-screen messages useful for those who need to interact at a deeper level. An effective user interface is the result of a clear understanding of the cognitive psychology of users at all levels and requires the combined skills of a programmer, psychologist and artist amongst others, together with an active involvement of users.

What are the most important qualities of a good interface from your personal point of view?

An effective user interface

So, what do we consider to be a good user interface? Humans interact with a computer via input and output devices. The design of a keyboard or mouse has a direct effect on the level of comfort experienced by the user. For speech activated input, the quality of speech recognition is not only vital for the functionality of a system, poor speech recognition can result in considerable user frustration. The same is true for output devices because the level of user experience depends greatly on the performance of these devices. Due to the current debates on health and safety, much work has been done on the physical design of computers and peripheral devices. However, the usability of a computer depends to a large extent on the quality of the software running it. For example, when we enter a command to print a document, a well designed program displays messages using text and graphics to keep us informed of the progress of the task. This way if a large document has to be printed which takes a long time we can tell at what stage the process is at, at any point of time. Error messages using text and sound (normally a beep) when incorrect steps are taken (for example, clicking on an inappropriate icon) is another example of useful feedback from a system. The most important user interface is the top layer of a program via which a user communicates with the computer, for example Windows-based applications programs with buttons and menus designed with user perception in mind. A common example of good interface design is the prompt on a bank cash machine which asks users to collect their card before their money is delivered. This was initiated by frequent cases of users leaving the cashpoints without collecting their cards.

Can you think of any interface designs used in the service industries which are either good or bad examples for effectiveness?

Let us now take a brief look at the characteristics of a well designed graphical interface. By now, even the newcomers to computers amongst you must have gained some experience of using modern windows based programs. These are typical examples of 'user friendly' interface design, although as we get increasingly more used to good interfaces, we become educated in detecting weaknesses in such designs. This in turn, drives the initiative for even better designs. The characteristics that today's users seek could be summarized as follows:

- *simple* – uncluttered and 'clean' design aids user perception;

- *self-explanatory/intuitive* – naturalistic use of menus and icons reduces learning time. This is achieved by finding metaphors which help to explain real life activities through objects. The use of folders for saving files and wastepaper baskets for deleting (throwing away) files in current Microsoft Windows programs are good examples of this;

- *adaptive* – a user should be able to adjust the interface to suit his or her own level of expertise. For example, an expert user may wish to use commands rather than windows for improved user control and speed;

- *standardized* – a common look for different applications aids familiarity thus reducing learning time. This principle is often followed by commercial software developers for their applications programs;

- *transparent* – an interface should hide the complications of a task by providing tools for the most common functions;

- *creative use of colour, sound and animation* – this plays an important role in the way we perceive, remember and learn things. Computer games are good examples of the way this can be used to improve a user's ability to engage in and enjoy an application;

- *on-line help* – a well designed help program can use text, graphics and animation to provide general and context-sensitive (linked to the task in hand) help at different levels of detail to suit users with different needs. For example, many modern windows based software packages include step-by-step animated demonstrations of tasks in their help programs to provide maximum clarity of explanation.

How does this list of characteristics compare with your personal views on the qualities of a good interface?

The main ideology behind the current thinking in interface design is to make it user centred. Designing an interface is a part of software development which in turn is a part of systems design. An interface that seeks to meet its guiding principles of usability, safety and functionality is a result of an iterative process that takes a flexible approach to design and follows the principles of socio-technical or user oriented system design as described in Chapter 9.

One aspect of human computer interaction left out in the discussion so far is the physical appearance of a computer. They no longer have to come in grey shells and sit on ugly grey trolleys. Computers now reflect the way people live and work; they can be made to match the decor of a room and come with colourful keyboards, monitors and mice to liven up an office. The driving force behind the study of human computer interaction is to change the image of a computer from an unfriendly, complex machine to an everyday object of enjoyment and fun and this can only be achieved by paying attention to all aspects of computer usage. Recently some colourful and modern designs have been introduced by PC manufacturers, notably the new desktop called imac by Apple which has attracted a large amount of consumer interest.

Summary

The use of computers has been associated with a number of health and safety hazards. These range from stress caused by long sessions in front of a computer and other office equipment to possible effects of VDU radiation on human tissues. Studies have been carried out to establish the relationship between the use of computers and human health; some concerns have been proved to be justified whereas others cannot yet be proved one way or the other. However, increasing complaints by users have resulted in a number of recommendations by the Health and Safety Executive for ergonomically safe offices with regard to equipment, the working environment, the responsibilities of employers and employees and the quality of software. The effect of software design on human activities has given rise to the study of human computer interaction and a move towards software design based on the principles of usability, safety and perceived functionality. Attempts are being made to create user centred interfaces which are modelled on the way humans process information with a view to making computers a natural extension of human activities. A well designed user interface has the characteristics that make it easy to learn, use and remember as well as being flexible and enjoyable. User centred interface design is part and parcel of the current philosophies of soft systems methodology.

Further reading

Fitting the Task to the Man: An Ergonomic Approach by E. Grandjean, Taylor & Francis Ltd, 1982. Despite the some what sexist title, this book gives a general discussion of the adaptation of work conditions to the physical and psychological nature of human beings.

For a detailed look at all aspects of the design of a workstation and the working environment read *The VDT Manual* by A. Cakir, D. J. Hart and T.F.M. Stewart, published by IFRA (Inca-Fiej Research Association in Germany), no date given.

A Practical Introduction to the Human-Computer Interface by Stephen Hill, DP Publications Ltd, 1995. This book gives an overview of the theoretical and practical aspects of HCI.

Read *The Art of Human-Computer Interface Design* edited by Brenda Laurel, Addison-Wesley, 1990 for a comprehensive look at the guiding principles of interface design.

'VR: hazardous to your health? Scientists sound safety alarm over virtual reality' by Johnson, R. C. in the *Electronic Engineering Times*, 5 June 1995, p.1 is an informative article on the effect of HMD design on our health.

The article by J. Seymour mentioned on page 238 of this book gives valuable information on safety around computing.

Revision questions

1. Summarize the possible effects of the following on human health:
    (a) use of keyboards;
    (b) design of workstations;
    (c) quality of screen display;
    (d) VDU radiation;
    (e) working environment (light, atmosphere, etc.);
    (f) design of software.

2. Describe an ergonomically safe office.

3. Discuss the role of users and employers in minimizing the hazards associated with the use of computers.

4. What are the goals of a well designed user interface?

5. Discuss the main concepts which underpin the design philosophies used in creating modern graphical user interfaces.

6. What are the characteristics of a good user interface?

7. Using the above list of characteristics, assess the interface of one item of software that you use. Discuss how the design of the software affects your ability to use it.

Food for thought

CTD Resource Network, Inc. 1998–1999

Ergonomic inaction: Congress puts OSHA's ergonomics standard on hold

Vernon Mogensen

While Congress consumes itself with the impeachment and trial of the president, many Americans are becoming increasingly frustrated as the nation's policy problems go unaddressed. Of special interest is the tremendous growth of repetitive strain injuries (RSIs) among office workers using video display terminals (VDTs). RSIs affect millions of workers with workers' compensation costs estimated at $20 billion annually. When lost work time, lost productivity and retraining are factored into the equation, the total bill rises to an estimated $80 billion a year.[1] Carpal tunnel syndrome, a type of RSI, is so debilitating that it results in more lost workdays (a median of 30 days per case) than any other occupational illness. The Occupational Safety and Health Administration (OSHA) calls RSIs 'the most important occupational safety and health problem in the United States today.'[2]

According to the U.S. Bureau of Labour Statistics (BLS), the reported incidence of RSIs have skyrocketed from only 18 percent of all occupational illnesses reported in 1981 to 64 percent today. But even this dramatic growth underestimates the scope of the problem. Many cases of RSIs go unreported as workers try to 'work through the pain' in order to keep their jobs, others are not reported by employers, and BLS data does not include self-employed workers or federal, state, and local government employees.

Private industry voluntarily reported 276,600 RSI cases in 1997 [3] but OSHA put the number of RSI cases at nearly 650,000 for 1996,[4] and the American Public Health Association estimated the number at more than 775,000 cases in 1997.[5] While RSIs afflict many types of workers doing repetitive tasks from postal workers using zip code sorters to automobile assembly line workers, the biggest variable during this time span has been the introduction and widespread use of VDTs. Most VDT workers are women and the federal government has long conducted a policy of not so benign neglect towards women and office workers' health problems. The federal government's 'Invisible Woman' policy is reflected in the fact that even in this day and age of the computer, the BLS does not collect data on the incidence of RSIs among the predominantly female VDT workers. Nevertheless, OSHA acknowledges that much of the increase in RSIs since 1981 is due to the proliferation of VDTs in the workplace.[6]

With more than half of America's workforce using computers, this has become an increasingly important and politicised story. Organised labour has been pushing for regulation of the growing RSI problem since the early 1980s. In 1994, OSHA released its proposed ergonomic standard that would have required employers to re-engineer the work process to limit the amount of time workers could spend at five repetitive tasks considered RSI risk factors: doing the same motion or motion pattern; use of vibrating or impact tools; forceful hand exertions; unassisted frequent or heavy lifting; and working in fixed or awkward postures. But OSHA's work

▶

received little support from the Clinton administration, even before the President's legal problems overwhelmed the White House's policy agenda. However, the Republican controlled Congress has taken a more proactive stance in its opposition to any effort to regulate the RSI problem. While VDT workers' hands become crippled, congressional Republicans, like majority whip Tom Delay (Republican, Texas), have put their faith in the invisible hand of the free market. When the Republicans took power in Congress in 1995 for the first time in forty years, Delay, whose Houston-based pest control company was fined by OSHA, put the safety agency's proposed ergonomics standard at the top of his party's regulatory hit list. In the hopes of saving some semblance of an ergonomics standard, OSHA voluntarily narrowed the scope of its proposal to apply only to workplaces where two workers were diagnosed with the same type of RSIs within a year of each other (the original proposal would have applied to a broader range of workplaces).

But Delay, whose nickname in business circles is 'Mr. Dereg,' was not to be placated; OSHA must be punished for 'flouting the will of this Congress,' he said. House colleague Cass Ballenger (Republican, North Carolina) seconded Delay's sentiments and displayed his disregard of the issue when he proclaimed: 'no one ever died of ergonomics.'[7] Punishment came in the form of Congress prohibiting OSHA from conducting research on the RSI standard, and cutting its already meagre budget by close to $20 million to preclude any possibility of the safety agency's interfering with the movement of the invisible hand.[8] However, supporters of the ergonomic standard won a surprising victory in 1996 with help from an unexpected source. Thirty-four moderate House Republicans committed the heresy of voting with the Democratic minority to permit OSHA to resume work on its proposed ergonomic standard. They were emboldened to cross the aisle by virtue of the fact that they held unsafe seats in an election year, and by then House Speaker's Newt Gingrich's declining popularity in the wake of his ethics violations and his embarrassing efforts to shutdown the federal government. But don't expect Congress to permit OSHA to promulgate its ergonomics standard just yet; the National Association of Manufacturers formed the National Coalition of Ergonomics, an imposing alliance of over 300 corporations and trade associations, just to oppose any such eventuality. Congressional Republicans are holding up the ergonomics standard asserting that OSHA lacks a scientific basis to proceed, despite the fact that the review of the literature they asked the National Academy of Sciences to prepare came to the contrary conclusion.[9]

The fight to have the ergonomics standard cover VDT workers (at present it focuses on manufacturing, construction and assembly line workers) represents the battle within the battle. This battle to include protections for VDT workers has been going on since OSHA first acceded to organised labour's calls for an ergonomics standard in 1990. The Republicans' laissez faire approach dovetails nicely with computer manufacturers, represented by the Computer and Business Equipment Manufacturers Association and a host of Fortune 500 corporations that rely heavily on VDTs. Since organised labour and women's groups like 9 to 5: The National Association of Working Women first proposed regulations in the early 1980s, corporate interests have pursued a strategy of redefining the VDT health and safety crisis (which, of course also includes vision, stress, reproductive and other health problems) as a little more than an employee 'comfort' problem that government bureaucrats best leave to employers to deal with on a voluntary basis. Their strategy has been successful in large part because it resonates so strongly with the individualist, 'get the government off my back,' philosophy that has been prevalent in American society since the 1980s.

Computer manufacturers received a major assist in opposing VDT regulation from the corporately owned major print and electronic media. The newspaper industry was one of the first industries to convert to VDT use, and the American Newspaper Publishers Association, which fought some intense battles with the Newspaper Guild during the 1970s, encouraged its members to downplay VDT stories. There were cases of outright censorship of VDT stories, but more commonly the major media just ignored it altogether. This latter strategy, much more subtle and successful than censorship, grew to such proportions that it prompted the media watchdog publication, *The Columbia Journalism Review* to publish an article entitled: 'VDTs: The Overlooked Story Right in the Newsroom.' This approach gave corporate interests the advantage of defining what the VDT debate was about and gave them the political momentum when organised labour called for regulation.

Federal and state government officials have been reluctant to regulate information industries that are seen as the engines of growth (i.e., a major source of new jobs and tax revenue) in the post-industrial economy.[10]

The labour movement has been in a state of steady decline, losing its predominantly male, blue collar membership as its base in manufacturing shrank since the 1950s. Labour unions, which long ignored the plight of women workers, were slow to organise the predominantly female office workforce. The majority of VDT workers are women in low-paying, non-unionised, dead-end jobs – increasing prospects for safe and healthful workplaces for those who work with VDTs in unorganised settings depends largely on the labour movement's ability and willingness to relate to the problems facing this post-industrial workforce.

Congress should permit OSHA to promulgate its ergonomics standard, and allow it to include provisions to protect VDT workers. But in order for safety and health regulations to be effective, workers must be included in the drafting process. Not only do they have first hand experience with the problems that many so-called 'experts' lack, but studies show that workers are more likely to follow regulations that they had a hand in crafting.

Roger Stephens, OSHA's chief ergonomist, has found that VDT workers are more likely to follow ergonomic instructions if they are included in their preparation.[11]

Finally, workers – especially office workers – are forced to check many of their democratic rights at the door when they enter the workplace. Worker participation is a means of promoting both safety and health rights and the practice of participatory democracy. Larry Hirschhorn argues that workers must be given greater responsibility in the postindustrial workplace. Since no manager or planner can anticipate all the problems that will occur in the work process, this includes the necessity that workers be free to learn from their mistakes. These 'control system failures,' as he calls them, not only create more productive and stimulated workers, but 'may help to bring out in the culture a developmental concept of the self, a concept that leads people to seek out learning opportunities throughout their lives.'[12] Carole Pateman states 'that it is possible for the authority structure in industry to be considerably modified, for workers to exercise almost complete control over their jobs and to participate in a wide range of decision making, without any loss in productive efficiency.'[13] She adds that giving employees a voice in workplace decision making contributes to a greater feeling of efficacy on their part in the political arena. This ▶

point is reinforced by Benjamin Barber who states that a strong civic democracy depends on the development of workplace democracy: 'The sharing of decision-making by workers and management . . . not only serve economic egalitarianism but foster civic spirit.'[14] These recommendations have implications that go beyond the prevention of occupational safety and health hazards to the very relationship between capitalism, work and democracy. Taken as a whole, they implicitly challenge traditional, hierarchical assumptions about the organisation of work, and, in effect, recommend greater workers' participation in the postindustrial workplace.

Vernon Mogensen is Assistant Professor of Political Science at Kingsborough Community College, The City University of New York, in Brooklyn, NY, 11235. He has written extensively on the public policy implications of RSIs and other health and safety issues, and is the author of Office Politics: Computers, Labour, and the Fight for Safety and Health (*Rutgers University Press*).

Notes

1. Charles N. Jeffries, Assistant Secretary for Occupational Safety and Health, speech to National Coalition on Ergonomics, Washington, D.C., April 29, 1999.
2. Quoted in Marvin J. Dainoff, 'The Illness of the Decade,' *Computerworld*, April 13, 1992, 27.
3. U.S. Department of Labor, Bureau of Labor Statistics, *Workplace Injuries and Illnesses in 1993, 1994; and Illnesses by type of illness – rates, numbers, and percent – 1993–1997*, December 1998.
4. Statement of Charles N. Jeffries, Assistant Secretary for Occupational Safety and Health, speech to National Coalition on Ergonomics, Washington, D.C., March 4, 1999.
5. American Public Health Association, Press Release, 'Leading Public Health Scientists Urge Congress to Allow OSHA to Develop Safe Workplace Standard,' Washington, D.C., July 11, 1997.
6. See the testimony of Lawrence J. Fine, M.D., Director, Division of Surveillance, Hazard Evaluations, and Field Studies, NIOSH, in House of Representatives, Committee on Government Operations, Dramatic Rise in Repetitive Motion Injuries and OSHA's Response: Hearing before the Employment and Housing Subcommittee, 101st Cong., 1st sess., June 6, 1989, 116. Also the BLS verified that they do not keep data on VDT-related CTDs, telephone interview with Larry Drake, July 19, 1990. Peter T. Kilborn, 'Rise in Worker Injuries Is Laid to the Computer,' *New York Times*, November 16, 1989, A24. For more on the federal government's 'Invisible Woman' policy, see Vernon L. Mogensen, *Office Politics: Computers, Labour, and the Fight for Safety and Health* (Rutgers University Press, 1996), 76–79.
7. Quoted in Frank Swoboda, 'OSHA to Defy House Ban With New Workplace Rules,' *Washington Post*, March 20, 1995, A1.
8. Quoted in Cindy Skrzycki, 'OSHA Abandons Rules on Repetitive Injury; Opposition by GOP, Business Cited,' *Washington Post*, June 13, 1995, D1.
9. National Academy of Sciences, *Work-Related Musculoskeletal Disorders* (Washington, D.C.: National Academy Press, 1999).
10. Jeff Sorensen and Jon Swan, 'VDT's: The Overlooked Story Right in the Newsroom,' *Columbia Journalism Review*, January/February 1981, 32–38. See also, 'The VDT Story: Why We Stick With It,' *Columbia Journalism Review*, November/December 1984, 19.
11. 'Adapt Work Stations to Workers' Needs, Experts Encourage Industrial Hygienists,' *Occupational Safety and Health Reporter*, November 5, 1986, 599–600.

12. Larry Hirschhorn, *Beyond Mechanization: Work and Technology in a Postindustrial Age* (Cambridge, MA: MIT Press, 1986), 4.

13. Carole Pateman, *Participation and Democratic Theory* (Cambridge, U.K.: Cambridge University Press, 1970), 62.

14. Benjamin R. Barber, *Strong Democracy: Participatory Democracy for a New Age* (Berkeley, University of California Press, 1984), 305.

Discussion questions

1. Search for information on reported cases of RSI in countries outside the USA. How does the information compare with the statistics quoted in the article and what does this demonstrate?

2. As the article states, most cases of RSI remain unreported because employees feel intimidated in various ways. What can they do to overcome this?

3. Find out how computer users in the UK have been dealing with the problem of RSI.

4. Discuss and critically review the author's views on why RSI has not yet been recognized as a serious issue for VDT users.

5. How can we proceed to change the situation?

CHAPTER 11

Security of computer systems

Objectives

At the end of this chapter you should have some understanding of:

▶ the security hazards related to a computer system;
▶ how computerized data can threaten individual privacy;
▶ the steps organizations and individuals can take to minimize the risks.

Introduction

Maintaining security is a major consideration for any business system. Hazards associated with the physical security of the components of a system are relatively easy to envisage and therefore not difficult to safeguard against; in the same way, computer hardware can be made secure by following well established procedures. However, the security of electronic data is more difficult to handle because it is not visible to the human eye and any damage done to it is not instantly detectable.

Whereas loss or theft in any business has obvious consequences, computer systems are unique in that they often hold personal data on individuals; inadequate security means inadequate privacy for those people. In this chapter we are going to discuss the main reasons for the loss or theft of computer equipment and data and what can be done to minimize the risks. We will also look at how lack of security can contribute to loss of privacy.

What can go wrong with computer systems

Damage to computer systems can be placed in two categories: accidental and intentional.

Accidental damage

Although the threat from criminal activity has dominated public discussions on security, a large amount of data and equipment are damaged by accident due to inadequate physical safeguards. Natural disasters such as fire and flood can cause unlimited damage and power failures can destroy ongoing work. Also, incorrect data entered at the input stage or undiscovered errors in a computer program can produce unreliable information. Such errors are difficult to deal with because they may not affect the output for a long time. When they do, however, they can create panic and take a long time to locate.

Intentional damage

Although a computer system consists of expensive items, theft of equipment for its resale value is only a small part of computer crime (although theft of chips has become common). It is also relatively easy to deal with by utilizing the safety measures applicable to any piece of equipment used in business systems, for example the safeguarding of locations, insurance cover, and so on. The growing problem for computer systems is in the security of information. In a study carried out in North America in 1994, 82% of the companies surveyed said that information risks were increasing at least as fast as their computing resources resulting in many companies losing large amounts of money (Buckler, *Newsbytes*, 21 Dec. 1994). Although the survey included natural disasters as well as computer crimes, the majority of losses were due to inappropriate access to information. This may be an employee in an organization using his or her legitimate rights of access to pass on information to third parties, an individual or an organization tampering with computer programs, or a hacker getting into a computer system illegally to cause damage.

As computer systems become increasingly powerful, the sophistication of the techniques used to break into them is growing accordingly, forcing many IT managers to address the question of security. Before we can discuss how security may be improved we need to understand what can go wrong with computer systems and why organizations become victims of computer related crimes.

Find examples of damage done to computer systems by fraudulent activities.

Techniques used to invade a computer system

Computer crime is often committed by the employees within an organization. People can use their legitimate rights of access for illegitimate purposes, such as passing information on to external interested parties, or altering information for personal gain. An example of this is the case of two bank employees (reported in the news a few years ago) who altered a computer program that calculated interest payable to customers. Instead of rounding the last pennies up in certain calculations, the employees made the program round them down and transfer the difference to their own accounts. The difference this made to each customer's total balance was unnoticeable, but when accumulated from a large number of customers added up to a considerable sum. This continued until other staff noticed the frequent withdrawal of large amounts from their accounts and became suspicious.

Cases of employees setting up 'Trojan horses' have also been heard of. This is when someone writes a program to imitate the screen display for entering a system. When users try to use it to log in (in vain), the procedures result in writing the user ID to a file which is later used by the culprit to gain access. Organized software piracy is another common offence: this happens when an organization buys software from a company and re-engineers it to claim it as its own.

Can you find some examples of damage done to a company's computer system by employees of that company? What methods did they use?

Outsiders can gain access to a computer system by somehow acquiring a password, perhaps from an employee of the organization who could be an unsuspecting friend or a disgruntled member of staff. There are also examples of outsiders collecting vital information on computer systems, including lists of passwords, which have been left carelessly in easily accessible places.

Another way that access can be gained is by guessing at passwords (because people often make very predictable choices), by using the access to one network to get into others (for example, the Internet), or by watching someone logging in. One publicized case was that of a gang of people who took photographs of the hand movements of cashpoint users and then used the information to deduce their pin codes. Companies that outsource their computer operations (employ another organization to run their system) are often vulnerable. For example, the outsourcing supplier may run a client's database on a computer connected to the Internet, which makes it vulnerable to hacking. There have also been cases of hackers being hired by large organizations determined to gain access to vital information on rival companies: this makes it very difficult to trace culprits.

Find some recent examples of hacking. What damage did they do to the computer system?

The most high profile crime against computer systems is that of electronic vandalism. This occurs when outsiders (hackers) access computer systems illegally with an intention to steal or damage data. Their motives vary: sometimes it is the challenge of simply being able to break into a system; sometimes it is for personal gain such as blackmailing an organization or selling information to third parties. For a number of years hackers have been active in introducing viruses to computer systems. A virus is a program stored on a floppy disk which when used on a system can access other programs and corrupt them. It is called a virus because it can copy itself into the programs it attacks, which then become virus programs themselves. Often this is merely a nuisance which, with good data back-up policies, can be adequately dealt with. Also anti-virus programs have been written that can detect a virus on a disk before it can attack the system. However, there have been cases of more harmful viruses which affect programs, sometimes on preset dates, and halt the working of large systems.

Have you experienced the phenomenon of virus attack? How did this happen and what did you do to get over it?

The root of the problem

Companies are often reluctant to report computer crimes because of the concern they might invoke amongst customers and business partners. In spite of this, there was a 183% increase in the number of reported crimes between 1990 and 1993, according to a report published by the Computer Audit Commission in 1994. Further reports since then reflect a continual deterioration of the situation. This shows that even in the face of such a growing problem managers are not doing enough towards security. The greatest threat comes from easy access to computer systems which leads to the problem of information getting into the wrong hands. Studies made by the Audit Commission have shown that the main impediment to combating abuse of information has been the lack of awareness amongst users and the lack of procedures for internal audit. Many organizations do not have an understanding of the role of formal policies on internal audit and risk analysis procedures. Traditionally, many of them have depended on the security procedures built into network software and have trusted those employees with supervisory access rights to the network. It has been proven by the Audit Commission report that only 15% of the total amount of computer abuse comes from external break-ins; the rest is rooted in the organizations themselves. High turnover of IT staff has been stated as one of the main problems.

In recent years hackers have become a serious problem. It is very difficult to catch the culprits because the virus programs they introduce often affect a system afterwards. In fact, very few hacking incidents get reported and even fewer of the hackers get caught. According to the San Francisco based Computer Security Institute (CSI), only about 17% of companies report hacking incidents because of the fear of adverse publicity, copycat hacking and loss of customer confidence (Didio, L., *Computerworld*, 27 April 1998, p.6).[1] Out of those reported cases, normally an infinitesimal number of those responsible are caught. Hacking has only recently become a criminal offence but that has not deterred experienced hackers. A few years ago hacking used to be a pastime for whizzkids; now the offenders have become smarter and more financially motivated. Some companies now hire experienced hackers to test their systems for security and, in some cases, for reasons of industrial espionage, and a number of grown-up hackers have found respectable careers as security consultants. Although in some cases

---

1   The full report of a study carried out in March 1998 by the CSI in conjunction with the FBI is available on the website http://www.gocsi.com

hacking needs a high degree of technical skill, hackers also depend on the ignorance and lack of awareness of the users of data. Some hackers have been known to collect all the information they need to get into a computer system from the wastepaper bins in offices. This proves the importance of paying attention to simple routine precautionary measures as well as maintaining security at a more technical level.

What is your experience of the behaviour of computer users in relation to the safety of a computer system?

Even after a number of well publicized cases of theft and fraud, many companies fail to recognize the seriousness of the problem. Some have suggested the following reasons for this:

- Many managers are not directly involved in the handling of data and, as a result, do not relate to the risks of data loss or damage.
- Many computer systems are left in the hands of a few technical people thus giving a limited number of employees too much power over technology.
- The benefits of security measures are not tangible and are therefore difficult to justify – especially to managers with non-technical backgrounds.

How to make a system secure

The UK Department of Trade and Industry and the European Commission use the following criteria as the measure of a computer system's security:

- **Confidentiality** – Is the system able to prevent unauthorized disclosure of information?
- **Integrity** – Is the system able to prevent unauthorized alteration of data?
- **Availability** – Is the system able to prevent unauthorized withholding of data, information or resources?

These qualities ensure that correct and up to date information is available to authorized users but is out of the reach of anyone else.

So, how do we safeguard our computer systems? The most important criterion for security is also the simplest: limited physical access to computer equipment and data. This involves such measures as restricting access to computer rooms by anyone other than those with permission; using electronic locks; keeping disks and other removable hardware in safe locations; limiting the extent of hard (printed) copies of data and ensuring that any such copies are destroyed when no longer required; spot checks in computer rooms, and so on. In addition, the following measures can be taken to minimize the risk of loss or damage.

Backing-up data

Back-up copies of files should be made at regular intervals to limit damage caused by systems malfunction and power failures, and duplicate copies of disks should be kept in a disaster-proof safe.

Keeping a secondary provision

Some large organizations have fault-tolerant systems consisting of duplicate hardware, software and power supply. The secondary system maintains background processing and, in case of failure, control is automatically passed on to the secondary system. Damage caused by the loss of power supply can be limited by installing an uninterrupted power supply (UPS), a secondary source of power which takes over only if the main supply fails. UPS can maintain the system for long enough to close the running jobs properly without loss of data.

Setting up disaster recovery procedures

Some companies provide back-up computer services to subscribing client organizations. They either run critical systems in parallel as a back-up for their clients so important jobs have a duplicate output or establish a system whereby processing is passed on to the servicing company during an emergency.

Setting up control

Formal procedures set up to avoid errors are called controls: these are measures incorporated in computer programs and operations to ensure that all errors are trapped before they can affect processing. Amongst common controls against accidental damage are the following:

● thorough testing of the programs before a live run;
● procedures to check for data entry errors;

- codes used in programs to trap invalid data, such as 30 February for a date or 10 for the age of an employee;
- facilities for audit trails throughout the system; these are procedures which allow one to trace the complete path of a system;
- the use of computer readable input media (data entry at source as described in Chapter 3) to minimize manual data entry;
- the use of regular checkpoints during processing to verify the consistency of data.

It is not enough to establish the procedures at the beginning of a new computer system; it is of vital importance that they are maintained throughout its life cycle. It may also be necessary to review the effectiveness of the procedures at regular intervals and update them when necessary.

Interview an IT manager of your university or place of work. How many of the above safety measures are followed by your organization?

Most organizations are aware of the steps to be taken to prevent accidental damage. How successful they are in making their systems secure depends on the awareness of the IT managers and the success of the IT departments in maintaining security procedures.

Keeping data and information out of reach of hackers is more difficult. Access to networks is the main concern of security experts because most hacking takes place via networked systems. In a report published in 1995 the Computer Security Institute recommended the following steps for maintaining the safety of network systems (*PC Week*, 25 April 1995):

1. Insist that users choose alphanumeric passwords (a mixture of letters and numbers) rather than just alphabetic thus making them difficult to guess.

2. Install anti-virus software in both servers and workstations.

3. Use encryption software to scramble data sent via a network which is unscrambled at the receiving end. Following complaints about the use of the Internet by individuals and groups for improper purposes (as discussed in Chapter 8), much debate has been going on on the role of encryption in the security of electronic data communication. Read the article mentioned in the Futher reading section for more information on encryption.

4. Monitor remote access by limiting access time and duration.

5. Put firewalls in place before allowing Internet access. Firewalls are electronic barriers designed to insulate an organization's internal systems from external networks.

6. Install access control programs and physical security devices on all mobile systems. Access control programs run extra checks on users before allowing access. Physical security devices include biometric scanning devices fitted to a computer which check a user's face, retina, fingerprint, hand, voice, typing rhythm, signature, and so on, against a set of stored data for all legitimate users.

7. Check security logs and audit trails regularly.

8. Conduct a thorough risk analysis of the system.

9. Develop and enforce comprehensive security policies.

10. Eliminate disk drives from network terminals in order to prevent the spread of viruses.

As mentioned above, some organizations hire security experts (who are sometimes ex-hackers) as consultants and allow them to try to break into their systems. Also, various electronic devices are now available to secure networks, for example, 'smart badges' containing infrared transmitters to be carried by all users. Sensors in all computer rooms keep tabs on where people are and give only legitimate users access to their nearest terminals which are automatically configured to their personal preferences and set according to their previous log-in. When the user walks out of the room the terminal shuts down.

   How many of the above steps are taken by the organization you surveyed?

As the dangers to data security increase, so new safeguard devices and methods are invented. However, no system can be made 100% safe. One of the reasons for this is that most danger comes from the users within organizations. And with the increasing sophistication of security related technology, the knowledge and innovativeness of hackers improves as well. Organizations need managers who believe in the importance of IT security and users who are made to understand the need for following security procedures. However, various regulations are now in effect to safeguard users and punish those who misuse electronic data.

The Computer Misuse Act

The Computer Misuse Act (CMA) was introduced in 1989/90 to tackle the problem of crimes such as hacking and the misuse of computerized data. Under this act it is an offence for a person to perform any function with the intent of securing unauthorized access to any program or data held on a computer. The law covers the misuse of data accessed via any type of computer or even bank cash dispensers. It also covers data obtained by using a legal password, thus trying to prevent the misuse of data by employees in an organization. However, although the introduction of the act has made it easier to punish a proven hacker, very few people have been prosecuted because of the difficulty in catching the guilty persons.

Using articles in newspapers, magazines and on the Internet, find some examples of cases of culprits who have been caught and punished for computer misuse.

Privacy of data

Most of us are used to getting junk mail from organizations we have never contacted ourselves: where do they get our names and addresses from? When we buy a new car on hire purchase our credit worthiness is checked by the dealer: how do they assess our situation? If we are stopped by the police for a traffic offence, they can run an instant check on our driving record. It is obvious that data on us is held by many organizations and others can get access to it by using a few key facts such as our name and address, national insurance number, credit card number, car registration number and so on. They can use any one of these to search large centralized databases to receive a variety of information on us.

So, who are the main holders of personal data on individuals? Normally they are banks and building societies, credit card companies, the Inland Revenue, our employers, doctors, the Department of Social Security and the DLVA office (which deals with our car registrations and driving licences), because we have to supply them with information to get the services they provide. It is possible for other organizations to access such data either by tapping into other's systems illegally, or because the holders pass it on. Now, with the widespread use of the Internet, nearly all networks can be connected to each other, thus making it easier for one organization to acquire information from another.

This raises the question of privacy. Almost anyone with access to a large network and some technical know-how can acquire data on other people. This amounts to an invasion of an individual's right to privacy when personal data held for a particular purpose is passed on to someone else, used for a different purpose or becomes inaccurate. To safeguard data subjects (those on whom data is stored) from such invasion the Data Protection Act (DPA) was introduced in 1984.

Think of some more examples of the use of centralized databases by service providers.

The Data Protection Act

The UK Data Protection Act of 1984 provides rights for individuals and regulates the way computerized information is stored and used. The act also brought the data protection laws in this country in line with Europe, thus allowing the free flow of data between countries. The act is administered by the Data Protection Registrar, an independent officer who reports directly to parliament. It concerns 'personal data' that is 'automatically processed' meaning data on individuals held on and processed by computers. With a few exceptions, anyone holding personal data on computers must register with the Data Protection Registrar. Failure to do this is a criminal offence and can attract a fine of up to £5000 in a Magistrates court and, in exceptional cases, an unlimited amount in a Criminal court. The registrar has the power to investigate whether or not a data user is registered. By 1995 there were 180,000 entries in the DP register, which seems a very low number given that there are 900,000 limited companies and 2.5 million other businesses in the UK (*PC Pro*, Sept, 1995). The reason suggested for this is that the resources available to the registrar are too limited to investigate cases of non-registration.

The data protection (DP) register, which is available for inspection at no cost, contains data users' (those who collect, use and control data on others) names and addresses together with broad descriptions of:

- the data held;
- purposes for which the data can be used;
- the sources from which information can be obtained;
- the people to whom information can be disclosed;
- any overseas countries or territories to which data may be transferred.

There are eight principles of good practice that data users must comply with. They are:

1. Data must be obtained and processed 'fairly' and 'lawfully'. This means that the data holder can only take data from those who are entitled to have it and/or are required to supply it by law, for example, those holding the electoral list.

2. Data must only be held for specific purposes, which must be the ones for which the data user has registered. Thus, a bank must not hold data which is not related to its customers' financial affairs.

3. Data must only be used for the purpose for which it has been registered. For example, a bank must not use its data on customers to obtain information on how much money they spend on holidays.

4. Personal data must be adequate, relevant and 'not excessive' for the purpose registered. Thus, it is an offence for a bank to hold data on the political affiliations of its customers.

5. Data must be accurate and, where necessary, kept up to date.

6. Data must not be kept for longer than necessary.

7. Data must be made available, on request, to data subjects in a form that they can understand, within a reasonable period of time and at reasonable cost. Individuals are entitled to have data corrected or erased where appropriate.

8. Appropriate security measures must be taken against unauthorized access, alteration, accidental loss or deliberate destruction.

These principles refer to information about people and not on organizations. Data subjects, on making a written request, are entitled to be supplied with a copy of any information held on them. An individual can appeal to the DP tribunal if he or she considers that breaches of principles have occurred. The DP registrar can then investigate the data users and, if necessary, serve them with notice to take appropriate corrective action. Failure to respond to this constitutes a criminal offence and also leads to a deregistration of the offender. However, very few cases have been taken to the tribunal (fewer than 12 in over 10 years according to *PC Pro*, September 1995). This is mainly because the principles are so broad and imprecise that it is difficult to prove an offence. For example, it is very difficult to prove how much data is 'adequate' or what constitutes 'appropriate' security. Another reason for the low rate of prosecution is that although the registrar has a duty to consider any complaints, he or she has no powers to initiate an investigation of registered data users nor the ability to enforce payment of compensation to data subjects.

Data subjects are entitled to seek compensation if it is proven that damage has been caused. However, it is up to them to exercise their rights. Because most of the general public are not aware of how privacy is invaded and what they can do about it, most cases of improper use of data remain unnoticed.

What, in your view, are the main reasons for there being so few reported cases?

Exemptions from the DPA

The situation is also made difficult by exemptions from the DPA which free many data holders of the restrictions of the act. Organizations holding personal data under certain conditions are not obliged to register with the Data Protection Registrar and are thus exempt from the DPA. These are:

1. All records held in the cause of national security.
2. Personal data held only for accounting and payroll purposes.
3. A small amount of personal data (usually names and addresses) for mailing lists held with the permission of the data subjects.
4. Data held solely for domestic and leisure purposes, for example for sports, social or leisure clubs.
5. Personal data which is required to be made public, for example data on the electoral register or a company list of shareholders.
6. Data held for the purposes of preventing or detecting crime. This allows the police, tax and immigration authorities almost unlimited power to hold and use personal data.
7. All data held in a 'manual' form, for example handwritten or typewritten on cards or paper.

In October 1992, the Commission for the European Communities published a general European Directive in an attempt to bring the data protection laws in EU countries into line with each other. However, this still did not eliminate some of the anomalies of the UK DPA, for example, the exemption of non-computerized data. In 1995 the EU ruled that all member states should adopt the EU directive on data protection by October 1998. Only a handful of member states actually met the deadline. Although a revised version agreed by the Commission to close some loopholes was expected to become law by 1999, this has not yet been achieved in the UK.

What do you feel about the above exceptions and why?

Summary

A computer system needs to be protected against damage caused by accident as well as criminal activity. The damage can be of two kinds: loss or theft of the physical components and the misuse of data. Although complete security cannot be guaranteed, steps can be taken to minimize the risks. Routine precautionary measures and good user habits can improve security by a considerable amount; formal procedures and controls built into computer systems are required for the rest. Managers in an organization need to understand the importance of security and devote resources to safeguard equipment and data.

Many organizations hold personal data on individuals. Lack of security can lead to the misuse of such data and consequently the invasion of privacy for its owners. The Data Protection Act attempts to regulate the way data is obtained, held and used and gives the DP registrar the power to investigate when breaches are considered to have been made. This law is not perfect and the resources given to the registrar are limited. However, revisions of the legislation introduced recently may close some of the loopholes.

Further reading

Computer Viruses and Anti-virus Warfare by Jan Hruska, Ellis Horwood, 1992 gives basic information on how a virus is introduced into a PC, how to eliminate/avoid them and so on.

Computer Security Solutions by J. Hruska and K. M. Jackson, Blackwell, 1990 includes a thorough coverage of the security of stand-alone as well as networked systems.

A set of booklets published (and updated when necessary) by the Data Protection Registrar called *Data Protection Act 1984* give the guidelines on the various aspects of DPA.

An article by Bill Machrone in *PC Magazine*, 14 June 1994, p.87, discusses encryption is some detail.

There are many articles in magazines and on the Internet on security and privacy. Look at *Computer Select*, the CD-ROM of computing publications, and on the Internet for information and discussion of these topics.

An article by John Lamidey in *PC Pro*, September 1995, p.173 discusses the weaknesses of the Data Protection Act well.

The articles mentioned on page 257 by Buckler and on page 260 by Didio give valuable information on security of data.

Revision questions

1. Discuss the ways in which a computer system can be damaged.

2. What are the main reasons behind computer crimes?

3. Describe some of the techniques commonly used by vandals and hackers to steal or damage data.

4. How can computer systems be secured against accidental loss or damage?

5. How can a computer system be protected against vandals and hackers?

6. Discuss how our privacy may be invaded by computerized data.

7. Discuss the role of the Data Protection Act in fighting to maintain privacy of data subjects.

8. Discuss the weaknesses of the above act and suggest ways to overcome them.

9. Using examples from your own experiences, discuss how modern day living contributes to data on us being easily available to others.

10. Discuss how the lack of awareness of computer users, data holders and data subjects can contribute towards the invasion of individual privacy in the situations mentioned above.

Food for thought

Computer Weekly, 18 June 1998, p.38(1)
Reed Business Publishing Ltd (UK)

They want to be safe

David Bicknell

The issue of Internet privacy is shaping up to be the biggest IT headache of the future, with different countries and continents failing to agree on a common standard.

Justice Louis Brandeis' landmark definition of privacy was delivered in 1928, but it is no less relevant in the Internet era: 'The right to be left alone – the most comprehensive of rights, and the right most valued by a free people.'

Our privacy is significantly under threat and it is this, rather than the issue of security, that could prove to be the real thorn in everyone's sides. According to some academics, intelligent highway systems like the Internet are creating an all-seeing society – something akin to a circular arrangement of prison cells – with the guards' tower set at the centre of the circle, allowing them to see what goes on in every cell.

Last week, the US Federal Trade Commission issued a devastating report on industries' efforts at privacy self-regulation of their Web sites, disclosing their information collection policies and the safeguards for users.

The report pointed to a complete disregard for privacy. Only 14% of Web sites polled disclosed their security policies, with little improvement between any of the industries surveyed which included retail, financial services and health.

The move sparked condemnation from the White House, which accused the industries of a lack of leadership. A further report is now being prepared for the White House and a privacy summit will be held at the end of the month to thrash out the issues, chaired by vice-president Al Gore.

Conflicting views

Meanwhile another problem has emerged: a conflict between the US view of personal privacy, and the more stringent one adopted in Europe.

At the heart of this is a European directive on privacy, first approved in 1995 and due to come into force in October, under which European member states have to bring into line their various national policies.

The problem for the US is that not only does the directive toughen liabilities, it also gives them a global reach. According to the Forrester research group, data identifying any individual gathered from any equipment in European Union territory is covered by the directive. So US firms must comply or risk a lawsuit in Europe.

A number of Asian countries, including Japan, are likely to adopt the European measures, which have strict protection of personal data, such as basic demographics, race, politics, finances, religion and health. This leaves American corporations wanting to trade in Europe having to adopt privacy standards they are not used to at home, and needing to take into account the differences in individual countries.

▶

The prospect has not gone down well with some, who feel Europe should adopt the US system, not vice-versa.

In summary, the European directive seeks to accomplish a series of policy objectives regarding users' personal privacy protection. For example, companies with an international presence must ensure that personal data on the Internet is:

- processed fairly and lawfully
- collected and processed for specified, explicit legitimate purpose
- accurate and current
- kept no longer than deemed necessary to fulfil the stated purpose.

Also included are user rights to:

- access
- correction, erasure, or blocking of information
- object to usage
- oppose automated individual decision
- judicial remedy and compensation.

Equally, before transferring information, companies must ensure an 'adequate' level of protection in the recipient country. The only exceptions are consent by the user; a contract with the user; information that is in the public interest; or legal claims.

Adaptability

Forrester believes that although privacy protection will be a burden for most Web sites, requiring major revisions of their transaction processes, those that adapt to the more rigorous demands will see increased traffic in the long term.

It also believes Europe's radical approach to privacy could ultimately help its Net economy, bringing more unified approach, which will satisfy the public's privacy concerns notably in states such as Sweden and Germany. This will contrast with the various, though worthy, privacy initiatives being adopted by disparate US pressure groups such as Truste, and the Direct Marketing Association.

In fact, the poor state of US efforts at self-regulation of privacy – an approach generally favoured by the Clinton administration and enshrined in its Framework for Global Electronic Commerce – has already prompted many observers, like the Electronic Privacy Information Centre, to recommend direct government action.

The approach is backed by the public, if recent research information is to be believed. In a survey carried out for Louis Harris/Westin last year, of those not currently using the Internet, 52% said they would be more likely to start if the privacy of their personal information and communications could be protected.

In addition, of 1,000 users questioned, more than half said they were concerned the Web sites they visit could be linked to their E-mail address and disclosed to third parties without their consent.

On the issue of cookies – a file transferred to your computer's hard drive which enables a Web site to track your activities – 87% of Net users surveyed said such Web sites with cookies should identify themselves and obtain users' permission before placing the identifier.

There is a flip side to this. If you visit a greengrocer's shop regularly, and the shop assistants notice what you buy, the next time you visit they may point our some particularly delicious apples to you. So they have made a point of personalising your trip to the store. In their equivalent good use on the Web, cookies can be morally permissible. But not when they generate information that leads to advertisements tracking your progress across the Web.

The problem with most of these privacy instances is that you could argue the Internet is a public place, and you can only expect reasonable privacy there. The argument has a long way to run yet!

Guide to online privacy

- Read the privacy policy of individual Web sites
- Check that it has an opt-out which allows you to prevent solicitation or sharing of personal information with third parties
- Guard your password and don't give it to anyone online who asks for it
- If performing credit card transactions via your browser, check for icons, such as unbroken keys or closed padlocks, which depict the secure transmission of data. If you do not see the icons, consider avoiding making the transaction
- Check software suppliers for any tools that will provide an additional layer of privacy protection. Examples include cookie cutters or anonymisers
- Use discretion in the data you give out. If you would not give out personal information to a stranger in the offline world, adopt the same safe guards in online.

Discussion questions

1. What are the privacy risks for users of the Internet?

2. Why is it necessary for different countries to agree on a common standard for privacy on the Internet?

3. What do you think industries can do by self-regulation to improve the privacy of the users of their websites?

4. What could be the problems for industries if the European Directives became law?

5. Surf the Internet to find out what functions are performed by a 'cookie'.

6. Some would argue that it is not always possible to follow the 'Guide to online privacy' given in the article. What do you think are the reasons behind such perception?

7. How could an employer or an organization encourage people to follow the guidelines?

CHAPTER 12

Computerization of our society

Objectives

At the end of this chapter you should have some understanding of:

▶ how the proliferation of information technology affects our lives in general;
▶ how different groups of people are specifically affected;
▶ some controversial social issues surrounding the use of computers.

Introduction

Thirty years ago, science fiction writers dreamed that by the turn of the century we should all live in a fully automated world with large display screens, control buttons and flashing lights on machines we could talk to. Judging by the science fiction films of today, soon we ought to be able to move between times and planets all dressed up the same way in an integrated world where men and women of all races participate equally in matters of interplanetary communications.

This vision, if and when it becomes a reality, brings many questions to mind. Although we have not yet reached the stage predicted, technology exists to fulfil at least some of the dreams of the authors. What we cannot do in reality we can achieve in the virtual world of simulation. We can cross gender and racial barriers on the Internet; disabled people can take part in simulated adventures in equal partnership with others; and we can fulfil our fantasies on a computer screen.

Every aspect of our lives is influenced by computers. At home, we are surrounded by electronic gadgetry with advanced microprocessors controlling their functions. We can work, shop, bank and entertain ourselves without leaving home; at work we can communicate and hold meetings without leaving the office. Highly sophisticated software giving us the benefits of artificial intelligence and virtual reality combined with worldwide communications networks have made the world a small place. But what are the real long term consequences? Are there differences in the way the IT revolution affects the lives of different people? Are there issues of ethics and justice that should concern us?

There are many conflicting ways in which information technology affects our lives: in this chapter we will look at these conflicts and address the concerns and hopes expressed by people over recent years.

The opposing effects of information technology

The diffusion of information technology has aroused views from two opposite quarters – the optimists and the pessimists. The optimists suggest that information technology is the key to future prosperity and well-being; the pessimists, on the other hand, argue that it creates further divisions in society and causes the dependence of technologically 'backward' communities and countries on a handful of technologically advanced ones. Whichever group gains prominence in the overall debate, information technology is here to stay and an awareness of the possible impact on society is important.

 Which group do you put yourself in – the optimists or the pessimists – and why?

It is a truism that when new information technologies are introduced into a business or other milieu, they often introduce new disruptions, anxieties and uncertainty. From the workplace to the marketplace to the home, new technologies are transforming familiar practices and challenging received norms of law and social ethics – while offering little guidance about what new norms should prevail.

(Firestone, Conference Report, Dec. 1992)

The controversies

Centralization versus fragmentation

New technologies allow those in power to centralize control over information, while on the other hand, they also enable the dissemination of information. With the increasing use of widespread telecommunication links it is possible for organizations and governments to hold information on others and create an environment of surveillance. Again, the same technology can be used to empower people by giving them easy access to information.

Hierarchy versus democracy

The introduction of email and the World Wide Web can open doors to communication between people in all walks of life. This can encourage a democratic ethos by giving employees at all levels access to each other, but on the other hand, it can be seen as undermining hierarchy. Bill Gates of Microsoft can be accessed via email by all his employees: does this give his employees a say in the way the business is run?; does it hinder the position Bill Gates has as the leader of the company? The answer lies in how much notice is taken of the contributions employees make and how the leadership responds to their increased exposure to the workforce. It also raises the question of how much public intervention is desirable and how it affects the process of decision making by management.

Isolation versus community spirit

Information technology can give people access to the outside world from within the boundaries of their homes. They may be teenagers in their bedrooms surfing the Internet, or telecommuters working from home: either way, this eliminates the need for personal contact and can cause isolation. However, the same technologies can create new communities, connecting their users via electronic mail around which relationships and support systems can be built. They may be people with disabilities taking part in international debates, or religious fanatics spreading messages of hatred through the Internet.

   In the following sections we are going to look into some of the facts behind the controversies in an attempt to form a view on the consequences of information technology in our lives.

Information overload

It is more common to hear people complaining about not getting enough information than about information overload: at least, this was so until the days of the Internet. But now, the Internet enables users to transmit information through the electronic superhighway. Much of the information available through the Net is useful and users can choose which information they want to receive. However, not all information available is either correct or useful and, in some cases, users do not have a choice. For example, many user groups have a system where each message sent by any member of the group is automatically sent to all other members. Also, communication through the Internet is easy, which means that rumours can spread fast and get out of control. How the availability of information affects individuals and businesses depends on the corporate culture adopted by the organization in transmitting and receiving information as well as the habits and integrity of the users.

What has been your experience of using the Internet? Have you found it useful?

Information technology and the nature of work

Pundits have been forecasting fully automated offices for a long time, but such automation has been slow to come. The reasons for this are partly technical and partly social. Articles written even in the late 1980s and early 1990s expressed cynical views on the idea of the worldwide use of video-conferencing and electronic mail even though the technology existed for such services. This was because the monopolistic telecommunication services available in most countries resulted in high costs and, in some cases, unsatisfactory technical standards and protocols, which prevented organizations from making full use of the technology. However, since then much has changed. Telecommunications have been liberalized in many countries, the cost of technology has come down, widespread communications infrastructures have been set up and new software has emerged. This, coupled with the vigour with which life in cyberspace has captured people's imagination, has created a culture, at least in the developed world, in which the boundaries between work and home are blurred.

Restrictions such as distance between colleagues and the time of day have disappeared: people are now able to conduct business with each other from anywhere in the world, at any time of the day or night. This can have profound consequences for both employers and employees.

Many people are working harder, for longer hours and are in constant competition with those who can deliver more. Organizations are developing new ways to structure work out of which two trends have developed in recent years: 'hotelling' and 'telecommuting'. Hotelling reduces business overheads by eliminating office space for all but a few members of staff. Most workers are mobile, working in the 'field' in close contact with customers, using their laptops and keeping in touch with their organizations via email and voice mail. When they need office space they send a message and space is made available for them.

Telecommuting allows employees to work at a location other than the traditional office, either at home or at a telecommuting centre close to where they live. Both these methods can increase productivity and reduce expenses for the employers. They can also offer employees flexibility, allow them to work in an environment of their own choice and save commuting time. However, this has had some negative effects on the employees' support infrastructure: they have become more isolated, which has led to a reduction in their collective strength in the workplace. Some employees, although able to maintain work relationships through the network, have lost the social interaction with colleagues. This can be counterproductive for business performance as well since personal contact and companionship score highly in people's reasons for working. Organizations are now beginning to see the benefit of flexible work patterns as well as the need to set up strategies for supporting mobile and home workers.

In some cases information technology has also changed the way people work together. The use of groupware and email, and instant access to centralized information have improved the scope for user participation in decision making. To achieve the best possible benefit from such developments, conventional structures of hierarchies and boundaries have, in some cases, given way to teams of people working together as self-directed and empowered individuals. However, for some employees, such disruption of the old power structure may create a sense of insecurity. Good management involves channelling the range of skills available in the workforce wisely and allowing the new information-rich employees to make a contribution. One of the effects of the introduction of information technology in many organizations has been the loss of the layer of middle management who had the knowledge and interpersonal skills necessary to work with people in the lower ranks. The gap so created can be filled by allowing employees with increased access to information to make local decisions. This can, on the one hand, decentralize power, while on the other, allow senior managers to hold central control via existing information networks. Eventually, how information technology affects a business and its workforce depends on which route the management takes in utilizing the opportunities available to them.

Talk to some people working on the administrative side of an organization and find out how/if their jobs have changed since the introduction of computers.

Information technology and jobs

Innovations and the introduction of new technology have always threatened job security; the industrial revolution in the middle to late nineteenth century aroused the same fears. Yet the number of jobs rose in the textile, railway and chemical industries during these periods (Jenkin, 1988 – see Further Reading section). This was owing to improved productivity which resulted in higher demands for goods, better competitiveness and hence higher demands for a workforce trained to operate and maintain the new technology.

Our experience with information technology has been more complicated. As usual there have been two opposing views from optimists and pessimists: both have produced reports and statistics to prove their points. Both sides agree that technology which can perform tasks previously done by humans can replace people, the difference in opinion has occurred in estimating the extent of this effect. Optimists have calculated that each robot, for example, can replace two people's jobs on a factory floor, but for those two jobs another new one is created for maintaining the robot. They have argued that information technology creates new jobs by improving the overall performance of a business, by creating more demand and by encouraging newer technological innovations as well as creating new jobs in the information industry.

Pessimists, on the other hand, have cited many examples of job losses due to automation. The printing industry, the automobile industry and banks are some of the sectors in the UK where many employees have lost work to information technology. Many jobs have also disappeared from the computer industry, mainly because of the trend amongst businesses towards using packaged solutions and outsourcing projects rather than in-house developments. In the views of the pessimists, innovations have not been adequate to replace the jobs lost.

Studies have shown that while new jobs have been created in the electronic, manufacturing and distribution (mainly supermarkets and chain stores) industry, jobs have been lost in many other areas. Skilled manual and lower paid white collar workers have been the hardest hit. Also, the new jobs created often involve working with new technology which requires new skills, thus giving young and technically able workers some scope for entrance into the job market whilst causing de-skilling and job losses amongst other groups. Many skilled typists have had to make way for those with expertise in the use of PCs and current software packages; there is less demand for office filing and store keeping because records are kept on computers and operated by a small number of trained staff; a number of clerical and secretarial functions are now performed by the managers themselves in a fraction of the time. All this has affected women, the low paid and the older workforce more than others. Those who are in employment have, in many cases, found greater fulfilment and involvement at work but it has become increasingly difficult for low or traditionally skilled people to find employment.

Read some recent publications to find out how jobs in different industries are affected differently by automation.

Women and information technology

The trend towards de-skilling and unemployment caused by the introduction of information technology has had more serious effect on women than men. The optimists' forecast of technology creating new jobs may have come partially true for men but has opened up opportunities for only a very few technically qualified women. A study by a college in the USA confirms that 'the more technologically intense the industry, the greater the occupational segregation by gender' (Pinola, C.E., *Data Based Advisor*, May 1994, p.18).

Various reasons have been suggested for the absence of women from the higher paid jobs in information technology: women neither know how nor like to play the corporate game and deal with a company's political infrastructure; there is an absence of women role models; girls tend to drop out of science and maths at the middle school level; family commitments; lack of parental support; social stereotyping, and so on. Some researchers have suggested that biological differences in the way the two parts of the brain work for men and women are the reasons behind women's lack of interest in computers. These reasons point to girls and women as being the source of the problem. Other researchers have focused on society and studied various aspects of computer development, production and use in order to explain the differences between women and men working in the computing and IT fields. They have examined the development of computers and the design and manufacture of technical products such as microwaves and smart houses (houses equipped with automatic gadgets) to identify the processes that lead to the association of certain technologies with men. They have explored the experience of boys and girls in education, noting differences such as boys having more access to computers both at home and at school. Researchers have also shown how, in the employment market, the jobs that are open to women are those that are defined as low skilled and low status such as data entry. This means that women are, in effect, excluded from the higher paid and higher status computing and IT jobs (Webster, 1996). See the section on Further reading for more information on the subject.

There are some highly placed women computer scientists, academics and even board directors in technology firms. However, the number of women who have achieved such positions of authority is very low. A survey performed in the USA in 1994 showed that out of a total of 11,790 board seats, only 814 were held by women (Bellinger, June 1995 – see Further Reading section). One of the reasons for this was that there were very few women in high positions in the industry out of whom board members could be selected. A 1992 survey showed that in the UK, only 5.9% of all managers in computing were women, compared with 6.6% in France and 8.7% in Spain (Haughton, E., *Computer Weekly*, 23 April 1992, p.26). By comparison 64% of the help desk workers in computing were women. The situation hasn't changed much since then. Women working in computing in general, earn between 2% and 10% less than men; women start their working lives at lower pay than men and the difference grows as the workers progress through life and ranks.

The bleak statistics produced by various studies on women's performances in computing careers have discouraged other women from considering such careers: thus the trend has carried on. The picture is slightly distorted by the fact that the number of computer literate women is maintained at a reasonably high level by the participation of a large number of women in jobs involving the use of application software such as wordprocessing and databases. Thus, while women have moved on from typewriters to PCs, men are employed to do work defined as more technical and offering higher salaries and career prospects.

Find out from some organizations you have made contact with, how many women work in the IT department and what their positions are. How do your findings compare with what has been said in this chapter?

It is not only in the job market where information technology affects women differently from men. Computers are seen mainly as men's toys by most software developers of whom the majority are men. As a result computer games, program interfaces, on-screen graphics and messages are developed from a male perspective for a male audience. The images produced and the icons used are often alienating to women. Pornography and violence in video games and on the Internet often offend women's values and reinforce their positions in society. Such images also contribute towards the stereotyping of male and female roles. More games are made with boys in mind, thus maintaining male domination in the use of new technology. 'What kids are learning is that girls are expected to be passive, decorative and quiet, and boys are expected to be active, aggressive and smart' (Frayer, 1995 – see Further Reading section). There are divisions of opinions in this area and computers are not the only media exploiting sex and violence. There have been calls from different groups to combat sexist games, and some companies are developing software with female characters in positive roles such as maths experts or as strong and smart fighters. However, such programs need careful marketing to make them attractive to both boys and girls, otherwise the message to the future generation remains incomplete.

What is your opinion about the quality of computer games in relation to their social value?

Computers and education

It is a recognized fact that many children prefer a computer keyboard and monitor to reading and writing. They are fast to accept technology, whether through playing games or surfing the Internet to chat with their favourite pop stars. It has been suggested by many educators and politicians that children's fascination for computer games can be utilized by making computers a learning tool for all subjects. Traditional teaching methods have often failed to motivate children on many occasions. In large classes with students of a varied range of abilities and interests, computer software can be used to allow children to learn at their own speed. Interesting multimedia techniques and virtual reality software can make learning fun and challenging at the same time. However, although many educational programs are available, unfortunately very few schools can afford to buy enough computers to allow their integrated use in all classrooms. Traditionally, computers in schools have been restricted to computer courses and for limited use by the members of staff. Some schools have run after-school computer clubs but these have offered little more than entertainment for children and were used mainly by boys. Recently, however, the UK government has started a number of initiatives to promote the use of CD-ROMs, multimedia technology and the Internet as teaching and learning aids. According to media reports it is the government's intention to provide a computer for each child in a class but it remains to be seen whether resources can be found to facilitate this.

Education in all sectors can benefit from the use of technology. Traditional classroom teaching in some higher education courses is making way for open and distance learning. This involves the use of networked computers and educational software together with high quality multimedia course material which allows students to learn from a place of their choice, at their own speed and keep in touch with tutors at the same time. This has brought education within the reach of those with special educational needs: mature students who come back to education after a long gap can use this to adapt to higher education, students who are housebound due to domestic problems or disability can learn from home, people at work can study in their spare time, the problem of large class sizes can be overcome by introducing virtual classes and so on. To use the full potential of technology for education, society needs to invest in improving the communications infrastructure and the quality of hardware and software suitable for such provisions.

However, some would argue that by allowing computers to take over some of the roles of a teacher, we are losing the benefits of traditional teaching methods. Many children are now leaving school with inadequate abilities in literacy and numeracy, they often have very short concentration spans and little interest in reading books. As with all other areas in life, the final result depends on how the power of technology is controlled to achieve the most possible benefits.

What do you think a classroom for 15 year old pupils will look like in the future? What do you think about the educational value of such a classroom?

Computers and the disabled

We have already seen how innovations in input and output device technologies can work for people with disabilities. The use of networked computers and especially the availability of the Internet allow some people with restricted physical abilities to take equal part in education as well as in social interactions.

'Cyberspace is a great leveller, where no-one is identifiable by anything but the thoughts they put up on-screen – a playing field that gives freedom to those who may be confined or restricted elsewhere' (Fowler, *Computer Shopper*, March 1995, p.586). There are many bulletin board services (BBSs) run by different groups catering for a number of disabilities. These are mainly in the USA but the trend is catching up in the UK as well.

However, one group of people who have lost out are the blind and partially sighted. Windows and other GUI based software have excluded them from a large number of activities in the workplace. Although some attempts have been made to service these people through the introduction of voice input and output, Braille keyboards, scanners for Braille text and so on, there is still a long way to go before blind people can make use of information technology at the same rate as the rest of society.

Do you think enough has been done to make computer technology useful to disabled people?

The ethics of the Internet

The Internet has broken down barriers between cities, countries and continents. Users can now access information on almost any issue, create web pages on any subject and join in discussions on any topic. The Internet is an anarchistic world, no one owns it and no one controls it, thus giving users enormous freedom of speech and access. Consequently, it carries with it the danger of misuse and exploitation. A debate is currently going on about the promotion of pornography and violence on the Internet. The same is true for other media but while it is possible to control the distribution of printed material or underage sex rackets by law, it is difficult to pass any law which can effectively control the Internet. If we wish to utilize the exposure to the world that the Internet offers we may have to rely on a shared sense of decency and responsibility of its users. However, governments in some countries do not allow the use of the Internet or filter its contents in an attempt to avoid the above problems. At the time of writing, an Internet committee is being set up in this country to control the publication of child pornography through the medium.

On the one hand the anonymity of the medium enables people to take part in discussions at equal level with each other regardless of gender, race, class, or level of physical ability; on the other, this also allows them to engage in unethical discussions and activities protected by the privacy of their own desktops. Children can now access violent images on their computer screens even if their parents refuse to buy them such games on disk; political groups can distribute speeches inciting hatred without the fear of consequences. The debate on how we can control this or whether it is right to do so is likely to go on. Read some of the articles and discussion documents available on the Internet on this subject.[1]

Where do you stand in the debate on the Internet and civil liberties?

Information technology and developing countries

People have different views on the contribution information technology can make to economic development. Some would say that poor countries should try to meet their basic needs, such as health, literacy, essential facilities and domestic infrastructure first, before embarking on expensive items such as information technology. Others would argue that one of the means these countries can use to achieve the above goals is information technology. Developing countries are often 'information poor' as well: gathering information and giving people access to it is difficult because of problems in transport, funding, expertise and so on. Information technology can play an important role in helping them to overcome these barriers. For example, in rural areas technology can be used to facilitate basic education in agricultural, social and health matters; use of IT in the health service can save lives; technology equipped to predict famine, flood and other disasters can limit damage; effective communications networks can improve national and international cooperation. However, developing countries must set up efficient power supply and telecommunications infrastructures in order to access the full potential offered by technology.

There are some countries, sometimes referred to as the newly developed countries (NDCs), where governments have made large investments in IT. Through such investments as well as the liberalization of economic policies, countries such as South Korea, Taiwan and Singapore have established themselves not only as

---

1   Electronic Frontier Foundation (EFF) based in the USA is active in the debate on this topic and has published many articles on the Internet.

technologically self-sufficient but also able to export hardware and expertise to the rest of the world. These countries are prime examples of how IT can be adapted to suit the unique needs of relatively poor countries. The low labour costs of developing countries often combined with a large population of technically qualified and highly motivated people can be used as a sound foundation upon which development can be built.

In recent years India has made an enormous impact in the international market as a software exporter. A number of computer systems operating in western countries are run by software written in India. Amongst organizations using Indian software are American Airlines and Swissair, American Express and Citibank. A large number of Indian programmers are now being employed by American companies, either by subcontracting work to Indian software houses or by giving short term visas to Indian citizens to work in firms in the USA. The diffusion of IT in government, private and educational organizations in India has also been impressive. Again, reasons are the highly skilled workforce pool combined with labour costs which are low by international standards.

Some would argue that the developed countries are exploiting the less developed by taking advantage of cheap labour. However, the skilled workforce in most developing countries are 'typically highly paid professionals in their own countries; it is merely that the rate of exchange gives less developed economies a significant cost advantage when they are trading internationally' (Cast, M., *Computer Bulletin*, published by the British Computer Society, Oct. 1995, vol 7, part 5, p.14). The question of exploitation cannot be ruled out but although this may be the case at the beginning of a country's journey along the technology route the situation can change when it establishes its strength in the field.

The proliferation of IT in the developing countries has been blamed by critics for widening the gap between the rich and the poor. Some have referred to the Internet as not so much a 'global village' but more a 'middle-class suburb' because typically the well-off have access to such facilities. However, this is true for both developed and developing countries. How the opportunities presented by the new technology can be taken advantage of is determined by the efforts made by people in positions of authority in this field.

Find out by looking at the sources of information made available by the Internet, how developing countries not mentioned here have used information technology to their benefit and what price, if any, they had to pay for it.

The future

During the mid-1970s to the mid-1980s the terms 'paperless office' and 'cashless society' came up in many writings. Pundits predicted that soon we would be rid of filing cabinets and archives because all storage would be done electronically. We were told that cash transactions would be eliminated because electronic money and smart cards would take over. Neither of these has come true even though the technology required to achieve them has been available for some time. In fact, rapid technological progress has been made: fast processors, multimedia technology, highly sophisticated software, and above all communications links, are able to provide what we need to make the dream come true. What has stopped us from fulfilling the vision is a combination of factors foremost of which is people's natural resistance to change. Most of us still prefer to read a sheet of paper rather than a VDU screen; many people choose to use cash rather than plastic cards and many small businesses simply do not have the technology required to perform electronic fund transfer. Some visionaries now predict that in the next 25 years the concept of desktop PCs will be replaced by a computer in everything we use. However, 25 years later we may have to give the same reasons for not getting there.

Summary

Like all new technologies, the introduction of computers has attracted opposing reactions: some people see it as the gateway to prosperity, freedom and empowerment of individuals; others fear job losses, invasion of privacy and divisions in our society. IT affects our lives at home, at work, in schools and colleges and in our personal and leisure activities. Different groups of people are affected differently. People with traditional skills such as printers, typists and car assembly workers have lost jobs due to automation; women have failed to gain access to well paid computer-related jobs at the same rate as men; whilst the gap between rich and poor countries has become wider, in many cases poor countries have made incredible achievements through their investment in information technology; and people with disabilities have managed to benefit from the use of computers. The widespread use of the Internet has enabled people to achieve enormous flexibility and empowerment in work and social functions, whilst at the same time it has given rise to concerns in the areas of security and ethics. Although IT has the potential to fulfil the optimists' aims, its ultimate effects depend on how the power of technology is utilized.

Further reading

Read the report by Charles M. Firestone available from EDGE Publishing, 908-852-7271 (USA), and any updates available, for useful information on how the information revolution brings in changes in every aspect of our lives.

Read *Shaping Women's Work: Gender, Employment and Information Technology* by Juliet Webster, Longman, 1996, for information on how computers have affected women's lives.

R. Bellinger, *Electronic Engineering Times*, 5 June 1995, p.125 has a good discussion on women and computing.

Governance of Cyberspace: Politics, Technology and Global Restructuring, edited by Brian D. Loader, Routledge, 1997 covers the social aspects of the Internet well.

Information Technology: Social Issues – A Reader edited by R. Finnegan, G. Salaman and K. Thompson, Hodder & Stoughton, 1991 is a collection of articles covering all aspects of the effect of information technology on society.

New Technologies in the 1990s: A Socio-Economic Strategy, OECD, 1988 is a collection of reports by experts working on the national and international implications of new technologies on society.

Sexism and kids' software, Frayer, B., PC World, 1995, **13**:12 p.406 (Frayer, B. 1995).

The implications for the use of computers on jobs are discussed well in the article 'Automation is good for us' by Patrick Jenkin in a book called *The Information Technology Revolution*, edited by Tom Forrester, Basil Blackwell, 1988.

There are many articles available on the web which discuss the politics of the Internet.

For further information on the weekly magazines mentioned in this chapter, see the Further reading section of Chapter 1.

You may like to read the article by Pinola mentioned on page 280. *Data Based Advisor* is available on the CD-ROM *Computer Select*.

Revision questions

1. Discuss the opposing views on the effects of information technology in our society.

2. Discuss the effect of IT in the following areas:

    (a) the nature of work;   (c) the lives of different groups of people;
    (b) availability of and opportunities at work;   (d) the use of the Internet.

3. Some developing countries are making remarkable progress in the use of IT when they have not yet met the basic needs of all their people. Discuss your own views on this subject.

4. Discuss how, on the one hand, the Internet has given us access to an enormous amount of information and, on the other, it has opened doors to some who abuse the freedom.

Food for thought

BYTE, June 1997

RIP: anonymous user
Mark Schlack

'Howdy, stranger' is being replaced by 'Identify yourself' on the Net. Should we worry?

Face it: Digital IDs will mean the end of anonymity on the Internet. I've written before (December 1996) on how people hide behind that anonymity to lob bombs on e-mail. But they also depend on it to maintain a level of irreverence and outspokenness that's valuable, fun, and worth preserving in some form.

In the future, people who want privacy to air their views may still use nicknames, but remaining truly anonymous to someone who really wants to identify you (say, because you owe them money) will get harder and harder. If you want to buy or sell, or even just download information, you'll have to say who you are.

Without the basic elements of identity, the Internet won't realize its potential as a universal backbone of commerce and communications. Neither big corporations nor individuals will want to expose themselves in an environment where they can be attacked by people wearing electronic ski masks.

But will the end of anonymity also mean the end of personal freedom? What if a government could find 'undesirables' instantly, correlate all their movements and purchases, and ensure that they're not able to hide behind aliases? Ultimately, computers will be able to do that. We should be worried about that kind of security. It's not needed for ordinary commerce and communications, and we shouldn't let governments hide behind the argument that it is.

That's just what the U.S. government is doing. The Clinton administration has consistently stood for an Internet where the government has the last word, whether on security or content. So far, U.S. courts don't seem inclined to agree on the content issue. And the international market is now making a sham of the U.S.'s stringent export restrictions on cryptography: The recent CeBIT show in Hanover, Germany, saw the debut of several Euro-grown 128-bit encryption products. If the U.S. couldn't keep the atomic bomb under wraps, it certainly can't make a secret of basic math.

So, security and freedom – how do we navigate these two sometimes contradictory goals?

▶

First, let's not go overboard. The noncomputerized world we've lived in for millennia has never been 100 percent secure. If someone steals your credit card, the issuer makes good on its promise to protect you and the merchant. These relationships – not some foolproof system of identity – are why it all works.

Let's emulate these kinds of relationships on the Web. Digital IDs should give us enough certainty to support our traditional notions of trust, but in a form that also respects privacy and is as unobtrusive as it is appropriate. I happen to favor strict checks on people who buy rocket launchers; I certainly don't favor them for people who buy shirts on-line.

Which brings me to my second point: personal freedom. Governments should play a role in digital security; someone, for example, should validate certificate authorities (but not as an excuse to monopolize encryption, as British authorities are attempting to do). Governments might ultimately need to regulate what can be done by various parties with your digital ID. It's far from certain that we all won't cry 'Uncle' after a few years under siege from 'targeted' marketing efforts that presume we want to receive hundreds of offers for vacations in Mexico just because we charged a burrito at the local tacqueria.

But my fond hope is that governments can be kept as far away from core security mechanisms as possible. Clipper chips, government key servers – these spell trouble for individual liberty. The usual arguments of crime and terrorism don't bear scrutiny: They're just lazy attempts to pull the trigger on expanded intrusion into all our lives, a temptation nearly irresistible to bureaucrats.

The libertarian idealism of the Internet is already strained. The end of anonymity is a reasonable price to pay for the expanded community that the Internet can bring. The end of liberty is not.

Mark Schlack is Editor in Chief of BYTE.

Discussion questions

1. Find out what is meant by 'Digital ID' and how it is meant to work.

2. Referring to the last paragraph of the article, discuss in what ways digital ID and other security measures imposed on the Internet affect anonymity and liberty.

3. Critically discuss the last paragraph of the article addressing both sides of the argument and explaining clearly why public opinion may be almost equally divided on the issues.

4. Search the Internet and other sources to find out what initiatives have been taken in the USA and Europe in controlling encryption (clipper chips and government key servers are elements of such initiatives).

5. The UK government has backed down on 'key escrow encryption' conceding that it is an unworkable solution (*Computing*, 25 March 1999). Search the Internet for information on what is involved in key escrow and what the situation is at the moment.